The Influence of the United States on Canadian Development: Eleven Case Studies

The Influence
of the United States
on Canadian Development:
Eleven Case Studies

Irving M. Abella, Robert Babcock,
Carl E. Beigie, Carl C. Berger,
Andrew Hill Clark, Robert Gilpin,
Alexander Hull, Carl F. Klinck,
Allan Kornberg and Alan Tharp,
Lawrence B. Lee, Richard A. Preston,
Mildred A. Schwartz

Edited by Richard A. Preston

Number 40 in a series published for the
Duke University Commonwealth-Studies Center
Duke University Press, Durham, N.C.

1972

Preface

The study of Canada has long been neglected in the United States. Many other countries further away and less important have attracted more American interest perhaps because they seemed more exotic. There may have been some feeling that research and writing on Canada should, or could, be left to Canadians: that which has been done has been largely the work of Canadian expatriates.

Past efforts to stimulate joint Canadian-American effort to remedy this deficiency have been only relatively and temporarily successful. Although often financed by American money, they have usually tended to be Canadian rather than American in content and personnel. This is one consequence of the great difference between the two countries in population, wealth, and responsibilities. The United States looms larger in Canadian eyes than vice-versa. Financial support in the United States has, therefore, not been sufficiently available for the study of Canada by American nationals.

It has also tended to dry up for Canadians resident in the United States. The Canada Council does not normally support research about Canada done by Canadians resident in the United States. The belief of some Canadians that American study of Canada is a form of imperialism helps to compound these tendencies. In some quarters there is resentment against American study of Canada.

A consequence of lack of support is that American writing about Canada tends to have serious limitations because, although almost always benevolent in intention, it is often based on inadequate knowledge or understanding. Yet American understanding of Canadian problems is of paramount importance. It is needed in order to help to preserve Canadian identity and interests as well as to increase American understanding of foreign societies. If Americans do not understand a society that is similar to theirs and close at hand how can they understand any other?

One explanation for inadequate study of Canada is the lack of a permanent American national organization to promote it. This was remedied during the winter of 1970–1971 when a group of scholars, Americans and Canadians resident in the United States, called together by Dr. Dale Thomson, Director of the Center for Canadian Studies at Johns Hopkins University's School for Advanced International Studies in Washington, D.C., formed the Association for Canadian Studies in the United States.

The aim of the Association is to encourage American interest in and promote American knowledge of Canada, not just of American-Canadian relations. Nevertheless, its inaugural seminar conference, open to all interested persons, which was held at Duke University in April, 1971, took as its theme the influence of the United States on Canadian development. This theme was adopted because of a belief that it would direct attention to the study of Canada rather than merely of relations between the two countries. The conference was made possible by the generosity of the following corporations: Alcan Aluminum Corporation, International Nickel, Metropolitan Life, Standard Oil.

This volume is a selection of the papers presented at the conference. Duke University's Center for Commonwealth Studies, which has long been engaged in teaching, research, and publication about Canada, has sponsored publication to help promote Canadian studies in the United States. The Association for Canadian Studies is therefore grateful for financial aid to make publication possible, to Dr. Ralph Braibanti and his associates on the Center's Committee, and to Dr. Craufurd Goodwin, Vice-Provost for International Studies. The Association is also indebted to those of its members who gave papers and who have agreed to publication in this form.

RICHARD A. PRESTON

October 1, 1971

Contributors

Irving M. Abella, Assistant Professor of History, Glendon College, York University, was born in Toronto in 1940. Professor Abella was educated at the University of Toronto, from which he received his doctorate in Canadian history in 1969. He served as a researcher for the Royal Commission in Biculturalism and Bilingualism and now teaches Canadian history at Glendon College. His special field of interest is the Canadian labor movement, and he has contributed articles on this subject to various journals. His book on the CIO, the Communist Party, and the Canadian labor movement will shortly be published by the University of Toronto Press. Professor Abella is also the founding chairman of the Committee on Canadian Labour History.

Robert Babcock is Assistant Professor of History, Wells College. Born in 1931, he was educated at the State University of New York at Albany and taught in public high school for several years. He completed his doctorate at Duke University in 1970 and was elected to Phi Beta Kappa. An Instructor of History at Duke during 1968–1969, he came to Wells in the latter year and is currently working on a study of the American Federation of Labor's activities in Canada.

Carl E. Beigie, Executive Director, Private Planning Association of Canada, was born in Cleveland in 1940. Mr. Beigie graduated from Muskingum College and did graduate work in economics at the Massachusetts Institute of Technology. He taught economics at the University of Western Ontario from 1966 to 1968. From 1968 to 1971 he served as international economist and assistant vice president at the Irving Trust Co. He is the author of *The Canada–U.S. Automotive Agreement: An Evaluation* (Montreal, 1970).

Carl C. Berger, Associate Professor of History, University of Toronto, was born in Manitoba in 1939. Professor Berger attended the University of Manitoba and received his graduate degrees from the University of Toronto. His special fields of interest are Canadian intellectual and social history, and his publications include *The Sense of*

Power: Studies in the Ideas of Canadian Imperialism, 1867–1914 (Toronto, 1970).

Andrew Hill Clark is Finch Research Professor of Geography, University of Wisconsin, Madison. Born in Manitoba in 1911, he received his first degree from McMaster University and graduate degrees from the Universities of Toronto and California. He taught at the Universities of Toronto and California, Johns Hopkins, Canterbury (N.Z.), Dundee (Scotland), Rutgers and Wisconsin, serving as Department Chairman in each of the last two. During World War II he served with O.S.S. in Washington and China. He has published widely, particularly in the Historical Geography of Canada and New Zealand. His *Acadia: The Geography of Early Nova Scotia to 1760* (Madison, 1968) received the citation of the Beveridge Award Committee of the American Historical Association as the best historical work about Canada published in 1968.

Robert Gilpin, Professor of International and Public Affairs, Princeton University, was born in Burlington, Vermont, in 1930. Professor Gilpin graduated from the University of Vermont in 1952 and earned his doctorate from the University of California, Berkeley, in 1960. He served as a U.S. Naval Officer (1954–57) and has taught at Columbia University and the London School of Economics. In addition, he was a post-doctoral Fellow at Harvard University and was a Guggenheim Fellow. His special fields of interest are international relations, Western European affairs, and the relationship of economics, technology and politics. His publications include *American Scientists and Nuclear Weapons Policy* and *France in the Age of the Scientific State.*

Alexander Hull, Associate Professor of Romance Languages, Duke University, was born in Portland, Oregon, in 1928. Professor Hull took his undergraduate and graduate degrees at the University of Washington. He also studied at the University of Michigan and the University of Paris. He taught at the University of Massachusetts and at St. John's College of the University of Manitoba before coming to Duke University in 1962. He served for several summers as the linguistics specialist for the Franco-American Institute at Bowdoin College and Assumption College (Worcester, Mass.). He has published articles on North American French and on the history of French phonology, and is the coauthor of several French textbooks.

Carl F. Klinck is Professor of English, the University of Western Ontario, London, Canada. Professor Klinck was born in Ontario in 1908, graduated from the University of Western Ontario in 1927, and received his M.A. and Ph.D. from Columbia University. He taught at Waterloo College (affiliated with the University of Western Ontario) from 1928–1947, and was Dean of Arts, 1942–1947. He became a Professor of English at the University of Western Ontario in London in 1947, Chairman of the Department, 1948–1956, and a Senior Professor in 1956. In 1961 he was elected a Fellow of the Royal Society of Canada. His special fields of interest are Canadian and American Literature, and his principal publications include *Canadian Anthology* (edited with R. E. Watters) (Toronto, 1955, rev. 1966), *William "Tiger" Dunlop* (Toronto, 1958), *Literary History of Canada* (general editor) (Toronto, 1965), and *The Journal of Major John Norton 1816* (edited with J. J. Talman) (Champlain Society, 1971).

Allan Kornberg, born in Winnipeg, Canada, in 1931, received his doctorate in political science from the University of Michigan in 1964. In 1964–65 he was a member of the Department of Political Science at Hiram College. In 1965 he became a member of the faculty of Duke University where he is professor of political science. Currently, he is engaged in an extensive cross-national study of political socialization and political recruitment that is funded by the National Science Foundation and the Canada Council. He is the author of *Canadian Legislative Behavior: A Study of the 25th Parliament* (1967) and coauthor and editor of *Legislatures in Developmental Perspective* (1970), and has contributed articles to professional journals, including *American Political Science Review, Journal of Politics, Western Political Quarterly, Midwest Journal of Political Science, Social Forces, Sociology, The Canadian Review of Sociology and Anthropology, Political Science, Parliamentary Affairs,* and *Journal of Constitutional and Parliamentary Studies.*

Lawrence B. Lee is Professor of History, San Jose State College (California). A native of Illinois born in 1917, Professor Lee graduated from Illinois Institute of Technology and received his graduate degrees from the University of Chicago. He taught at Fort Hays Kansas State College, the University of Detroit and Northwestern University before joining the staff of San Jose State College in 1957. He has taught summer terms at the University of Calgary and the University of British Columbia. His field of interest is American history with his specialty in comparative frontiers and agricultural history. He has been on the executive committee of the Agricultural History Society and on the editorial board of the California State Colleges Press as well as the *Pacific Historical Review*. He has contributed articles and reviews to numerous professional journals.

Richard A. Preston is William K. Boyd Professor of History, Duke University. A native of England, born in 1910, Professor Preston received his B.A. and M.A. degrees at Leeds University and his Ph.D. degree at Yale. He was lecturer at the University of Toronto and at University College, Cardiff, and during World War II served in the Royal Air Force. He then served as an assistant professor at the University of Toronto until 1948 when he became professor of history at the Royal Military College of Canada. He came to Duke University in 1965. He is a Fellow in the Royal Historical Society, a former president of the Canadian Historical Association, the founding president of the Association for Canadian Studies in the United States and Chairman of the Canadian Studies Committee at Duke University. President Preston's publications include *Gorges of Plymouth Fort: A Life of Sir Ferdinando Georges* (Toronto, 1953), *Men in Arms: A History of Warfare and Its Inter-relationships with Western Society* (with S. F. Wise and H. O. Werner) (New York, 1956 and 1962), *Canada in World Affairs, 1959–1961* (Toronto, 1965), *Canada and "Imperial Defense"* (Durham, N.C., 1966), and *Canada's R.M.C.* (Toronto, 1969). He is presently on sabbatical leave as a Guggenheim Fellow.

Mildred A. Schwartz, Professor of Sociology, University of Illinois at Chicago Circle, was born in Toronto. Professor Schwartz graduated from the University of Toronto and earned her doctorate from Columbia University. Prior to coming to Chicago, she taught at the University of Calgary. Among her publications are *Public Opinion and Canadian Identity* (Berkeley, 1967), *Political Parties and the Canadian Social Structure* (with F. C. Englemann) (Scarborough, 1967), now being revised, and "Canadian Voting Behaviour," forthcoming in Richard Rose, *Comparative Electoral Behaviour* (New York). Also forthcoming is a book tracing the significance of regions in the political life of Canada, *Politics and Territory*.

Alan Tharp was born in Roanoke, Virginia, in 1944, and is a graduate student in political science at Duke University. He is the author of "Whose Southern Strategy?: Nixon, the South, and School Desegregation," in *Trying Times: American Politics in the 1970's* (1970).

Contents

The Influence of the United States on Canadian Development: Eleven Case Studies

Introduction

A Plea for Comparative Studies of Canada and the United States and of the Effects of Assimilation on Canadian Development

Richard A. Preston

The essays in this book are offered as a contribution to the extension of understanding of the influence of the United States on the development of Canada and of its great significance.

Use of the word development calls for preliminary discussion. The Oxford and Webster dictionaries both define development as advance or growth through progressive changes; and they both emphasize gradual growth from within. For social scientists and public administrators, however, development has acquired a special meaning that in some ways conveys ideas contrary to its earlier general usage. The *International Encyclopedia of Social Sciences* defines "modern economic growth *or development*," which it dates from the 18th century, as "a *rapid* and sustained rise in real output per head and attendant shifts in the techno-logical, economic, and demographic characteristics of a society."[1]

Interest in fostering economic growth, or development in this more specific sense, was evident from the 14th century on. It increased greatly towards the end of the 19th century and even more after the socialist experiments in Russia and elsewhere. Yet it was not until the extensive decolonization following the Second World War brought the emergence of many new nations and the revelation of vast disparity between the productivity and well-

1. David L. Sills (ed.), *International Encyclopedia of the Social Sciences*, LV (New York, 1968), 395.

being of developed and underdeveloped countries that the revolutionary practice of international aid for development was initiated. Intensive study of the developing process—much of it theoretical in nature, followed. It showed that economic growth depends on social and political change, a process collectively described as "modernization," or sometimes as political development.

The capture of the word development by social scientists has brought wide acceptance of a narrower meaning which in some ways contradicts the original definition. Development has come to imply economic growth and related social and political change; it is believed capable of being achieved with outside aid, perhaps even quickly.

Neglect of lessons that can be drawn from an understanding of the older concept of development is responsible for some anomalies in current experience with the application of developmental theory. Despite programs of international aid for development, the gap between rich and poor nations is still widening rather than narrowing. An attempt to distinguish between underdeveloped societies which are in process of development (or which wish to be developed) and developed societies, therefore, comes up against the awkward fact that the latter are still developing more rapidly than underdeveloped societies despite all national and international efforts.

Part of the difficulty in fully understanding the development process in the narrower sense of the word is caused by distinctions made between underdeveloped nations on the one hand and developed nations on the other. Developmental theory has all too often been related to, or built upon, the situation and experiences of underdeveloped states in Asia and Africa and has paid insufficient attention to relevant lessons from Western Europe, North America, and related societies. For instance, the conditions suggested by Lucien Pye to possibly be essential for political development have been shown to be not applicable to the growth of two Canadian provinces where the developments that actually occurred in particular circumstances were precisely the opposite of those he postulated.[2] There is, therefore, need for more attention to the process of economic growth in countries now classed as developed; there is need for acceptance of the fact that development is a complex and lengthy ongoing process rather than one that can be induced and completed in a relatively short time; and there is need for more study of economic growth in relation, not merely to social and political development as has already been suggested by sociologists and political scientists, but also to the whole process of history.

In the title of this volume the word development is used in its wider sense to mean the process of overall change that has produced the community known as Canada. An important part of that development has been vast economic growth, including technological innovation and related social and political change, that is to say the development of Canada in the narrower sense of the social scientists. In addition there are less tangible aspects of national development, sometimes grouped together as cultural, including not merely art and letters but also ideology, and especially the concept of national identity. The sum total of all these parts is national development in the sense used earlier by historians, namely the evolution or history of a national community with distinguishable characteristics and interests.

Economic growth and the evolution of conscious national identity do not necessarily go hand in hand. Nationalism can lead to the rejection of, or abstinence from, economic advantage even when it claims, sometimes with truth, that national assertion and independence are necessary for national well-being. Attempts to induce economic development by external aid may run counter to forces which serve to fashion national identity. Development in the historical sense may or may not coincide with economic growth, that is with development as now used by the social scientists.

The story of the development of Canada with which these essays are concerned provides a vast storehouse of information

2. S. F. Wise, "Conservatism and Political Development: The Canadian Case," *South Atlantic Quarterly*, LXIX (Spring, 1970), 229–243.

about the developing process, and about the way in which it comes about, which should have useful general application. The two most powerful factors that fashioned Canada were, on the one hand European influences from two mother countries by the transfer of people, institutions, and ideas, and through domination, and on the other the North American environmental factors. Different schools of history have put more or less emphasis on one or the other of these. The presence of two distinctive cultures within a single polity, the constitutional protection given to the minority group, and an approximate coincidence of geographical regions and boundaries, have led to an increasing assertion of provincial autonomy and have thus contributed to Canada's distinctiveness. Another factor now coming to be recognized as a further explanation of divergence of Canadian from neighboring American society is a stronger tradition of governmental direction and initiative.

Yet perhaps the most interesting formative factor in Canadian development has been the influence of the United States. This was exerted from the colonial beginning of Canadian history and it has steadily increased with the passage of time, with the improvement of communications, and with the emergence of the United States as the leading world power. In this respect the story of Canadian development differs appreciably from that of most other countries. In few cases has a foreign neighbor exerted as much an influence as the United States has exercised on Canada. (Parallels might be Britain's influence on Ireland and the Soviet Union's on Finland.) American proximity helped to further some aspects of Canadian development in the narrower sense, much in the way that international aid furthers the development of new nations by the provision of capital and of technical know-how. Canada received these stimuli for development from the United States in addition to those she received from the mother country. However, the American influence not only expedited the growth process but also served to decrease dependence on Britain. It has been suggested that it helped in the attainment of Canadian independence, first by a threat of attack that encouraged a trend towards self-reliance if not self-sufficiency, and later, when autonomy was achieved, by American willingness to arbitrate disputes.[3] American influences have in fact also affected almost every aspect of Canadian life.

What now bothers many Canadians is that political and economic dependence on Britain has been replaced by economic dependence on the United States with a more subtle threat to Canada's national identity and autonomy. A preponderant part of large sectors of the Canadian economy is not merely owned, but also controlled, by Americans. Many Canadians therefore believe that Canada is being taken over lock, stock, and barrel and that political annexation in the future may become a mere formality or an unnecessary step. On several occasions in the past, e.g., in 1849, 1891, and 1911, the idea of annexation contributed to Canadian political crises. Some Canadians believe that Canada can still preserve the essentials of her own identity and well-being by political action. A few fear that Canada's efforts to postpone absorption may actually mean eventual American control on less advantageous terms for the unfortunate victim, or the acceptance of a substantially lower standard of well-being as the condition for nominal independence. Many Canadians believe that living next to a giant neighbor may mean the destruction of Canada. Further American aid to Canadian economic development is therefore widely considered a mixed blessing because it appears to threaten the development of Canada as an independent nation.

What complicates the question of American domination is that American social and cultural influences, their effect accelerated by modern communications, are "Americanizing" many other aspects of Canadian life in more subtle ways than by the obvious one caused by the growth of economic control. Because of the lead of the United States in so many spheres, it is difficult to distinguish between modernization and Americanization; and the superficial evidence of the latter is often over-obtrusive. Similar evidence of modernization and Americanization can be found throughout the western and nonaligned worlds; it is only

3. Carl George Winter, *American Influence on Canadian Nationhood* (Washington, D.C., 1954).

more plentiful in Canada because contact there is closer and more prolonged, and the Canadian people, while very conscious of their differences from Americans, are also regularly impressed by similarities old and new.

In view of alarming evidence of an American take-over of the Canadian economy, of American infiltration (by invitation) of the educational system, and of American dominance of Canadian labor unions, and in view of assumptions of a pervasive American influence in many other aspects of Canadian life, it is not surprising that the debate about measures necessary to maintain an independent Canada has attracted much attention, has stirred much emotion in Canada, and has led to the wildfire spread of a nonpolitical or nonparty movement of resistance. Although in some cases modernization may not necessarily mean the further-ance of American control, much of the discussion about American economic domination and the infringement of Canadian sover-eignty takes for granted that a rapid process of cultural assimi-lation is expediting and will continue to expedite these unwanted phenomena.

Despite the importance of Americanization in this debate about the future of Canada, it is noteworthy that there has been only incidental scholarly study of this process. Canadian research and writing have been concerned chiefly with the question of sover-eignty and autonomy rather than with assimilation and its effects. Yet, as Dr. Schwartz points out in her essay in this book, influence can mean more than conscious or unconscious attempts to control. It can mean conscious or unconscious transference of ideas and institutions.[4]

Most Americans are either unaware that there is a problem, or are unable to understand what it is all about. Native Americans have rarely studied Canada intensively. There have been a few brilliant exceptions, from Francis Parkman to Seymour Lipset and Richard Caves. Otherwise, Americans have left the field to Canadians at home or to Canadians resident in the United States. Dr. Carl Berger shows in an essay in this book that the number of courses given on Canadian history in the United States a

4. See chapter 3, below.

generation ago was actually larger than the number given in Canada.[5] Nevertheless, it was still small in relation to the huge American system of higher education. By and large Americans were, and still are, unaware of, apathetic about, or unsympathetic towards Canadian efforts to preserve national identity and independence. They reveal more concern about such questions in more remote lands than they do in their immediate neighbor. When they think of Canada at all, they either note obvious differences as evidence of the resilience of Canadian nationalism, or they hail similarities as evidence of a close, beneficial relationship.

As Canada is only one of many external problems for the United States, and as most members of so vast a country are immersed in domestic and local matters, the problem of arousing American interest is complex. Yet it is becoming increasingly important. American influence has become a world-wide phenomenon exerted on all states in the free and third worlds and perhaps even behind the curtains, but the nature and results of this influence are not yet understood.[6] However, similar American pressures and influences have been exerted on Canada for two centuries. Canada is thus a kind of laboratory in which the processes of Americanization can be studied first hand. It has been largely ignored. Another point is that Americans are now beginning to talk of the need for abandoning the meltingpot in favor of a new "plural society" within the United States. There has been a plural society in Canada for nearly two centuries that can offer long experience of pluralism as a guide for future American policy, but it is virtually an unknown factor in the United States. Finally, some Canadians see the relations of Canada and the United States approaching a new form of international relationship which will bring greater closeness, yet preserve national identity.[7] This relationship might be a pointer for global international relations.

5. See chapter 1, below.
6. See for instance Jean-Jacques Servan-Schreber, *Le defi Americain* (Paris, 1967).
7. John Holmes, "Canada and the USA," *The Lamp* (Fall, 1971), p. 8. See also Professor Underhill's views below, pp. 22–23.

To achieve the greatest benefit from a study of American influences on Canada for these various purposes, a new approach is needed. In the past, interest has concentrated too narrowly on the story of Canadian-American relations rather than on the process of assimilation or Americanization. One obvious reason for this has been that, as it was Canadians who were more interested, the question of the preservation of Canadian sovereignty became the principle objective of research and writing. However, as it was virtually impossible to write about many Canadian topics without considering American experience, many Canadian scholarly works showed the extent of Americanization, or of parallel development, in Canadian society. For instance Delbert Clark's studies of religion, urbanism, and manufacturers' associations all revealed an awareness of the American presence. In his discussion of "Crestwood Heights," a sociological study said to be based on a Toronto suburb, Professor Clark speaks of "American" or "North American" problems without specifically mentioning or distinguishing "Canadian" problems.[8] In Canada, therefore, a start has been made towards exploring the nature and extent of American influence even though most general studies of Canada pass it off briefly or only relate it to the problem of the survival of Canadian sovereignty. A similar interest in comparative studies has, however, not emerged in the United States because consideration of American problems does not require a similar examination of Canadian influence on the United States or a discussion of parallel developments.

Before summarizing the contribution of these present essays to the study of American influence on Canadian development, a topic which is as wide as it is important, it is desirable to survey earlier collaborative and individual effort in the study of American-Canadian relations because this has already thrown some light on the nature and effect of American influences on Canada.

The most substantial attempt made so far has been the Carnegie

8. Samuel D. Clark, *The Suburban Society* (Toronto, 1966). See also Professor Clark's other works: *The Canadian Manufacturers' Association* (Toronto, 1939); *Church and Sect in Canada* (1942); *The Social Development of Canada* (1942); *The Developing Canadian Community* (1962).

series of studies edited by Dr. James Shotwell and financed by American money. This program demonstrates certain short-comings in the study of assimilation. Because the series figures prominently in a paper by Dr. Berger in this volume, it will not be dealt with at length here. It will suffice to say that there was a dichotomy of purpose. The study was described in a press statement in 1934 as "the history of two nations emerging side by side on a single continent . . . history collected and studied from the point of view of inter-relations in economic, political, and social spheres"; [9] and it proposed to offer "a unique record of the inter-relations of two modern nations." [10] When the proposal was discussed at a preliminary conference in 1933, however, Allan Nevins put his finger on a basic difficulty. Was this program to be a history of the two countries, in which case it would include material about each not related to the other, or was it to be restricted to Canadian-American relations as such? Shotwell's reply, that it had been agreed at an earlier conference at Banff that it would be a study of Canadian-American relations but not merely of the facts which deal narrowly with the inter-action of Canada and the United States, and that there should be enough of the comparative aspect to bring an understanding of the common North American elements, suggested that there might nevertheless be restrictions that would exclude important matter that would demonstrate differences.[11] Yet study of differences between the two countries would be the very material that would reveal to each country what the other was really like and so would facilitate a study of the process of assimilation and its effects.

Dr. Berger shows in his essay in this volume that Shotwell's aim was to portray Canadian-American relations as an example of internationalism in action. Some later volumes in the series concentrated on Canadian development in a way that was not at all congruent with Shotwell's ideas of either continentalism

9. *Toronto Globe,* May 7, 1934, clipping in Carnegie Series file, Trotter Papers, Douglas Library, Queen's University.
10. "Canadian-American Research Project, April, 1935," in *ibid.*
11. "Canadian-American Relations, [1933] Conference on Research," pp. 28–29, in *ibid.*

or internationalism. The original plan for the Carnegie series proposed about forty-five volumes.[12] Only twenty-six were actually completed. Nine dealt with political or diplomatic relations, and three or four of these had a virtually exclusive Canadian content. All these nine volumes had some bearing on the impact of the United States on Canadian development, but it was secondary to their main interest. The remaining four regional studies, three studies of population movements, one study of Canadian attitudes, and three comparative economic studies were somewhat more relevant to a study of American influences exerted on Canada.[13] However, it was clear in all of them that this was not the prime purpose of the series, and most of them threw only incidental light on the consequences of impact for the two societies. The Shotwell series had, in effect, been partially captured by Canadian nationalists like Harold Innis and Donald Creighton. They told only the Canadian side of the story of the two nations. As a consequence the value of the Carnegie series as a study of the influence of the United States on Canadian development automatically declined.

Much the same sort of things can be said about the series of conferences on Canadian-American relations held at Queen's University, Kingston, Ontario, and St. Lawrence University, Canton, New York, which was an outgrowth of the same movement that organized the Carnegie series of research studies. It, too, was largely concerned with cultivating good international relations and, as it came in the late thirties, in developing a common stand in face of a hostile world. It was not devoted to examining influences in the sense of either domination or assimilation.[14]

Another series of scholarly studies of Canadian-American re-

12. "A Survey of Canadian-American Relations" (Carnegie Endowment for International Peace, Division of Economics and History, June, 1935), in *ibid.*
13. See the list in the last volume that was published in the series, J. B. Brebner, *North Atlantic Triangle* (New Haven and Toronto, 1945).
14. See Reginald G. Trotter and Albert B. Corey (eds.), [*Fourth*] *Conference on Canadian-American Affairs . . . under the joint auspices of Queen's University, the St. Lawrence University,* [*and*] *the Carnegie Endowment for International Peace* (Boston, 1941). Previous conferences had been held alternately at Kingston, Ontario, and Canton, New York, in 1935, 1937, and 1939.

lations is now in process of production. It is the work of the Canadian-American Committee which is jointly sponsored by the Private Planning Association of Canada and the National Planning Association in the United States. This committee was set up in 1957. The first of these sponsors, the Private Planning Association of Canada, which was created for the purpose of undertaking independent and objective study of Canadian problems and policies mainly in the fields of economic affairs, and of Canada's international problems with other countries, was, however, actually not set up until a year later than its agent, the Canadian-American Committee; and once again the effort was largely financed by American money, this time from the Ford Foundation. A strong initiative therefore seems to have stemmed from the United States. The original incentive for the Canadian-American Committee appears to have come from business interests in both countries which were anxious to promote trade exchanges and to have been largely inspired by concern about the growth of Canadian restrictive protectionism.

Many of the committee's publications emanating from Washington have been anonymous "statements" or "staff reports" rather than academic research papers; but a substantial number of scholarly publications have been published under an author's name. As in the Shotwell series, the majority of these have been written by Canadians, including Canadians resident in the United States. The Canadian-American Committee series is narrower in scope than the Carnegie series in that its studies deal with Canadian-American trade relations and with industries of interest to both countries. Its studies therefore contain information relevant to only one aspect of the impact of the United States on Canada, economic domination; and again assimilation is discussed only incidentally. Some of the studies have referred to the difficulties Canada has in seeking to cooperate on equal terms with a more powerful neighbor. When this fact is taken into consideration along with the organization by the Private Planning Association of a Canadian Trade Committee to "examine Canada's international trading position and commercial policies" (which occurred in 1961),[15] this special concern for Canada's disadvantages indicates that, as in the Shotwell series, even though the Canadian economists associated with the program appear to be continentalists rather than nationalists, there is a trend towards exploring Canadian, rather than mutual, problems.

Some Canadian royal commissions are usually regarded as having been set up specifically to investigate the American impact on Canada. Foremost among these are the Royal Commission on National Development in the Arts, Letters, and Sciences, the Royal Commission on Canada's Economic Prospects, the Royal Commission on Broadcasting, and the Royal Commission on Publications. Although the terms of reference of only one of these commissions, that on publications, referred to the problem of American influence, and then only obliquely as "foreign," [16] it can be discerned between the lines that that question is their chief concern. Reluctance to admit the real objective of one of the commissions caused chapter 2 of the Massey report to be called coyly "The Forces of Geography"; but the index to the volume indicates more bluntly that it deals with "American influences." That chapter concluded that "American influences in Canadian life to say the least are impressive . . . a vast and disproportionate amount of material coming from a single alien source may stifle rather than stimulate our own creative effort. . . . We are now spending millions to maintain a national independence which would be nothing but an empty shell without a vigorous and distinctive cultural life." [17]

The commission reported on the generosity of American foundations to Canadian scholars and artists, on extensive Canadian use of American institutions of higher learning, libraries, and books, and on the American invasion by film, radio and peri-

15. See the information given about the Private Planning Association of Canada in its Canadian Trade Committee series. The parallel statement given in the Canadian-American Committee series conceals the fact that the committee was established a year before its sponsor in Canada.

16. [Canada], Royal Commission on Publications, *Appendices*, B, "Commission of Appointment."

17. [Canada], Royal Commission on National Development in the Arts, Letters, and Sciences, 1949–51, *Report* (Ottawa, 1951), pp. 11–18, 507.

odical, subjects investigated by other royal commissions. It then went on to suggest that the Canadian government should support cultural development in Canada. It noted elsewhere that, if it did, it would diverge from practice in the United States which was "the one conspicuous exception to the general rule that modern governments are increasingly becoming the principal patrons of the arts." [18]

The Massey Commission's report and the briefs and evidence presented to it, were constructive in the sense of encouraging Canadian development rather than merely blocking American importation. Yet it is noticeable that when the commission referred to Canadian identity it became vague and abstract rather than concrete and specific. "There are important things in the life of a nation which cannot be weighed or measured. The intangible elements [which] are . . . essential . . . give a nation not only its essential character but its vitality as well." [19] The Massey report did not give concrete examples or illustrations of Canadian identity and did not attempt to define or describe it. All it did in this regard was to refer to Mr. Churchill's invocation of the spiritual heritage of Britain in 1940, to the vitality of life which had made French-Canada survive, and to the adherence of United Empire Loyalists to a common set of beliefs. Apart from these references, it merely talked of "certain habits of mind and convictions which [Canadians] . . . shared and would not surrender." [20] It did not attempt to illustrate these more precisely.

An attempt to define national character, national spirit, and national traditions, the things that go to make up national identity, would indeed have led inevitably merely to an elaboration of clichés. The commission therefore wisely allowed its detailed proposals for the stimulation of the arts and letters to speak for themselves. It is noticeable that the commission's offspring, the Canada Council, has also not attempted to define Canadian culture. Nor has the council clearly indicated whether it regards that its task is to foster Canadian culture or culture in Canada, two things that may be quite different.

18. *Ibid.*, p. 273.   19. *Ibid.*, p. 4.   20. *Ibid.*

Inevitable vagueness in the Massey report about the makeup of national identity was accompanied by an inability to define fully and precisely the nature of the American influence upon Canadian culture which the commission had been tacitly established to offset. In the report and the briefs presented to the commission there are few specific references to American influence and its effects, apart from those noted above. One of the few specific references incidentally suggested a possible explanation of why they are so few. B. K. Sandwell wrote in his brief, "Present Day Influences on Canadian Society," "the culture of English-speaking Canada is so little differentiated from that of the United States that when the Americans are not dealing with their own politics they seem to be speaking with the same body of general assumptions as if they were Canadians." Indicating that in French-Canada, in addition to the language barrier, there was a quite different attitude and philosophy, he concluded that because of easy communication and a long boundary "the Canadian people, especially those of the English tongue, must inevitably be highly receptive to every kind of communication from the United States." [21]

Like the reports, the briefs presented to all the other aforementioned royal commissions speak positively of Canadian development rather than negatively of adverse American influence which, if referred to at all, is obliquely mentioned merely as "alien." Furthermore, like the reports, the briefs tend to interest themselves in aspects of control, penetration, and infiltration and have less to say about the borrowing or unconscious assimilation of American ways of life and ways of doing things. The large number of briefs about various industries and other aspects of the economy presented to the Royal Commission on Canada's Economic Prospects is particularly noteworthy in this respect. Although these conform to the usual theme of considering American influence in the sense of domination, they nevertheless contain considerable information that helps to throw light on the

21. [Canada], Royal Commission on National Development in the Arts, Letters, and Sciences, "Present Day Influences on Canadian Society," in *Royal Commission Studies: A Selection of Essays Prepared for the Royal Commission. . . .* (Ottawa, 1951), p. 6.

nature and extent of the Canadian approximation towards the American economic pattern. What they offer is, however, only a scattering of source material for a study of that aspect of the problem of Canadian-American relations. The Economic Commission's reports are not a comprehensive study of Americanization.

The amount of empirical evidence based on research about the assimilating effect of American influence on Canadian life is thus noticeably small. Everybody knows and says that American influence on Canadian life is very great; but little research has been done to substantiate this belief or to find out whether or not the American influence is actually greater or smaller than the average American and Canadian readily believes. One reason for the neglect of this kind of investigation is the vagueness of the question. Another is the vast extent of its ramifications. A third is the difficulty of disentangling environmental influences, influences from a common inheritance, and mutual interreaction. A fourth difficult problem is to distinguish between Americanization and modernization.

A few monographs and special studies must be mentioned. The earliest comprehensive examination of assimilation was by Sir Robert W. Falconer, President of the University of Toronto, in 1925. He pioneered by getting beyond governmental relations and by talking of "the world of the average man." There he found parallel causative factors in both countries, for instance Puritanism, and also the frontier spirit. He noted examples of direct copying or borrowing, for instance Canadian adoption of the American school system, and so many social influences that only a few could be included in his book, for instance service clubs, a superficial enthusiasm for comradeship and democratic friendliness, the media of communications, and the internationalization of sport. He commented on the inflow of American vocabulary, including some older words that had dropped out of use in Britain. He concluded that the average Canadian, while adopting much from his neighbor, has modified what he has received through his own individuality, and at the same time has "kept open the channels along which new power has been constantly brought from the British Isles to reinforce the ruling conceptions of his life."

In addition to the world of the average man, Falconer mentioned common elements of population, boundaries, fisheries, Canadian nationalism, trade and commerce, the world of higher education, and the concept of Canada as an interpreter, as topics that threw light on his study of the Canadians' view of the United States.[22] All of these bear on the problem of assimilation.

Four years later a rather deeper study by Hugh L. Keenleyside made a survey of these points of contact between the two North American peoples which he was to claim later to have been "the first published attempt at a comprehensive view." He came to the conclusion that it was probable that there was a more complete knowledge of the relations between Canada and the United States than of any other two countries in the world.[23] However, the subject had in fact not by any means been exhausted, or even as yet thoroughly researched as a question of cultural assimilation.

In the same year that Keenleyside's book appeared, there appeared another study that showed how particular aspects of the problem can and should be dealt with in greater depth. The Professor of American History and Government at Harvard, William B. Munro (who was born in Ontario), when lecturing at the University of Toronto on American influences on Canadian Government, indicated many analogies between American and Canadian government. Munro spoke approvingly of the high standards of English government and administration: free government, its enforcement of law, its administration of justice, and its encouragement of municipal home rule; and he urged Canadians not to give up this heritage lightly. He said, "There is no such thing as 'manifest destiny' as far as political standards are concerned." But he also showed that in many respects the American example, or the similarity of the common North Ameri-

22. Sir Robert Falconer, *The United States as a Neighbour from a Canadian Point of View* (Cambridge, 1925).
23. H. L. Keenleyside, *Canada and the United States: Some Aspects of the History of the Republic and the Dominion* (New York, 1929; and the revised edition coauthored by Gerald Brown, 1952).

can environment, had already wrought many changes. Thus he noted that Canada tended in theory to follow the British concept of political patronage but in practice adopted the American system. He also said that many other Canadian departures from time-honored British practice had been "smuggled" across the border, and had often become fully naturalized, before they were discovered. In this connection he instanced the partisan role of the speaker in the legislature, rigidity of the caucus, and gerrymandering of electoral districts. He commented that Canadian political parties had British names, but not the same principles. Despite variations from American electoral procedure and party discipline, Canadian political parties were akin to American parties in many ways, for instance in the interplay of economic and political issues caused by sectionalism, in the influence of the West and the frontier spirit, in the rise of new parties with idealist goals, and in the similarity between the influence of the "solid South" and the Province of Quebec.

Munro's belief that the Turner thesis of national development would be repeated in Canada does not now find many supporters, but his belief that city government in Canada has been even more susceptible than national political practice to American example stands up well. He declared that American practices would continue to flow in, especially when they came incognito. More important still, he showed that the Canadian concept of federalism, which was deliberately fashioned to put more strength in the central government than in the United States, had appeared just at the time when the Civil War had altered the American pattern. Since that time the strength of the central government in Canada had been steadily eroded by judicial practice. Munro noted that despite the intentions of the founders the two federal systems were steadily approximating towards each other, a situation that may no longer be true.[24]

One study originally planned for the Shotwell series appeared separately. It was an investigation of the mining industry by

24. William Bennett Munro, *American Influences on Canadian Government: The Marfleet Lectures delivered at the University of Toronto* (Toronto, 1929), pp. 3–7, 16, 71–92, 105, 141, *et passim.*

Professor E. S. Moore of the University of Toronto. Far more than any volume in the Shotwell series it emerged as a comparative study of both countries. Entitled *American Influence in Canadian Mining*, although the author found it impossible to discover the extent of American participation and therefore could not tell the full story of the influence in the sense of domination because records were either not available to him, were nonexistent, or were insufficiently revealing, he was able to give much evidence of the introduction of American capital, American personnel, American equipment, and American methods, and of their effect on the industry. Moore found that one reason for American influence in Canada was the fact that the United States was a world leader in the field. He showed that the trade in minerals between Canada and the United States was a great factor in Canadian development.[25]

American economic influence on Canada was also the subject of a seminar at the Commonwealth Studies Center at Duke University in 1958 which published a suggestive volume on the subject. The project was organized, edited, and published in the United States but the speakers in the seminar were all Canadians, mainly economists. It covered general American economic influences with a separate treatment for Quebec (done by Maurice Lamontagne, a political scientist) and also special studies of agriculture, investment, and labor organization. However, here again the chief interest was on government and business policy and their effects, rather than on assimilation.[26]

Despite the fact that the amount of empirical research has been very limited, interest in the influence of the United States on Canada has inspired many public lectures by distinguished academics who have made generalizations about the relationship of the two countries. Professor George M. Wrong of the University of Toronto lectured on *The United States and Canada: A Political Study*, as early as 1921 in order to promote "better understanding"; but his talk was very superficial and not as

25. E. S. Moore, *American Influences in Canadian Mining* (Toronto, 1941), pp. xvi–xvii, xix, 130–134.
26. Hugh G. J. Aitken, *et al., The American Economic Impact on Canada* (Durham, N.C., 1959).

valuable as Falconer's and Munro's.[27] Another lecture on this subject was given at Carleton University in 1958 by Professor Jacob Viner, a Canadian-born Professor of Economics at Princeton. He made particular reference to art and learning and not to "the different tribal rituals of dietary habits of the anthropologists." He said that he was not sure whether English-Canadian culture in this sphere was "substantially different from American culture" but he noted the effect of common linguistic origins, the effect of disparity in size, and the fact that Americans were "more cosmopolitan" than Canadians. However, here again a penetrating analysis was based on general observation by an intellectual rather than on a solid body of substantiated research.[28]

Senior scholars giving such ceremonial lectures in the neighboring country, which has superficially been one of the most fertile sources of publication about assimilation and differences, possess the balance, judgment, and wisdom, as well as the necessary experience and knowledge of the neighbor, to make useful statements. Younger scholars embarking on comparative research studies too often know only one side of the border and are governed by prejudice when they speak of the country they do not know. An extreme example of this is a Denver doctoral thesis in which the author concluded that during the 1950's the United States leaned over backward to accommodate a partnership with Canada but that Canada did not reciprocate.[29] But even excellent books by more mature scholars like Melvin Conant and Jon McLin on Canadian defense reveal that an American author often does not really know what makes Canada tick.[30] These scholars might now want to revise some of their conclusions of Canadian waywardness in the light of recent revelations about the conduct of American foreign policy.

27. G. M. Wrong, *The United States and Canada: A Political Study* (New York, 1921).

28. Jacob Viner, *Canada and Its Giant Neighbour* ([Ottawa], 1958).

29. James Richard Wagner, "Partnership: American Foreign Policy toward Canada, 1953–57," Ph.D. dissertation, University of Denver, 1966.

30. E.g., Melvin Conant, *The Long Polar Watch: Canada and the Defense of North America* (New York, 1962); and Jon B. McLin, *Canada's Changing Defense Policy, 1957–1963: The Problem of a Middle Power in Alliance* (Baltimore, [1967]).

This problem of the need to have sound knowledge of both countries explains why the most reliable comparative research that has been done has come from Canadian scholars resident in the United States. Now that the brain drain has been reversed, it may be that the future will bring more comparative studies by Americans resident in Canada who should become equally well qualified.

In the fifties and sixties, fear of American economic domination and also of the "Americanization" of Canadian universities (and therefore of much of Canadian intellectual life and thought) as a result of a great invasion of American professors, coupled with heightened Canadian nationalism, brought several books protesting against, or complaining about American influence. Cases in point are George Grant's *Lament for a Nation: The Defeat of Canadian Nationalism,* Walter Gordon's *A Choice for Canada: Independence or Colonial Status,* Donald Creighton's *Canada's First Century,* and Kari Levitt's *Silent Surrender: The Decolonization of Canada.*[31] Being consciously polemical, all these authors tend to write in hyperbole, to exaggerate, and to oversimplify in order to convince. They make the fullest possible use of the growing evidence of American economic domination and intellectual penetration, and also of the ordinary Canadian's apathy without, however, plumbing the depth of that mythical person's intense patriotism and basic anti-Americanism. American imperialism and continentalism are widely disparaged in Canada, and not only by intellectuals.

Nevertheless, intellectuals have been responsible for much of the present excitement. Frank Underhill wrote in his introduction to a series of essays on *Nationalism in Canada* edited by Peter Russell, "we cannot at present discuss our relations with the United States in a cool, rational frame of mind." He declared that the "cool rational intellectuals" who contributed the essays in the volume accepted assumptions about Americans "which are the precise twentieth century equivalents of those nineteenth century assumptions about our Canadian national superiority

31. Published respectively Toronto, 1965; Toronto, 1966; London, 1970; Toronto, 1969.

at which we all now smile with genial irony." As examples he noted the belief that the Canadian "mosaic" differs from the American "melting-pot," and that Canadian international policy is better for the world (he noted cynically that it is certainly cheaper) than American imperialist power politics. Underhill said, however, that he believed that ordinary Canadians, without in any sense being in danger of losing their Canadian identity, are subconsciously experimenting with some new form of international relations, and he wrote, "Our [Canadian] social scientists have not yet discovered the new categories of thought into which this merging new relationship may be fitted." With his usual flare for coining phrases, he said that Canada's alarmist intellectuals were "archaists suffering from hardening of the categories," and that it is the "mean sensual Canadians who are in the avant garde." [32] Although this point of view is, like that of the nationalists, based more on intuition than proof, it seems to contain a germ of truth; but it also overlooks the extent to which ordinary Canadians are conditioned to be anti-American.

A flood of books about various aspects of American "imperialism" or "continentalism," from James M. Minifie's *Peacemaker or Powder-monkey,* and *Open at the Top,* to Robin Mathews's and James Steele's *The Struggle for Canadian Universities: A Dossier,* and to Ian Lumsden's collection of essays entitled *Close the 49th Parallel: The Americanization of Canada,* [33] has helped to create an atmosphere in which impartial research has become difficult. Nevertheless, despite all the obstacles that have so far prevented it, there is need for a large program of comparative studies of Canada and the United States. The program laid down for the Carnegie series indicated the areas that must be explored. But a new program should not be aimed, like the Carnegie series was, at internationalist continentalism, and should not be allowed to diverge to one-sided studies of Canada. Comparative studies should necessarily be done by scholars with knowledge of both countries. They should avoid

32. Peter Russell (ed.), *Nationalism in Canada* (Toronto, 1966), p. xix.
33. Published respectively, Toronto, 1960; Toronto, 1964; Toronto; 1970; Toronto, 1970.

preconceived ideas about continentalism and American imperialism on the one hand, or about the essential similarity of Americans and Canadians on the other. What is needed is statistical and analytical study of ideologies, attitudes, institutions, and behavior in both countries, and in various disciplines, to discover the real extent and nature of American influence. We need to know whether American influence is greater or smaller than is generally believed, and whether it is increasing or diminishing. We must find out how fast it is changing and how far it affects the preservation of Canadian autonomy and the Canadian identity. Much work needs to be done in regard to ideological transfers, industrial and technical influences, the interchange of population, labor relations, the effect of the media, various regional exchanges, governmental and commercial practice, cultural influences, and in every other aspect of life. We need to discover where American influences have been strongest and where they have been weak. We need to know whether they operated by conscious American plantation, by conscious Canadian borrowing or imitation, or by unconscious assimilation. We need to know how assimilation relates to economic and political domination or influence. We need to know whether assimilation in certain fields coincides with or precludes the maintenance of a sturdy sense of Canadian identity.

The formation of a new Association for Canadian Studies in the United States in 1970 should serve to recruit laborers to work in this vast vineyard. At its first conference, held at Duke University in April, 1971, it took up the theme of the influence of the United States on Canadian development in order to pioneer the way. But the small number of studies presented at the conference and now published in this book can only touch slightly on this vast subject. They serve chiefly to show that, while the subject of Canadian-American relations appears to be shopworn or frustrated by polemics, comparative study of Canada and the United States is a vast unexplored field.

Most of the essays presented here deal with topics that are not necessarily being approached for the first time, but they have a different objective both from the one-time pious hope to promote good understanding and from the present pathological obsession with the alleged menace to Canadian existence. They seek to explore the actual nature of American influence in the belief that impartial scholarship will both promote good relations and at the same time help to preserve Canada's distinctive identity and interests. What the *Preliminary Report* of the Royal Commission on Bilingualism and Biculturalism experimentally called "the presence of the United States in Canada" [34] is not new. It is as old as Canada itself. Yet, though much is already known about it, much more remains to be discovered.

The essays that follow cast only a little more light on the nature of American influence on Canadian development. Being written by independent scholars each with his or her own point of view, they do not pretend to produce a consensus. Dr. Mildred Schwartz, a Canadian teaching in the United States, asserts that, while direct political influence on Canada in the sense of control is minute, by either conscious introduction or by subconscious imitation there is a complex form of adaptation in certain aspects of the political process that would be difficult to prevent, partly because it is a result of the bureaucratization of modern government. Hence, although direct influence in the sense of direct control may be moderate, influence on political development through assimilation may be even harder to counter than influence in other aspects of life. This could potentially have enormous implications for Canada's future awareness of a separate identity.

Dr. Kornberg, also a Canadian, similarly indicates that there is difficulty in distinguishing between Americanization and innovations that are natural developments on a universal or at least a general scale. As he is a behaviorist, he is not prepared to accept the thesis advanced by Ellen and Neal Wood [35] that the

34. [Canada], Royal Commission on Biculturalism and Bilingualism, *Preliminary Report* (Ottawa, 1965), p. 56. It is interesting that there is more direct reference to American influences on Canada in this investigation of internal difficulties than there is in the reports of the royal commissions to investigate American influence.

35. Ellen and Neal Wood, "Canada and the American Science of Politics," in Ian Lumsden (ed.), *Close the 49th Parallel: The Americanization of Canada* (Toronto, 1970).

adoption of quantifying techniques in Canada is Americanization and is also stultifying and conservative. The inflow of American political scientists into Canadian universities, deplored by Mathews and Steele, he shows to have been due to Canada's own problems and needs. He might have added that the inflow is partly caused by the attraction of higher Canadian salaries which are the result of taking advantage of scarcity in Canada. He produces statistics to show that the inflow of Americans has not led to a neglect of the study of Canada. His paper is much more than a study of American influence; it is a valuable contribution to the study of an important aspect of the intellectual development of Canada.

Robert Gilpin, an American studying the American economic impact on Quebec, starts with the premise that the American economy is dominant and exerts its influence in its own interest. He says that Canada is therefore internationalist in the sense of seeking an alternative to United States imperialism. But while economic forces are leading to integration of the two economies, political resistance to them leads to conflict. Professor Gilpin shows that Canadian problems arising from federal-provincial relations, and expecially from Quebec's aspirations, serve to weaken Canada in its struggle against American economic domination and therefore increase American influence on Canadian development.

On the other hand, in a specialized study of the Automative Agreement another American, Carl Beigie, asserts that in that important part of the industrial economy, Canada's political initiative succeeded in producing a unique agreement on cooperation, but that this was only because the United States did not realize its significance. He forecasts that the Automotive Agreement is therefore not a precedent that will follow in other industries, and he warns that Canada must therefore seek other means of protecting its interests, in his opinion by pushing for a beneficial general trade treaty with the United States. He thus shows that political action furthered Canadian interests in the past and he points to difficulties in the future.

Neither of these essays on economic relations discusses the

effect of multinational corporations, or how they can be controlled by government; and both tend to support the case made by the radical critics of those corporations in so far as they assert that political forces must be taken into account. They also suggest that the panacea of wide free trade advocated by some economists is a pipe dream. But as usual in this much debated area of Canadian-American economic relations, both essays concern themselves with domination and trade relations rather than with the transfer of methods of doing business, or of organizing production and their consequences. There is room for further study of the quiet impact of American dynamism and management technique as well as American capital on Canadian economic development.

The concept that "international" trade unions are a form of American imperialism and are made necessary because international capitalism (that is the multinational corporation) can only be opposed by large and powerful international unions, has long held sway in certain quarters in Canada. Although Dr. Babcock, an American scholar, subtitled his doctoral dissertation on the AFL in Canada "A Study in American Labor Imperialism," he produces evidence in the paper published here to prove that Samuel Gompers seized control of the Trades and Labour Congress in Canada merely as part of his bitter struggle against dual unionism in the United States. Dr. Babcock suggests that this led to lasting grievances and to nationalist countermovements on the part of Canadian Labor.

However, Dr. Abella, a Canadian from York University, argues that some of these Canadian countermovements were based on a mistaken belief in the value of American aid. He shows that a protesting CIO was "dragged unwillingly into Canada" because Canadian workers, impressed by its work in the United States, were blinded by its reputation. The real organizing was done by Canadians with money collected in Canada. Many of the Canadian organizers happened to be Communists. It was therefore the attitude of Canadian workers who believed, possibly wrongly, that CIO affiliation would get them a bigger wage packet, rather than the continentalist ideas of Canadian organizers or the ambitions of American trade-union leaders that, in Dr. Abella's opinion, allowed Canadian unions to become dominated by foreigners, a situation that is probably unique. The "invasion" of the CIO, as many Canadians have seen it, led to a pathological reaction on the part of Mitch Hepburn, premier of Ontario, and to drastic strike-breaking activities which even the multinational General Motors Corporation disliked; and Hepburn was motivated not so much by nationalism as by a desire to serve his capitalist cronies who feared unionization in Northern Ontario gold mines. Nationalism and anti-Americanism have thus served domestic Canadian special interests. However, it is clear that Canadian imitation and the adoption of association with American institutions can be as menacing to Canada's interests and identity as can deliberate American imperialism. What is not known is how far activity was generated simultaneously in Canada as a consequence of American example or as a result of parallel circumstances. This is one of the problems met frequently in the study of the American influence on Canadian development.

Only two purely regional studies are presented in this set of case studies. Dr. Lee, a Canadian teaching in California, shows that the Western provinces gained substantially from the adoption of American technical know-how in irrigation measures but that, in the period with which he deals, the question of water-sharing which is now an issue, was not raised as a by-product of that cooperation. The alternatives of public or private ownership were discussed, but the course followed was not dictated by American example. On the other hand, according to Dr. Clark, another Canadian who has taught for many years in the United States, although they had long suffered from innate disadvantages arising from their location and their lack of resources, the Maritimes were held back by their proximity to more prosperous American states. Both of these studies show that although the American impact differs considerably from one part of Canada to another, yet in each case it was powerful, perhaps dominant, in its effect.

Two studies in language and literature explore special problems in cultural assimilation. Dr. Klinck, from the University of Western Ontario, shows that in the early 19th century, although Canada was stimulated by both British and American influences, the latter flourished more vigorously in the North American climate. It is interesting that in that day, when communications were poorer and costs of production infinitely lower, competition with cheaper United States periodicals helped to develop literary effort in Montreal, a result not found today. Finally, Dr. Hull, an American linguist, points out that the Americanization of the French language in Windsor (he argues that it should be called "Americanization" and not "Anglicization" because Canadians are a small numerical minority in the region and the influence is therefore chiefly American) has served to isolate the Windsor francophones from the rest of French-speaking Canada. American influence and proximity thus has had important effects on the literary and linguistic development of Canada.

These papers, taken as a whole, suggest that there is much mythology in the formation of Canadian attitudes towards the United States, that American influence is encouraged and enhanced by Canadian weaknesses and difficulties as well as by her relatively small population and wealth, and that these problems have ramifications that may affect the establishment of a strong identity. There is, however, little here to help to prove or disprove the contention of Canadian intellectuals that the Canadian public, by its apathy, is selling away its birthright. There is also nothing to counter the fear that assimilation to American models might weaken resistance to American domination or control. All that is amply demonstrated is that political action is important and that at times it has been effective.

Nationalism is an emotional abstract quantity which cannot be measured. Its implications for Canadian-American comparative studies and for Canadian-American relations require a vast amount of further research in very many areas. It should be added that Canadian concern about American penetration is also related to circumstances in the United States. When things go well there, Canadians rejoice in the benefits they receive from a wealthy near neighbor. When the United States gets into difficulties, Canadians fear that Canada will become absorbed and want to tear themselves away.

These essays also reveal that several important questions remain to be answered before adequate generalizations can be made about the importance of Canadian assimilation to the American model and can be assessed properly in an attempt to show its significance for Canadian development. The first question is whether the nature of that silent impact is sufficiently simplistic to make any meaningful generalizations possible. American pressure, or what Canadians assume to be American pressure, is related to many extraneous factors such as America's problems of world leadership, Canada's desire to perform a distinctive role in world affairs, concepts of internationalism on a universal or regional scale, and above all the universal desire to follow the modernizing path trodden earlier by the United States. What must be discovered is how far these many irrelevant factors can be disentangled from the essential elements of the American impact on Canada in order to make useful deductions possible.

A second question is how far the Canadian view of the United States derives from conditions or ideologies in Canada rather than from the actions or intentions of the United States, that is to say from myth. This point was stressed in the late David Potter's comments on Professor S. F. Wise's paper published in *Canada Views the United States*.[36] Canadians tend to see in the United States, and to dislike, those things which they oppose in Canada; they are inclined to possess a mythical stereotype of the United States that serves their own ends. Furthermore, what must be also explored is how far Canadian anti-Americanism is based on Canadian desires to propagate doctrines of public ownership in Canada or to resist business rivalry. Walter Gordon, long associated with Toronto financial interests, Mel Watkins and Stephen Hymer, radical economists, and Donald Creighton, nationalist conservative historian, make strange bedfellows! Their common support of economic nationalism does not establish the validity of whatever is common in their doctrine. If subjective

36. S. F. Wise and R. Craig Brown, *Canada Views the United States: Nineteenth Century Political Attitudes* (Seattle, 1967).

ideology and unrelated interests can be removed, what empirical evidence can be found to demonstrate the nature and effect of the American impact on Canada, and what must be done to counter it?

The third of these questions is whether or not the present rise of anti-Americanism in Canada, while different in form and intensity, is merely part of a continuing theme in Canadian history that has frequently reached critical temperature in the course of two centuries. Only on one of these occasions did it lead to a real showdown, in the War of 1812. Current concern is different from much that went before in that it stresses the concept of a "silent take-over" due to increasing American control, as well as American ownership, of vital parts of the Canadian economy. Annexation, or political control, is believed to be now of lesser significance, though not impossible. What must be decided is whether Canadian willingness to use political power to resist an economic take-over is now being seriously eroded by cultural pressures on the ordinary Canadian to the point of destroying Canada's identity. As yet there is no clear answer to this all-important question. But the future of two distinctive free societies in North America may depend on an understanding of, and an answer to this question even more than on the intentions of government, capitalists, labor leaders, or professors.

What is most important of all, whatever may be the ultimate destiny of two nations in North America, is that their past and future relations, particularly the influence of the greater on the lesser but also the way in which different answers have been found in each country to similar problems, must be thoroughly understood. In a world that is becoming modernized—or Americanized—and where people everywhere wish to be able to preserve the essential elements of their own distinctiveness as well as to benefit by economic growth, Canadian experience must not be overlooked.

1

Internationalism, Continentalism, and the Writing of History: Comments on the Carnegie Series on the Relations of Canada and the United States

Carl C. Berger

The idea of Canadian-American relations as a field for historical study is now such an accepted notion that it is difficult to appreciate that it was once an exciting discovery. Interpreters of Canada, of course, had hardly been unaware of the ways in which the continental environment influenced Canadian history, society and culture, or of the enormous and continuous impact of the United States upon its neighbor, but it was only in the late 1920's that increasing numbers of historians and social scientists grew conscious of the need to explore this relationship in a systematic fashion, and only in the 1930's and 1940's that the concepts of Canadian-American relations, of American influence on Canada, and of continental comparative history were clarified, elaborated and widely applied. Though the most impressive example of this preoccupation was the twenty-five volume series on Canadian-American relations published under the auspices of the Carnegie Endowment for International Peace between 1936 and 1945,[1] the impulse to discover the continental affinities

The research for this paper was made possible by a C. D. Howe Memorial Fellowship and it has benefitted from the criticism of my colleagues, C. P. Stacey and G. M. Craig.

1. A list of these volumes, some of which are only generally alluded to in the following pages, is given at the end of J. B. Brebner, *North Atlantic Triangle* (New Haven and Toronto, 1945).

of Canadian experience represented a general shift of perspective in the way in which Canadian history was conceived. It is appropriate for the purposes of this conference and in the general interests of self-awareness that some of the reasons behind this concern be examined and that some of the leading themes running through the approach be subjected to analysis.

I

The interest in Canadian-American relations in historical writing was a reflection of the growing magnitude and complexity of those relations in the 1920's and 1930's. The statistics of American investment in Canada, the movement of people back and forth across the border, and the existence of similar outlooks in world affairs, were subjects of discussion in the popular mind sometime before they provided a series of insights into history. Observers sensed that these relations were altering in character and that the fear and suspicion which had been so pronounced as late as 1911 were remnants of the past. The belief that the tendency of history moved in the direction of trust and understanding, and the heightened appreciation for the historical importance of Canadian-American relations, were broad and general, but a group of Canadian-born scholars teaching in the United States made it a particular discovery of their own. They first suggested that the North American aspects of the Canadian past be explored and the Carnegie series was largely a product of their efforts.

The education of Canadians in the universities of the United States was an old and familiar pattern. The prestige of the German-inspired seminar was at its height in the years before the World War and advanced graduate training in history and economics was practically unobtainable in Canada until the 1930's. Canadian students still made their way to the seats of learning in Britain, but the United States was closer and graduate assistance generous. Not only were the Canadian social sciences professionalized under the influence of the United States but a substantial part of the pioneering work in Canadian history and economics was done in the American graduate schools. In 1927 the editor of the *Canadian Historical Review* listed fifty-seven doctoral theses being written on Canadian topics; forty-four of these were being done in the United States, thirty-two by students whose first degree was Canadian. By 1933 the number of Ph.D. theses on Canada in progress had increased to one hundred seven, and seventy were by students registered in American universities.[2] By the mid-1930's there were more courses in Canadian history being taught in the United States than in Canada.

The large number of Canadian students trained in the United States could not all be absorbed back into Canada. The university establishments were small and in some quarters there existed a preference for Englishmen, or at least for Canadians educated in England, and a snobbish opinion of the allegedly fact-grubbing, over-specialized and unpolished products of the American seminars. In 1925 there were nearly six hundred graduates of Canadian universities holding academic appointments in the United States.[3] While it would be impossible to draw a collective portrait of this generation of academic expatriates, there were some experiences and reactions that did affect the way they looked back upon the country which had no place for their talents. They were immediately made aware by their residence in the United States of how much Canadians and Americans seemed alike in their social life and aspirations and how essentially misleading were those images of the United States, based largely on constitutional and political differences, which appeared so credible at a distance. One student at Chicago typified this reaction when he told Adam Shortt that "I am beginning to realize the significance of what you often said to us—that the boundary line is imaginary, and that really the people of Ontario and New York State have far more in common than the people of Ontario and Quebec."[4]

2. *Canadian Historical Review*, VIII (March, 1927), 51–55; *ibid.*, XIX (Sept., 1933), 296.
3. Sir Robert Falconer, *The United States as a Neighbour from a Canadian Point of View* (Cambridge, 1925), p. 206.
4. W. Swanson to A. Shortt, Jan. 13, 1906, Adam Shortt Papers, Douglas Library Queen's University.

James T. Shotwell, who went from Toronto to Columbia in 1898 and was caught up in the vibrant intellectual world of Charles Beard and James Harvey Robinson, was not conscious of having crossed cultural boundaries. "I suppose," he later recalled, "that I think of the academic world as one that has no territorial frontier and that the chief thing is to have the opportunity to make one's full intellectual contribution to anyone, anywhere, who is interested in it." This migration involved a change of citizenship but that was only a recognition of what he called a "North American nationality."[5] John Bartlet Brebner, who had studied at Toronto and Oxford before going to Columbia, had the same internationalist view of the community of learning. The differences which he found in these three universities were minor and superficial; their essential tasks were indentical.[6] For some these experiences tended to strengthen an internationalist perspective; it stimulated others, however, to assume a rather patronizing attitude to those Canadians who had remained in Canada. "For some reason or other," one of them noted, "the expatriated Canadians in the colleges here whom I know seem to represent Canada as essentially a dependency of the United States."[7] The temptation "to put a tack under Canadians who had stayed at home," Brebner added, was one which a number of expatriates found impossible to resist.[8]

In spite of that, most of these men retained an abiding and affectionate interest in the country of their birth, and it was a measure of the hold that Canada had upon them that they sought to reveal the significance of Canadian history to their American students. Some found that this could best be done by comparative history; others were moved to emphasize the American influences. In 1929, in a discussion of the American influence on Canadian govenment, William B. Munro, the Canadian-born Professor of

5. Shotwell to H. A. Innis, Aug. 23, 1946, H. A. Innis Papers, University of Toronto Library; James T. Shotwell, "A Personal Note on the Theme of Canadian-American Relations," *Canadian Historical Review*, XXVIII (March, 1947), 42.
6. J. B. Brebner, "Oxford, Toronto, Columbia," *Columbia University Quarterly*, XXIII (Sept., 1931), 224–40.
7. A. Gordon Dewey to R. G. Trotter, Dec. 21, 1933, R. G. Trotter Papers, Douglas Library, Queen's University.
8. J. B. Brebner, "McLaren—Generally," undated manuscript, Box #10, J. B. Brebner Papers, Butler Library, Columbia University.

Government at Harvard, began with the observation that the boundary had no economic, physiographic, ethnic or linguistic reason for existence; in the same year, Hugh Keenleyside, a Canadian graduate of Clark University, published the first survey of Canadian-American relations and anticipated nearly all the themes later examined in a more comprehensive fashion.[9] In 1931 Brebner appealed for a "continental contours" approach to North American history and his paper struck a responsive chord in Shotwell, the Director of the Division of Economics and History of the Carnegie Endowment for International Peace.[10] The series, originally planned for no less than forty-five volumes, secured the financial support of the Endowment largely through Shotwell's efforts, and Brebner became his chief adviser and planner of the historical volumes. The writing of the series was paralleled by conferences held at Canton, New York, and Kingston, Ontario, which were intended to provide a forum in which scholars might discuss their work and also a meeting place where journalists, educators and public figures from both countries could discuss current issues. The conferences were suggested and later largely organized by two historians: Albert Corey, a Canadian graduate of Clark who taught at the St. Lawrence University at Canton, and Reginald Trotter, a product of Queen's who had studied under Munro at Harvard, taught at Stanford, and returned to Queen's. The studies on the economic relations of the two countries was partly supervised by Jacob Viner, a graduate of McGill and Harvard, and then teaching at Chicago. The whole project was initiated, largely supervised, and partly written by Canadian-born scholars in the United States aided by scholars who were American-trained and living in Canada. There were, of course, participants whose backgrounds were quite different and in any case it would be misleading to draw rigid correlations between academic experience and

9. W. B. Munro, *American Influences on Canadian Government* (Toronto, 1929); H. Keenleyside, *Canada and the United States: Some Aspects of the History of the Republic and the Dominion* (New York, 1929).

10. J. B. Brebner, "Canada and North American History," in Canadian Historical Association, *Annual Report* (1931), pp. 37–48; J. B. Brebner to J. M. S. Careless, April 21, 1954, copy, Brebner Papers.

precise historical views. But, in spite of certain exceptions, Canadian-born academics in the United States were most receptive to the idea of continental history because its truth seemed confirmed by their own experience. The discovery of North America was in a sense a discovery of themselves. Far from subordinating the importance of Canada in North American history there was a tendency to exaggerate it: they hoped that the continental approach would enable Canadian historical writing to escape from parochialism and that it would counteract the isolation of United States historical thought. Perhaps only a Canadian could describe Canada and the United States, as Brebner did, as "Rival Partners," for Americans have seldom, if ever, thought of their neighbor as a genuine competitor.

The determination to seek out the North American dimension of Canadian experience was powerfully reinforced by a general impulse to broaden the scope and enlarge the framework of Canadian history. The main historical concern in the 1920's was Canada's evolution from colony to nation: the history of Chester Martin, William P. M. Kennedy and, in part, George M. Wrong was severely constitutional and political in character and its burden was the steady extension of the principle of responsible government from its first anticipations down to the formal recognition of Dominion autonomy. Their history was imperial in focus and stressed that responsible government, a Canadian invention, was the device which had transformed the British Empire into a Commonwealth of equal and cooperating nations. It was also internationalist in the sense that its leading exponents were critical of the excessive claims of national sovereignty; they praised the Commonwealth as an institution which had successfully reconciled national independence with cooperation in a supranational framework; and they saw it as a model for the League of Nations. These historians believed profoundly that Canada was a nation within a community of English-speaking peoples which included the United States. Beyond the cultural and linguistic unity lay a common tradition of representative government and liberty which expressed itself in different ways. There was therefore nothing incompatible between seeking out the similarities between Canada and the United States and still emphasizing the Commonwealth orientation in Canada's past and present. Indeed, it was necessary to reveal these affinities because it bolstered what many Canadians regarded as the mission of their country in the world—an interpreter within the Anglo-American universe. This idea of Canada as an interpreter was at least as old as the notion of the unity of the English-speaking community; it has been revitalized by the war and internationalist thought in the 1920's. It accorded Canada a strategic place in relation to the United States just as the record of constitutional progress placed her at the very center of the emergence of the Commonwealth. The first tentative steps in the exploration of Canada's relations with the United States were made by scholars like Wrong, who developed this conception of the moral unity of the British Commonwealth and the American Republic in his *Canada and the United States: A Political Study,* published in New York in 1921.

At the end of the 1920's and in the early 1930's this preoccupation with constitutional evolution was criticized by young historians who were inspired by the newer modes in American historical writing and urged a reinterpretation of Canadian history in the light of geographic, economic and social forces. American historical ideas left a large imprint on Canadian historical thought in these years, but from the point of view of the emergence of the conception of North American history Turner's frontier thesis was perhaps the most suggestive. Turner's legacy was ambiguous and diffuse but the core of his statement was that the United States was settled by wave upon wave of European peoples, that European habits of thought and institutions were altered in adapting them to unfamiliar locations, and that this process of transformation in the continuous westward movement was a major but not the only determinant in the development of a distinctive American nationality. To Canadian historians like A. R. M. Lower who were attracted to the approach, the frontier thesis was not so much a precise instrument of analysis as simply a general alertness to the ways in which the continental environment shaped the evolution of the nation.[11] It stimulated the tendency to take the European heritage for granted and to explore the ways in which it had been changed in the new world. The Liberal editor, John Dafoe, in his *Canada: An American Nation* (1935), three lectures delivered at Columbia University in 1933–34 and dedicated to Shotwell, suggested how the central problem of the constitutional historians could be reformulated in environmental terms. The foundations of both Canada and the United States, he contended, were laid by colonists who had lived in America for four or five generations divorced from English influences and confronting problems upon which European experience threw no light. The founders of both countries had brought the ideal of self-government from Britain but it was in America that the tradition of English liberty evolved into a genuine social democracy. That development was a joint achievement of the North American people and at bottom it was considered to be due to the indigenous environment which broke down European notions of class and aristocracy and favored individualism, equality and freedom.[12] For Dafoe the transformation of the British Empire into a free Commonwealth was largely the result of this dynamic North American force. It seemed that in this march of liberty Canada and the United States had common history. The crucial events in Canadian experience appeared as analogies of crucial events in American experience: the rebellions of 1837, for example, were parallels to the Jacksonian assault on privilege. Canadian political parties, despite their British labels, were the same conglomerations of sectional, economic and class interests as American political parties as depicted by Beard and Turner.[13] The immediate effect of looking at Canadian history in terms of these identities was to blur the dis-

11. A. R. M. Lower, "The Origins of Democracy in Canada," in Canadian Historical Association, *Annual Report* (1930), pp. 65–70; and his *My First Seventy-Five Years* (Toronto, 1967), p. 152. On the place of environmentalism in Canadian historical writing see J. M. S. Careless, "Frontierism, Metropolitanism, and Canadian History," *Canadian Historical Review*, XXXV (March, 1954), 1–21.
12. J. W. Dafoe, *Canada: An American Nation* (New York, 1935). For a similar view, see J. T. Shotwell, *The Heritage of Freedom: The United States and Canada in the Community of Nations* (New York, 1934).
13. F. H. Underhill, "The Development of National Political Parties in Canada," *Canadian Historical Review*, XVI (Dec., 1935), 367–87.

tinctions that Canadians had traditionally made between their "British" political and constitutional system and the republicanism of their neighbors. The word "Americanization" was neutralized: the developments to which it had referred were now regarded not as matters of unfortunate imitation or influence but rather as similar responses to the same pervasive environment.[14]

While the Turner thesis was nationalistic in origin and isolationist in implication it contained an insight which was applied on a much broader front. Herbert Bolton of the University of California, a former student of Turner and one of those who participated in the early stages of the planning of the Carnegie series, generalized the frontier thesis to apply to the entire western hemisphere. The western hemisphere idea, or the belief that the nations of North and South America were united by a common history and commitment to liberty, had a respectable ancestry running back to the eighteenth century; in the 1920's Bolton popularized the notion of hemispheric solidarity as a challenging field for historical attention. All the countries of this hemisphere, he argued, had shared in a profoundly significant historical experience. They had been colonized and settled by Europeans; in all of them European culture had been adjusted to different conditions and there had been struggles between the reactionary forces and the defenders of democracy; and all had revolted against European domination and achieved independence. This process, the real "Epic of Greater America," had stretched over centuries and though Bolton conceded that it was marked by unique adjustments he insisted that there nonetheless existed a pattern to which the histories of individual nations, including Canada, conformed. It was therefore just as reasonable to think of the countries of the hemisphere as having a common history as it was to conceive of a history of Europe which was more than the sum of its parts.[15]

14. J. B. Brebner, "The Interplay Between Canada and the United States," *Columbia University Quarterly*, XXVI (Dec., 1934), 335.

15. Herbert Bolton, *History of the Americas: A Syllabus with Maps* (Boston, 1928); and his "Epic of Greater America," *American Historical Review*, XXXVIII (April, 1933), 448–74. Arthur P. Whitaker, *The Western Hemisphere Idea: Its Rise and Decline* (Ithaca, 1954) sets Bolton's ideas into the general development of the theme.

A rather mutilated version of Bolton's hemispheric history supplied the framework for the study of Canadian and American relations. It was applied, rather parochially, exclusively to the continent north of Mexico, and the main themes which Bolton had found linking the histories of all the nations of the hemisphere were seen to be at work only in relation to Canada and the United States. Brebner, who was not convinced of the extensive claims made by the disciples of Turner, found Bolton's suggestions far more valuable.[16] The editor of the Carnegie series frequently proclaimed that its aim was to describe the real epic of America on a larger canvas, in terms of the spread of civilization westward and the conquest of the continent. There were, of course, sceptics, usually Canadian historians of the old school, who protested against the attempt to separate Canadian history too sharply from the history of the old world. But the popularity of the idea of environmentalism did much to rivet the attention of historians upon those processes which made the two nations of North America so alike and so different from Europe.

For Shotwell, the examination of Canadian-American relations was intended to serve a further purpose which overshadowed the simple historical satisfaction of describing the past. Shotwell's main concerns were world peace and internationalism and it was these twin goals that in his mind justified the financial support that the series received and constituted its chief relevance for world history. In terms of his own life and interests the series was a climax to his career and it constituted another argument that could tip the scales against the drift to irrationality and war. His concern with peace was nurtured in the Quakerism of his family, Gladstonian liberalism which he described as a "lasting heritage," and the prewar progressive movement.[17] A colleague of Robinson and Beard at Columbia, he sympathized with their efforts to reform historical writing in order to make history a more effective instrument of reform, and he was committed to the view that progressive history could serve the cause of peace and world order. He accompanied the American delegation to the Paris Peace Conference as an

16. J. B. Brebner, *Explorers of North America, 1492–1806* (London, 1933).
17. J. T. Shotwell, *Autobiography* (New York, 1961), p. 29.

advisor, was profoundly moved by the challenge of Woodrow Wilson, and was an enthusiastic supporter of the League of Nations. From 1914 to 1928 he directed the writing of the economic and social history of the World War under the auspices of the Carnegie Endowment. That history, itself a monument to the progressive faith in education and the role of experts in the cause of reform, eventually comprised one hundred fifty volumes written by two hundred collaborators from fifteen countries. It described in complex detail the social costs of war and its chief lesson was that, in the industrialized and interdependent modern world, war could no longer be regarded as a legitimate instrument of national policy because its consequences and ramifications were uncontrollable and unpredictable. Once that lesson was understood by public opinion, it would, Shotwell hoped, force governments to renounce the use of force.

Soon after the Carnegie history of the World War was completed Shotwell realized that the study of Canadian-American relations could be used for the same purposes. The history of the recent conflict had shown the horrendous costs of war; the study of the relations of the two North American countries, at peace with each other since 1814, would reveal the positive foundations of international understanding and peaceful cooperation.

There was nothing novel about looking at these two countries in this fashion: the myth of the unguarded frontier had been a cliché for at least a generation and the isolationist reaction to the World War gave it renewed vitality.[18] During the 1920's Canadian representatives at Geneva never tired of reminding Europeans of this singular tradition. Neither Shotwell nor any of the scholars later involved in the series, however, accepted the notion that the border had been unguarded and that relations

18. One of its most fulsome expressions was *The North American Idea* (Toronto, 1917), by Rev. James A. Macdonald, editor of the *Toronto Globe* and a director of the New York based World Peace Foundation. Mackenzie King frequently invoked it; see particularly his "One Hundred Years of Peace," an address delivered at Harvard in 1909, in his *The Message of the Carillon and Other Addresses* (London, 1927), pp. 163–178. Its uses in the isolationist armory of the 1920's is brilliantly traced by James Eayrs, *The Defence of Canada From the Great War to the Great Depression* (Toronto, 1964), "Introduction."

had been tranquil and undisturbed. That myth had been laid to rest by the historians and one of the projected volumes in the series on armaments and disarmament in North America bore the ironical subtitle, "The Military History of the Century of Peace between Canada and the United States." The myth of the undefended border, moreover, rested on the conviction that there were exceptional and unique circumstances in North America, the implication being that it could not therefore convey any meaningful lessons to the old world. Shotwell's point of departure was quite different: he recognized that throughout much of the 19th century Canadian-American relations were characterized by friction, suspicions and controversies. Peace had been preserved, not because it was never tested, but "in spite of grievances unredressed, of threats and policies filled with menace and of almost constant economic strain." [19] There had been many occasions when war might have broken out, but it never had, and despite some lingering tension and a subterranean anti-Americanism in Canada, the two countries had come to understand each other better, had cooperated more effectively than any other two states, and had ceased thinking of each other in military terms. With the breakdown of collective security in the world outside, the answer to how and why this had happened became urgent and, to Shotwell, Canadian-American history took on a universal interest because it contained the secrets for solving the most pressing problem of the time.

Participation in the project did not signify complete acceptance of Shotwell's purposes and in fact few, if any, of those involved shared his motives or explicitly endorsed his vision of the larger significance of Canadian-American relations. The twenty-five volumes which eventually appeared were not bound together by a homogeneous conception of history or an identifiable ideology to which each and every contributor subscribed. The Carnegie Endowment functioned as a combined Social Science

19. J. T. Shotwell, "The International Significance of the Canadian-American Peace Tradition," in R. L. Morrow (ed.), *Proceedings* [of the Conference on Educational Problems in Canadian-American Relations Held at the University of Maine, Orono, Maine, June 21–22, 1938] (Orono, Maine, 1939), p. 8.

Research Council and Canada Council to Canadian scholars in the 1930's and early 1940's; it advanced research funds and subsidized the publication of books which might not otherwise have appeared. Nearly every Canadian historian was at one time or another involved in the project, and the series embraced a number of works which were conceived independently, calculated to answer different questions, and appeared under its auspices mainly because of convenience. The design moreover was planned and launched in 1934 at the high-tide of North American isolationism, and completed during the early 1940's when world events made it impossible to conceive of continental relations in exclusively continental terms.

Individual scholars produced works which were more far-ranging than the title of the series suggested: A. L. Burt's *The United States, Great Britain and British North America* (1940) was a study of Anglo-American, not merely Canadian and American, diplomatic history; Harold Innis's *The Cod Fisheries* (1940) traced the complex history of an international economy involving Western Europe and North America over five centuries. The Carnegie enterprise also represented an alliance of historians, economists, sociologists and legal scholars who brought quite different approaches to bear; those historians who were suspicious of the present-minded new disciplines were wary of accepting the task of dealing with the antecedents of problems that were defined in terms of immediate needs. In his editorial prefaces Shotwell tried to fit these individualistic studies into his thesis about the universal significance of Canadian-American relations. In doing so he did not distort the essential conclusions of these books. While it should be repeated that the majority of the scholars saw themselves as working on precise questions and may have been indifferent to the wider ramifications of their research, most of their works did support the generalizations which Shotwell sought to establish. It is in this limited sense that the series—again with some exceptions—may be said to contain a certain unity of argument and a coherence of purpose.

II

The most persistent theme running through these volumes was the determination to reveal those processes of civilization which transcended national units and bound Canada and the United States together. There were two such elements which were regarded as particularly central—the interpenetration of economic activity and the interchange of populations. The volume on Canadian-American industry was the first of the series to appear and in his explanation of the project Shotwell invariably accorded large space to this aspect of the relationship. "From the standpoint of economic interest," he wrote in 1934, "the most important foreign relations of the United States are those with Canada. Not only is our trade with Canada larger than with any other single nation, but we have almost four billion invested in Canadian industries." One of the most urgent reasons for the series was to promote understanding and goodwill at a time when what Shotwell called "maladjustments," by which he probably meant economic nationalist solutions to the depression, threatened to disrupt the smooth interdependence of the 1920's.[20] The enormous growth of American investment, particularly during the World War and the ensuing decade, was invariably explained as natural and normal, a result of geography, culture, opportunity and the fortunate absence of government interference. It was considered inappropriate to refer to this as "economic imperialism" and even the word "penetration" was considered slightly provocative in some quarters. Though most analyses conceded that the impact of American capital had distorted Canadian economic development in certain directions and retarded the emergence of industrial science in Canada, the process was regarded as generally beneficial in accelerating growth and increasing prosperity. American direct investment did not constitute control over the Canadian economy,

20. "Outline of Plan: Survey of the Economic, Social, and Political Relations of Canada and the United States, May 12, 1934," p. 12, Trotter Papers.

and it did not imply a loss of political independence because the banks, press and transportation interests remained in Canadian hands. And, above all, it was widely believed that the relative extent of American investment was destined to decrease. Canada was rapidly becoming a creditor nation and Canadians had more invested in the United States on a per capita basis than Americans had in Canada. The actual decrease in the number of American companies set up in Canada during the early years of the depression also seemed to confirm that foreign investment would level off. The sober conclusion was that "in the future Canada will depend less and less on capital imports for its national development. It is possible that capital imports by Canada on a large scale are entirely a thing of the past . . ."[21] The size of American investment, in short, should cause no concern; and even if it did, it was bound to decrease anyway. The extent and historical character of this economic interdependence were further illustrated by studies of the development of the forest industry, labor relations, and railway interconnections, and the cumulative impression was to underline the essential unity of the continent and the superficiality of merely political designations in North American affairs. The existence of substantial economic interests of Canadians in the United States and Americans in Canada, furthermore, was said to constitute a basis of trust and a guarantee of good relations. Canada's Deputy Minister of Finance, W. C. Clark, voiced the almost universal opinion when he told the assembled scholars in 1935 that "these financial ties should contribute to a better understanding and a closer fellowship between the two countries."[22]

The historical and statistical investigation of the movements of population in North America in almost complete disregard for political frontiers buttressed the same point. The migration of New Englanders to Acadia and Nova Scotia, Loyalists and

21. Herbert Marshall, Frank A. Southard, Jr., and Kenneth W. Taylor, *Canadian-American Industry: A Study in International Investment* (New Haven and Toronto, 1936), p. 295.

22. W. C. Clark, "Movement of Capital," in W. W. McLaren, A. B. Corey, and R. G. Trotter (eds.), *Proceedings* [of the Conference on Canadian-American Affairs Held at St. Lawrence University, Canton, New York, June 17–22, 1935] (New York, 1936), p. 66.

late-Loyalists to British North America, French-Canadians to New England, Maritimers and Upper Canadians to the Mississippi Valley, and American farmers to the prairies, were unplanned, haphazard, and prompted mainly by the search for economic opportunity. The American historian of immigration, Marcus Hansen, wrote that these people viewed the continent as a whole. "It was not the United States and Canada. It was all America to them." They had settled the continent jointly and in unison, not just in parallel movements, and they were, Brebner added, "capable of allegiance to one country one day and to another the next." [23] Their loyalty transcended nationality; their allegiance was to a common North American individualism. By the 1930's about one-third of Canadian-born stock lived in the United States; about one percent of American-born stock lived in Canada. It was estimated that there were over thirty million border crossings every year. This interchange of populations and the creation of a complex web of family ties reinforced a better understanding and mutual sympathy.

The five studies in diplomatic history bolstered this optimistic impression in a different way. They were based upon a wealth of fresh archival material, dealt for the most part with discrete questions in a technical fashion, and generally satisfied even the most fastidious adherents of "objective" history. Far from dilating upon the mythology of the undefended border, historians like Max Savelle, A. L. Burt, A. B. Corey, L. B. Shippee and C. Tansill concentrated upon episodes and issues where conflicts of interests had been sharp and intense. They ranged from the drawing of the boundary in the period 1749–1763 to the Revolutionary Settlement and the War of 1812, from the crisis of 1830–1842 to the unsettled period of Civil War and Confederation, and to the rancorous dispute over fisheries and trade policy

23. M. L. Hansen, "A Resumé of Canadian-American Population Relations," in R. G. Trotter, A. B. Corey, and W. W. McLaren (eds.), *Proceedings* [of the Conference on Canadian-American Affairs Held at Queen's University, Kingston, Ontario, June 14–18, 1937] (New York, 1937), p. 106; M. L. Hansen and J. B. Brebner, *The Mingling of the Canadian and American Peoples* (New Haven and Toronto, 1940), p. x. This volume was supported by two statistical studies: L. E. Truesdell, *The Canadian Born in the United States* (Toronto and New Haven, 1943), and R. H. Coats and M. C. Maclean, *The American Born in Canada* (Toronto and New Haven, 1943).

down to 1911.[24] The overall impression which emerged from these studies was that the Canadian-American relationship was born in civil war and was characterized for almost a century afterwards by tension, suspicion and hostility, and that gradually issues had been peacefully resolved and arbitrated until an unparalleled cordiality and friendliness prevailed and the two nations were united in defense of a common liberal democratic tradition. This pattern of progress was attributed to a tradition of realism in politics, to the spaciousness of the continent, and particularly to the application of arbitration and conciliation techniques.[25] The development of self-government enabled Canadians to see that their interests were similar to those of their neighbors and it gave them a measure of self-confidence which in turn undermined their traditional suspicions of the United States.[26] But, above all, this long progressive change was directly related to the intermingling of people and particularly to economic interdependence.

The series not only strengthened the assurance that relations between Canada and the United States had over the long run become more friendly and cooperative; it was dedicated to the purpose of making them better still. It appeared ridiculous in light of common interests that attitudes born in another day should still survive to distort the way these peoples looked at each other. The director of the study of Canadians' attitudes toward their great neighbor, the Columbia sociologist Robert M. MacIver, who had taught at Toronto from 1915 to 1927 and admitted in his autobiography that he had developed no affection for the country,[27] revealed this bias against an exaggerated

24. M. Savelle, *The Diplomatic History of the Canadian Boundary, 1749–1763* (Toronto and New Haven, 1940); A. Burt, *The United States, Great Britain and British North America From the Revolution to the Establishment of Peace After the War of 1812* (Toronto and New Haven, 1940); A. B. Corey, *The Crisis of 1830–1842 in Canadian-American Relations* (Toronto and New Haven, 1941); L. B. Shippee, *Canadian-American Relations, 1849–1874* (Toronto and New Haven, 1939); C. Tansill, *Canadian-American Relations, 1875–1911* (Toronto and New Haven, 1943).
25. P. E. Corbett, *The Settlement of Canadian-American Disputes* (Toronto and New Haven, 1937).
26. A. B. Corey and R. G. Trotter, in W. W. McLaren, A. B. Corey, and R. G. Trotter (eds.), *Proceedings* [of the Conference on Canadian-American Affairs Held at St. Lawrence University, Canton, New York, June 17–22, 1935] (New York, 1936), pp. 139, 148.
27. R. M. MacIver, *A Tale that is Told* (Chicago, 1968).

nationalism more fully than any other participant in the series. While Brebner recognized that anti-Americanism, that faithful consort of Canadian national feeling, was permanent and in-eradicable, MacIver saw it as an infantile disorder and attributed it to insecurity and jealousy. It was not clear where he drew the line between anti-Americanism and Canadian national-ism; in fact he rejected both when he wrote in 1938 that "we are still children when we think of ourselves in national terms." Nationalism, invariably fostered by "vested interests," warped the ways in which people viewed each other and messianic nationalism once again threatened the peace of Europe. Inter-national conflict, he argued, was not caused by economic inter-ests or different faiths but by false images. These had to be de-stroyed before men could understand the real world and control it.[28] The examination of Canadians' opinions of the United States conformed to this prescription; negative views were under-estimated and explained away. The parallel study of American national attitudes affecting Canadian-American relations was never made. The volume which dealt with Canada's rejection of reciprocity in 1911 took a similar view of nationalism: the defeat of that mutually advantageous measure was traced in large part to the opposition of "vested interests" which magnified and cul-tivated unfounded nationalist fears for selfish reasons.[29] The temptation to treat ideas, especially ideas which were so out of harmony with the purpose of the series, as rhetorical subterfuge and rationalization, was a common tendency of historians nur-tured in the progressive history and determined to get behind all facades to the economic "reality." It also conformed to the needs of the internationalist outlook.

Shotwell drew these themes together and stated their meaning for a larger constituency. In doing so he was moved by impulses which the majority of contributing scholars perhaps did not share, but he remained faithful to the history they had written. To him, the really creative forces in history were science, tech-nology, and liberal capitalism, and they were knitting the two

28. R. M. MacIver, "Introduction," in H. F. Angus (ed.), *Canada and Her Great Neighbor* (Toronto and New Haven, 1938), pp. xxv–xxvi.
29. L. E. Ellis, *Reciprocity, 1911* (Toronto and New Haven, 1939).

North American nations and indeed the whole world into one interdependent community. There was a lag, however, between these progressive forces and the regrettable tendency of mankind to think in terms of national categories, and it was because of this failure of intelligence to deal with the real world that international conflicts arose. Just as a number of American historians in the 1930's explained the Civil War as the result of emotionalism and hysteria, Shotwell believed that all international conflicts were the consequence of the failure to remove the exact issues in dispute from the abstractions and emotions which made rational appraisals of differences impossible. "We have the feeble instrument of intelligence," he wrote, "to battle with the old appetites, with claws that have become hands, with minds that are the museums of long antiquities . . ."[30] The role of history and the social sciences was to reveal those processes of civilization which made all peoples one, and to destroy the outdated conceptions of national sovereignty which were the causes of war. For Shotwell, the history of Canadian and American relations became a testament to the internationalist faith— that economic interdependence and the unrestricted flow of the forces of liberal capitalism, the interchange of populations, the embedding of parts of one nation within another, and the growth of a rational and nonideological approach to problems, were the sources of peace. This was the great theme which was revealed in the history of Canadian and American relations and which conveyed a lesson to the whole world.[31]

III

History has not been kind to Shotwell's optimistic vision. In the years after 1945 it was not favorable to some of those

30. A. B. Corey, R. G. Trotter, and W. W. McLaren (eds.), *Proceedings* [of the Conference on Canadian-American Affairs Held at St. Lawrence University, Canton, New York, June 19–22, 1939] (New York, 1939), p. 230.

31. J. T. Shotwell, "The International Significance of the Canadian-American Peace Tradition," *op. cit.;* and "North America and the World Today," in R. G. Trotter and A. B. Corey (eds.), *Proceedings* [of the Conference on Canadian-American Affairs Held at Queen's University, Kingston, Ontario, June 23–26, 1941] (New York, 1941), pp. 5–7.

assumptions about Canadian history which lay behind the conception of the project. The majority of Canadian historians had never forgotten that Canada's past had to be seen in an imperial perspective, that it had to answer the question of how Canada survived as an independent state in North America, and that it could not be reduced to "a series of footnotes and appendices to the history of the United States." [32] The Second World War stimulated an enormous emphasis upon the transatlantic dimension. Canada and the United States still had a common history: its framework, however, was not the continent but the Atlantic community. Historians, of course, had never really been oblivious to this fact, but in 1934 when Brebner laid out the plan which the historical volumes of the series were to follow, only the interplay between Canada and the United States was included. He grew conscious of the need to expand this framework in the late 1930's; by 1945, when his *North Atlantic Triangle* appeared, the focus had been altered to include Great Britain as well as the "Siamese twins" of North America. This rediscovery of the Atlantic world, partly provoked by the war, was sustained in the late 1940's and 1950's by the commitment to the North Atlantic Treaty Organization and the requirements of the free world alliance.

Still another approach to Canadian history which appeared within the context of the series was a direct rejection of the earlier emphasis that had been placed upon the geographical coherence of North America and the meaninglessness of the boundary in economic terms. The work of Harold Innis had demonstrated that the Canadian economy had developed along very different lines from that of the United States and that the boundary of Canada coincided with a natural division of the continent and generally conformed to the pre-Cambrian Shield and the drainage basins of the rivers which the fur traders had

---

32. R. G. Trotter, "The Appalachian Barrier in Canadian History," *Annual Report of the Canadian Historical Association, with Historical Papers* (1939), p. 9. For the insistence on the European dimension see Trotter, "Which Way Canada?" *Queen's Quarterly*, XLV (Autumn 1938), 289–299; and George Brown, "Have the Americas a Common History? A Canadian View," *Canadian Historical Review*, XXIII (June, 1942), 132–139.

explored. The most effective statement of this contention was D. G. Creighton's *The Commercial Empire of the St. Lawrence, 1760–1850* (1937), which carried the Carnegie imprint and originated, rather ironically, as an investigation of the Canadian business community and the "development of Canada as a field for foreign investment." Innis's own participation in the series was ambivalent. He was the editor of the books on Canadian economic history and he was a jealous guardian of the independence of Canadian scholarship. He was a nationalist who was aware of the ways in which nationalism perverted history, and his essays were peppered with ironical comments on the excesses of the Canadian variety. But he could not help but regard the American economic impact upon Canada as disturbing. In his scheme of things the east-west economy, which had been built upon the export of fur and wheat to Europe, was being eroded in the 1920's and the 1930's by the exploitation of staples which found their markets in the United States. This north-south pull on an economic and institutional system designed on different patterns was, in his opinion, one of the main causes of instability and aggravated regionalism within Canada.[33] In its implications, his views were radically different from the opinions of those economists who were more certain of the generally beneficient nature of economic interdependence based as it was on the north-south contours of the continent.

In the 1950's this rejection of the North American approach, which had inspired the Carnegie series but was only partly confirmed by it, was carried one stage further. In that decade the concern with "cultural nationalism" among Canadian intellectuals was pronounced and intense. The Massey Commission report on Canadian culture depicted the inundation of "American" mass culture as alien and threatening; Canadian comment on Canadian-American relations was sharp and critical and complaints relating to economic, military, and Cold War policies

---

33. H. A. Innis, "Economic Trends in Canadian-American Relations," in R. L. Morrow, (ed.), *Proceedings* (Orono, Maine, 1939).

bulked large.[34] In this atmosphere, which was so different from the easy acceptance of war-time cooperation, Canadians came to look upon Canadian-American relations more critically. The little interest shown by the Carnegie series in cultural relations seemed ominous to Innis. "We must rely on our own efforts," he wrote in 1952, "and we must remember that cultural strength comes from Europe. . . . We can only survive by taking persistent action at strategic points against American imperialism in all its attractive guises."[35] The dominant form of Canadian historical writing in these years was biography and the pioneer of the new biography was the most forceful critic of the Canadian-American relations series. In 1957 Creighton contended that the stress upon continental affinities and trust "was irrelevant to our circumstances, alien to our tradition, and useless for our fundamental purposes." This Rotarian version of Manifest Destiny and bogus internationalism, as he termed it, had prepared the way for Canada's subservient acceptance of American leadership in the Cold War. At a time when Canadians were growing uneasy about the survival of their country the appropriate historical question was not the identity of interest with the United States, but Canada's historical struggle for survival in North America.[36] Not all historians went this far, but they were all affected, as the preoccupation with biography and the continuing search for the Canadian identity suggested, with the unique and distinctive elements in the Canadian past, concerns which were not exactly central to the Carnegie series. The awakening of French Canadian nationalism made them very aware of the inwardness and persistence of cultural individuality. The reorientation of Canadian historical thought involved a new appreciation for personality and traditions, the conservative elements in Canadian experience, and the role of rivalry and

34. Michael Barkway, "Canada Rediscovers Its History," *Foreign Affairs,* XXVI (April, 1958), 409–417; Merrill Denison, "4000 Miles of Imitation," *Saturday Review,* XXXV (June 7, 1952), 25, 56.
35. H. A. Innis, *The Strategy of Culture* (Toronto, 1952), pp. 2–3, 20.
36. D. G. Creighton, "Presidential Address," Canadian Historical Association, *Annual Report,* 1957, and his "Introduction," in J. B. Brebner, *The North Atlantic Triangle* (Toronto, 1966), pp. xiii–xxiii.

conflict. Surveys of Canadian-American relations in these years concluded with descriptions of the hard, outstanding issues, not with salutations to their international significance. In a general sense the Carnegie series reflected an optimism about Canadian-American relations in the age of the reciprocal trade pact of 1935 and the Ogdensburg Agreement of 1940; by the 1950's and 1960's Canadians were disturbed about the continental integration and historians naturally shared these worries. There was a fine irony involved when a Canadian philosopher in 1965 contended that liberal capitalism and technological progress, the very forces which a generation before Shotwell saw as the sources of understanding and international goodwill, had undermined the Canadian state.

The conception of Canadian-American relations in historical writing, then, was born at a particular time and in special circumstances. Once an exciting discovery, it has since ceased to be so and has become only one among many approaches to the past. It inspired scholars to reveal a fundamental dimension of Canadian experience and their works have enormously enriched Canadian historical literature. But we are also conscious now of reading most of these volumes as documents illuminating the particular period in Canadian-American relations in which they were conceived and written. The Carnegie series, and the idea of Canadian-American relations upon which it rested, have passed into history and have become a part of the intellectual history of the relationship which the series originally set out to describe and appraise.

2

The American Impact on Canadian Political Science and Sociology

Allan Kornberg and Alan Tharp

The Problem

That Canadians, especially Canadian intellectuals, have been concerned with the reality of a Canadian nation is not especially noteworthy. What is worth noting is a relatively recent tendency to structure their nationalism more, or at least as much, in terms of fear of intellectual, as of economic, inundation by the United States. Obviously, this paper cannot begin to treat so complex a phenomenon. However, we will try to focus on how some of these fears are manifested in the attitudes of some Canadian academicians toward Americans and the American influence on teaching and research in two of the social sciences, political science and sociology.

An inspection of much of the literature concerned with the "Americanization" of Canadian universities reveals its tremendous diversity, but a majority of the arguments made are variations of three more-or-less common themes. Thus, with regard to the teaching of political science and sociology, the first claim is that American social scientists, because they are American,

This is a revised version of a paper prepared for the Annual Meeting of the Association for Canadian Studies in the United States, Durham, North Carolina, April 2–3, 1971. We are grateful to Mildred Schwartz, Barry Cooper, David Hoffman, Zack Kay, Howard Lentner, John Meisel, John Wilson and Mike Whittington for a careful and critical reading of an earlier draft of this paper. Although their observations have been extremely helpful, we naturally absolve them of responsibility for any errors of fact or interpretation in this paper. Donald Walker deserves special thanks for his assistance in collating some of the data that are presented.

tend to be woefully ignorant of Canadian history and the social and political institutions of Canadian society. Because they are, they tend most often to structure their courses in terms of United States political and social institutions and processes. Whenever Canadian society, its institutions and processes are examined, the comparison is always with their United States counterparts. Further, these comparisons are invariably invidious; implicit and frequently explicit is the assumption that Canadian society and Canadian institutions somehow are inferior. Thus, a whole generation of Canadian university students is being subtly and not so subtly brainwashed. Butler and Shugarman state, "A nation of people is not an automatically enduring reality but rather it is like an organism—a learning organism whose culture existence is contingent upon compliance with certain requisites: especially with regard to the experiences it undergoes and the necessity of keeping the national memory and feedback channels clear. If the experiences presented to it are primarily those of another culture and if the structures for communicating the national memory . . . are weak, then the nation will tend inexorably to assimilate to the alien culture . . . the problem is more serious than many realize or will admit . . . because the process by which the university is a socializer and interrelates with other key socializing agents indicates that inadequate Canadian content can have widespread societal ramifications reaching to the core of the national edifice."[1]

A second theme is that American social scientists tend to be positivists and empiricists and show little respect for "traditionally Canadian" methods of political and social inquiry. Again, Butler and Shugarman warn that "we are in danger of abandoning the Canadian tradition of scholarly research and values in favor of one of uneven and disputable merit."[2] They urge Canadian scholars to take as their models C. B. Macpherson, James Eayrs and Donald Smiley, presumably be-

1. Michael Butler and David Shugarman, "Americanization and Scholarly Values," *Journal of Canadian Studies*, V (1970), 24–25.
2. *Ibid.*, p. 18.

cause the scholarship of the three gentlemen reflects the standards toward which current students in political science and in
the social sciences, generally, should strive.

A third theme is that the presence of United States nationals
on social science faculties in Canadian universities has distorted,
nay perverted, Canadian research priorities. Because American
political scientists and sociologists tend to be concerned with
"methodological gimmickry," because they seemingly are ob-
sessed with quantitative methods, and because it is well known
that really significant political and social problems ordinarily do
not lend themselves to study with these methods, it follows that
scholarly attention has been directed away from the study of
significant problems to those that can be operationalized and
quantified but which invariably are trivial. Ellen and
Neal Wood, for example, object to the "simplicity, restricted and
shallow conception of science and scientific methods"[3] which
they see in American political science. They argue that not
only have human goals been forgotten but often the content of
research itself has been sacrificed to techniques and methodology.[4] Thus, "the elevation of techniques to an end in itself,
the cult of methodology, means that political science has forgotten almost all the other goals and concerns with which political thinkers have traditionally occupied themselves, including
the humanistic concern for the quality of human life."[5] Perhaps
the substance of all three themes is most succinctly stated by
Steele and Matthews: "The attitude that invites Canadians to
consider United States information as 'universal,' 'non-national-
istic,' and 'cosmopolitan,' is a product of United States nationalism and 'manifest destiny,' linked to the so-called 'objective'
ideology of the behavioural sciences."[6]

3. Ellen and Neal Wood, "Canada and the American Science of Politics," in
Ian Lumsden (ed.), *Close the 49th Parallel: The Americanization of Canada*
(Toronto, 1970), p. 182.
4. *Ibid.*, p. 184.   5. *Ibid.*, p. 183.
6. James Steele and Robin Matthews, "The Universities: Takeover of the
Mind," in Ian Lumsden (ed.), *Close the 49th Parallel: The Americanization of
Canada*, p. 175.

In this paper we will try to evaluate, as best we can, the validity of these assertions with data that are derived from: (1) responses to questionnaires that were sent to the several departments of political science and sociology in Canada; (2) a classification of articles that appeared from 1935 to 1970 in the *Canadian Journal of Political Science* and its predecessor, the *Canadian Journal of Economics and Political Science;* (3) a classification of the articles that have appeared in the *Canadian Review of Sociology and Anthropology* since its beginning; and (4) a collation and classification of political science doctoral dissertations in progress or completed by students in Canadian universities as well as those on Canadian topics completed in universities outside of Canada.

One of our three principal data sources, the aforementioned questionnaires, was divided into three sections. The first section deals with the national origins and educational backgrounds of departmental members. The second section is concerned with the number of Canadian courses taught, the national origins of those teaching in major subfields, and the methodological and philosophical orientations of departmental members. The third section is concerned with the distribution of departmental members along the instructor-professor continuum and the ages and national origins of individuals in each rank.

Our unit of analysis generally is the department, at least as it is seen through the eyes of our respondents—*the several department chairmen.* Unfortunately only 43 percent of the chairmen of sociology departments responded to the questionnaire, but fully 67 percent of Canadian political science departments are represented in the data. Although we certainly would not claim that the returns are completely representative of the universes of which they are a part, they are sufficiently representative (e.g., we received at least one completed questionnaire from a sociology and political science department in each of the Canadian provinces) to make their analyses worthwhile. Finally, it should be noted that a number of the departments of sociology for which we have data are "joint" departments (i.e., they are composed of both sociologists and anthropologists).

Political Science and Sociology in Canada:
An Overview

The growth and development of political science as a discipline in Canada in a very real sense is reflected in the content of two recent advertisements for textbooks; one from the University of Toronto Press, Canada's foremost academic publisher, the second from a Canadian division of a major American commercial publisher, McGraw Hill.[7] The former announces that a "completely revised and updated version" of the 4th edition of *The Government of Canada* will be "ready for fall courses." According to the advertisement, "Norman Ward's revision brings the text up to date incorporating the many changes in government since the last edition of 1963, and *restructuring it to accord more with the increased interest in the processes of government now*" (our emphasis). The McGraw Hill advertisement informs readers of the March, 1971, edition of the *Canadian Journal of Political Science* that the *Canadian Political System: Environment Structure and Processes,* by R. J. Van Loon and M. S. Whittington, will be published in July, 1971. With typical Canadian understatement and good taste it notes that, "At one time, political science was viewed as an isolated discipline in which the emphasis was on form and structure. However, the *emphasis in contemporary political science has shifted to the functional relationship of political institutions to society*" (our emphasis). Thus, two special features of the text are: (1) "it provides considerable original material on the policy process and on political socialization and political culture," and (2) "the authors use modern techniques of political analysis and up-to-date reference data." Not wishing, perhaps, to irritate some potential adopters or to give the impression that the textbook departs too "radically" from the Dawson tradition, the advertisement also points out that "forms and structures of political in-

7. The fact that in 1946 a textbook in political science had such a small prospective market it had to be published by a university press whereas commercial publishers now vigorously search for authors of potential textbooks is in itself a rather dramatic illustration of the growth of political science in Canada.

stitutions are discussed" and (in an advertisement that appeared in the previous issue) "the text will emphasize behavioural rather than institutional analysis but not to the exclusion of the latter."

It is readily apparent from the most cursory inspection of the first four editions of Dawson's book that Canadian political science historically has been concerned almost entirely with the description of the form and structure of governmental institutions. For example, in the fourth edition, revised by Norman Ward in 1963, political parties are treated in only 71 pages—the same number that had been allocated to the topic in the first edition published in 1946. Terms such as "interest group," "political culture," and "political socialization," although they have been widely used for at least a decade, cannot be found—even in the index. Rather, all four editions focus on the achievement of Dominion status, the historical development of the constitution, changes in legal and financial arrangements between the federal government and the provinces, and the formal rules and procedures under which the executive, the legislative, and the judicial branches of the federal government operate.

In part, Professor Dawson's tendency to limit himself largely to a description of the formal structures and processes of national government was a function of the contemporary lack of research. Thus, he observed in the preface to his first edition, "Until a year or two ago no comprehensive book on the government of Canada had ever been written"; and again, "The great obstacle in the way of preparing a more ambitious account of Canadian government has been dearth of specialized studies on various phases of the subject." And, although Professor Ward's preface to the fourth edition of 1963 observed with some satisfaction that "a small but respectable literature on Canadian politics now exists," the number of political scientists actively engaged in ongoing research at that late date still was relatively small. By way of illustration, of the 107 articles, notes, and review essays published in the *Canadian Journal of Economics and Political Science* between February, 1961, and August, 1963, only 25.2 percent were concerned with what might loosely be termed politics.

Further, in the entire period, 1935–1967, during which economics and political science articles were published in the same journal, only 36 percent of all published pieces were in "political science," broadly defined. More important (in the sense of being illustrative of the smallness of the discipline and the limited amount of basic research carried out), a significantly large number of these articles were written by a relative handful of men, the majority of whom were affiliated for the greater part of their professional lives with three elite Eastern universities. Specifically, one quarter of all political science articles published in the *Canadian Journal of Economics and Political Science* during the period 1935–1959 were written by Professors R. M. Dawson (10); C. B. Macpherson (8); H. M. Clokie (7); H. G. Angus (6); A. Brady (6); J. R. Mallory (6); E. Forsey (6); J. A. Corry (5); S. D. Clark (4); and J. E. Hodgetts (4) (see Table 1). In addition to their own distinguished contributions to the journal, Professors Dawson, Clokie, Corry, Hodgetts and Clark also were closely associated with its publication and at various times served on the *Journal's* editorial board. Also, Professor Clark, long-time member of the Department of Political Economy of the University of Toronto and the first chairman of the University's Department of Sociology, served as managing editor of the *Journal,* as did his departmental colleague, James Eayrs. In fact, every editor of the *Journal* during this thirty-two year period was affiliated with the Department of Political Economy of that great University: V. W. Bladen (1935–1946); G. A. Elliott (1947–1952); S. D. Clark and W. Hood (1953); G. A. Elliott (1954–1956); J. H. Dales (1957–1958); James Eayrs (1959); J. H. Dales (1960–1962); Jean Burnet (August, 1962–May, 1963); J. H. Dales (August, 1963–1966); and I. M. Drummond (1967).

It was not until the establishment of a journal devoted exclusively to the publication of research in political science that a member of another political science department, Professor John Meisel of Queen's, became managing editor. Concomitant with that change the proportion of articles published by scholars from the University of Toronto dropped sharply. Thus, although

Table 1. *Authors of Three or More Published Articles in the* Canadian Journal of Economics and Political Science, *1935–1959, 1960–1967, and the* Canadian Journal of Political Science *1968–1970*

	Number [a]				
Author	1935–1959	1960–1967	1968–1970	Cumulative total	Rank order
Angus, H. F.	6	–	–	6	5
Bladen, V. W.	–	–	–	3	8
Brady, A.	6	–	–	6	5
Clark, S. D.	4	–	–	4	7
Clokie, H. McD.	7	–	–	7	4
Coats, R. H.	3	–	–	3	8
Comeau, P.	–	–	–	3	8
Corry, J. A.	5	–	–	5	6
Crawford, K. G.	3	–	–	3	8
Curtis, C. A.	3	–	–	3	8
Dawson, R. M.	10	–	–	10	3
Dion, L.	–	–	3	4	7
Eayrs, J. G.	3	–	–	3	8
Forsey, E.	6	5	–	11	2
Fox, P. W.	–	–	–	3	8
Hodgetts, J. E.	4	–	–	6	5
Hoffman, D.	–	–	2	3	8
Laponce, J.	–	–	–	3	8
Lemieux, V.	–	–	3	3	8
Lipset, S. M.	3	–	–	3	8
Macpherson, C. B.	7	3	–	12	1
Mallory, J. R.	6	–	–	6	5
Qualter, T. H.	–	2	–	3	8
Rowat, D.	–	2	–	4	7
Scott, R. R.	3	–	–	3	8
Smiley, D.	–	4	2	7	4
Thorburn, H.	–	–	–	3	8
Watkins, F. M.	3	–	–	3	8
Wilson, J.	–	–	3	3	8

[a] All articles by an author are included in the cumulative total although they may not appear in the previous columns. Consequently, the cumulative total may be different from the total of the three columns.

Toronto-affiliated scholars contributed 20 percent of all the articles published in the *Canadian Journal of Economics and Political Science* between 1935 and 1967, since 1968 their contributions to the *Canadian Journal of Political Science* have declined to 5 percent, and Toronto's ranking among institutions in terms of the number of articles published by affiliated faculty has gone from first to fifth (see Table 2).

Table 3, which presents a distribution of the articles published in a major subfield during three time periods, points to

Table 2. Rank Order and Distribution of Political Science Departments in Terms of Institutional Affiliation of Authors in the Canadian Journal of Economics and Political Science, 1935–1959, 1960–1967, and the Canadian Journal of Political Science, 1968–1970

Institution	1935–1959 [a]		1960–1967 [b]		1968–1970 [c]		Total [d]	
	Percent	Rank order	Percent	Rank order	Percent	Rank order	Percent	Rank order
Toronto	20	1	20	1	5	5	18	1
Saskatchewan	7	4	4	5	1	8	6	4
Queen's	8	3	5	4	9	2	8	2
Univ. British Columbia	4	6	6	3	8	3	5	5
McGill	9	2	4	5	1	8	7	3
Dalhousie	3	7	–	–	–	–	2	8
Manitoba	5	5	1	7	–	–	3	7
Ottawa	4	6	7	2	7	4	5	5
Alberta	1	9	4	4	3	7	2	8
Sir George Williams	– [e]	10	–	–	–	–	– [e]	–
Carleton	2	8	6	3	4	6	3	7
McMaster	2	8	–	–	3	7	1	9
Acadia	– [e]	10	1	7	–	–	– [e]	–
Royal Military College	– [e]	10	–	–	–	–	– [e]	–
Windsor	– [e]	10	–	–	–	–	– [e]	–
Laval	– [e]	10	2	6	15	1	3	7
Memorial	– [e]	10	1	7	1	8	1	9
Montreal	–	–	7	2	3	7	2	8
Western Ontario	–	–	5	4	–	–	1	9
York	–	–	5	4	7	4	2	8
Waterloo	–	–	2	6	5	5	1	9
Quebec	–	–	1	7	–	–	– [e]	–
New Brunswick	–	–	1	7	–	–	– [e]	–
Calgary	–	–	–	–	3	7	– [e]	–
Simon Fraser	–	–	–	–	1	8	– [e]	–
Canadians not affiliated with academic depts.	14	–	–	–	1	–	10	–
U.S. institutions	15	–	16	–	13	–	15	–
Institutions outside of Canada and U.S.	4	–	1	7	10	–	5	–

[a] N = 255
[b] N = 82
[c] N = 75
[d] N = 412
[e] less than 1 percent

the shift that seemingly has occurred in the research interests of political science scholars in Canada. The most substantial change is the decline in the proportion of articles published on Canadian topics. Although at first blush these data would appear to support the claim that research on Canadian topics is

Table 3. *Distribution of Articles Published in the* Canadian Journal of Economics and Political Science, *1935–1959, 1960–1967, and the* Canadian Journal of Political Science, *1968–1970, in Terms of Major Subfields*

Subfields	1935–1959 (N = 255)	1960–1967 (N = 82)	1968–1970 (N = 75)	1935–1970 (N = 412)
Canadian	54%	51%	29%	49%
Comparative politics:				
Developed systems	18	12	19	17
Theory	18	18	19	18
International relations	6	1	4	5
Public law	1	–	–	1
Empirical theory	1	6	12	4
Comparative politics:				
Less developed systems	2	2	4	2
Political parties	1	9	13	5

being neglected, the figure is somewhat misleading. The category, "Comparative Politics: Developed Systems," for the period 1968–1970 contains a number of articles that focus at least in part on Canada. Further, the 1969 and 1970 reports of the co-editors of the *Canadian Journal of Political Science* make clear that Canadian politics continues to be the field of concern to a very substantial proportion of Canadian political scientists actively engaged in ongoing research. Thus, in their 1969 report Meisel and Dion state, "The field most widely explored was clearly studies in Canadian Politics," and in the 1970 report they state, "of the 103 substantive articles in English, 40 dealt with some aspect of Canadian politics, indicating that the strong preoccupation of the profession with Canadian subjects is undiminished." [8]

The shift in the analytic methods employed to pursue substantive interests is illustrated in rather dramatic terms in Table 4. We see that the proportion of published articles that are empirical in their orientation and that employ quantitative analytic techniques rises from 6 percent during 1935–1959, to 29 percent during 1960–1967, to 72 percent during the period 1968–1970. A reasonably valid inference that can be drawn from the

8. See John Meisel and Leon Dion, *Report of the Co-Editors January 1, 1969 to December 31, 1969,* and *Report . . . January 1, 1970 to December 31, 1970.*

Table 4. *Distribution of Articles Published in the* Canadian Journal of Economics and Political Science, *1935–1959 and 1960–1967, and in the* Canadian Journal of Political Science, *1968–1970, in Terms of Methodological Orientation*

	1935–1959 (Nᵃ = 207)	1960–1967 (Nᵃ = 63)	1968–1970 (Nᵃ = 50)	1935–1970 (Nᵃ = 320)
Institutional	48%	49%	22%	44%
Constitutional-legal	24	19	6	20
Historical	21	3	–	14
Quantitative-empirical	6	29	72	21

ᵃ N is not equal to the actual number of articles published during a particular time period, since articles classified under "Theory" are not included.

data in Table 4 is that the orientations of Canadian political scientists have shifted considerably and that this shift may lead or, perhaps, already has led to an accompanying change in the composition of the Canadian political science establishment. The latter change also may be reflected in the editorial policy of the discipline's most prestigious publishing outlet. Professor John Meisel, who in association with two French-speaking coeditors has borne major responsibility for the current editorial policy of the *Canadian Journal of Political Science,* in some respects occupies the position in Canadian political science in the 1970's that the late Professor R. M. Dawson held in the late 1940's and early 1950's; he is "setting the style" for a majority of the individuals most actively engaged in systematic research. A distinguished scholar[9] and teacher,[10] his prestige in Canadian political science derives in part from his close association with the American political science establishment, especially the Inter-University Consortium for Political Research. Meisel, more than any other political scientist, has been instrumental in making behavioral research in political science "respectable" in

9. See, for example, *The Canadian General Election of 1957* (Toronto, 1962); *Papers on the 1962 Election* (Toronto, 1964); and articles such as "Religious Affiliations and Electoral Behavior: A Case Study," *The Canadian Journal of Economics and Political Science,* XXII (1956), 481–496, and "The Stalled Omnibus: Canadian Parties in the 1960's," *Social Research,* XXX (1963), 367–390.

10. Professors Van Loon and Whittington, the authors of the textbook referred to above, both were students of Meisel at Queen's.

Canada.[11] For example, his paper on voting behavior was the first attempt by a Canadian political scientist to utilize both aggregate and survey data to systematically explore the effect of religious affiliations on variations in voting. He also has helped facilitate the recognition of the research of French-Canadian scholars and of a cohort of younger scholars, such as David Hoffman, John Wilson, Fred Schindeler and Gilbert Winham, most of whom are affiliated with departments of political science in relatively new universities in English-speaking Canada. Through the vehi-

Table 5. *Distribution of Political Science Doctoral Dissertations Completed in Canadian Universities, 1930–1960 and 1961–1970*

	1930–1960 (N = 40)	1961–1970 (N = 66)
Toronto	45%	32%
McGill	8	21
Queen's	–	14
Laval	–	1
Carleton	–	6
Alberta	–	9
Montreal	7	5
Ottawa	40	12

cle of the *Canadian Journal of Political Science* he has provided them with considerable visibility, both within and outside of Canada. If Canadian political science has experienced something of a behavioral revolution in the past decade, then Meisel must be regarded as its principal architect.

Two other indicators of the growth and development of Canadian political science, and, to a lesser extent, of its changing orientations, are the volume and distribution of doctoral dissertation research. Thus, with regard to growth, Table 5 indicates

11. One can speculate that a principal reason for Meisel's selection as editor of the new *Canadian Journal of Political Science* was that he was acceptable, despite his behavioral orientation, to the more traditionally oriented members of his discipline as well as to the behavioralist element. One can further speculate that a second reason was that he was highly visible and acceptable to French-Canadian political scientists—a very important consideration given the fact that the new *Journal* was to be the journal, in fact as well as in theory, of both the Canadian Political Science Association and the Société Canadienne des Sciences Politiques.

that of the 196 doctoral dissertations completed in Canadian universities in a forty-year period beginning in 1930 *fully 62 percent were written in the last decade.* Further, until 1960, 85 percent of all the political science doctorates obtained in Canada were awarded by the universities of Toronto and Ottawa. Table 6, which rank orders Canadian political science departments in terms of dissertations completed and in progress, makes clear that although the University of Ottawa's position as a prin-

Table 6. *Rank Order of Canadian Universities in Terms of Dissertations Completed and in Progress in Political Science*

	Completed	In progress
Toronto	1	1
Ottawa	2	6
McGill	3	2
Queen's	4	3
Alberta	5	4
Montreal	6	7
Carleton	7	5
Laval	8	8

cipal producer of Canadian Ph.D.'s is declining, the political economy department of the University of Toronto will continue to be the single largest grantor of Ph.D's in the immediate future.[12] But, despite Toronto's continued eminence, Table 7 points out that a number of recently established doctoral programs now have advanced to a stage at which students are engaged actively in preparing dissertations; 174 such dissertations currently are being written. We may infer from this statis-

12. Other data that we have gathered indicates that Duke University stands in somewhat the same relationship to United States universities as Toronto stands to Canadian institutions. That is, the greatest number of doctoral dissertations on some aspect of Canadian politics have been written at Duke University and the largest number of doctoral dissertations in Canadian politics currently are in progress there. Given the fact that Duke is a relatively small institution, and in comparison to giants such as Columbia and Michigan, does not produce a large number of doctorates annually, the contribution to the study of Canadian politics made by its Commonwealth Studies Center generally and by Professor R. Taylor Cole, in particular, is noteworthy.

Table 7. Distribution of Universities
With Regard to Dissertations Com-
pleted and in Progress in Political
Science

	Completed (N = 106)	In progress (N = 174)
Toronto	37%	44%
McGill	16	17
Queen's	8	8
U.B.C.	–	5
Laval	1	1
Western	–	4
York	–	3
Carleton	4	6
Simon Fraser	–	2
Calgary	–	1
Alberta	6	7
Montreal	5	2
Ottawa	23	3

tic that the number of dissertations that actually will be completed in the next five years will be equal to or perhaps even
exceed the number completed in the past forty years.

Insofar as shifting substantive and methodological orientations are concerned, an examination of the distribution of dissertations by subfield shows that over time approximately half

Table 8. Distribution by Area of Political Science Dissertations

	Political philosophy		Methodology		Canadian studies	
	1930–1960	1961–1970	1930–1960	1961–1970	1930–1960	1961–1970
Toronto	2	5	–	–	15	13
McGill	1	2	–	–	–	1
Queen's	–	–	–	–	–	6
Ottawa	3	1	2	–	6	4
Montreal	1	–	–	–	–	1
Alberta	–	1	–	–	–	2
Carleton	–	–	–	–	–	2
Laval	–	–	–	–	–	1
Percent	6.6	8.5	1.9	–	19.8	28.3

(48.1 percent) of the completed dissertations have been written on some aspect of Canadian politics. Sixteen dissertations (15.1 percent) were written in political philosophy; ten (9.3 percent) were in international relations topics; and twenty-three (21:6 percent) were in the field of comparative politics. Of the latter, ten were written during the last decade and focused on the politics of less developed countries. With regard to departmental distribution, McGill has turned out the majority of doctorates in comparative politics, whereas the bulk of dissertation research in Canadian politics, and to a lesser extent, political philosophy, has been carried out at Toronto (see Table 8). A comparison by subfield of dissertations written with those in progress indicates, as is the case with articles published in the *Canadian Journal of Economics and Political Science* and the *Canadian Journal of Political Science,* that the proportion of research being carried out in Canadian politics is declining. Doctoral research in political philosophy also is decreasing. Although the number of articles published in the *Canadian Journal of Economics and Political Science* and the *Canadian Journal of Political Science* on political parties is increasing, doctoral research in this area is declining somewhat. Most important, in that it bears on the claim that the study of Cana-

Completed in Canadian Universities, 1930–1970 [a]

Political parties		International relations		Comparative: Developed countries		Comparative: Less developed countries		Total percent	
1930–1960	1961–1970	1930–1960	1961–1970	1930–1960	1961–1970	1930–1960	1961–1970	1930–1960	1961–1970
–	1	–	–	1	–	–	2	45	32
–	–	–	3	2	3	–	5	8	21
–	2	–	–	–	–	–	1	–	14
–	1	4	–	1	1	–	1	40	12
–	–	–	1	2	1	–	–	7	5
–	–	–	2	–	–	–	1	–	9
–	–	–	–	–	2	–	–	–	6
–	–	–	–	–	–	–	–	–	1
–	3.7	3.7	5.6	5.6	6.6	–	9.4	100	100

[a] N = 40 for 1930–1960, N = 66 for 1961–1970
Source: *Theses in Canadian Political Studies* (Kingston, Ontario, 1970).

Table 9. Distribution by Subfield of Dissertations in Political Science Completed and in Progress in Canadian Universities

	Political philosophy N = 37	Methodology N = 15	Canadian studies N = 118	Political parties N = 10	International relations N = 31	Comparative: Developed systems N = 40	Comparative: Less developed systems N = 29
Completed (N = 106)	15%	2%	48%	4%	9%	12%	9%
In progress (N = 174)	12	7	39	3	12	16	11
Percentage difference	−3	+5	−9	−1	+3	+4	+2
Total percent	13	6	42	3	11	15	11

dian political institutions and processes is being neglected because of the Americanization of Canadian political science, it should be noted that Canadian politics remains the subfield in which the largest proportion of doctoral research still is being conducted (see Table 9).

Finally, Table 10, which compares the proportion of doctorates in political science completed in Canadian universities with the proportion of dissertations on Canadian topics written in American schools and abroad during two periods, 1930–1960 and 1961–1970, also illustrates the rapid growth of graduate pro-

Table 10. *Political Science Doctoral Dissertations Completed in Canadian, U.S., and Other Universities, 1930–1970*

Proportion of dissertations completed in:	Period 1930–1960 N = 74	Period 1961–1970 N = 106
Canadian universities	54.0%	62.3%
U.S. universities	40.6	31.3
Other	5.4	6.4

grams during the past decade. We see that the proportion of Canadian doctorates, whether the dissertations were written on a Canadian topic or in another subfield, has increased during the past decade. Further, of the 174 dissertations currently in preparation in Canadian departments of political science, fully 67 deal with Canadian politics, whereas approximately only 30 in this area are currently in progress in United States institutions and abroad. Given this fact, it seems reasonable to assume that in the near future teaching and research in the politically sensitive area of Canadian politics largely will be carried out by Canadian nationals trained in Canadian universities. Whether or not this will vitiate the so-called American impact on Canadian political science will be considered presently.

With regard to sociology in Canada, a number of studies [13]

13. See, for example, Frederick Elkin, "Canada," in Joseph S. Roucek (ed.), *Contemporary Sociology* (New York, 1958), pp. 1101–1123; Jean-Charles Falar-

indicate that its origins and especially its development as a discipline are even more recent than are those of political science. Although the first courses in sociology were taught at Acadia University in 1908 and at United College (now the University of Winnipeg) in 1910, development lagged in the Maritime and Western provinces and instead centered in Quebec and Ontario. Thus, l'Ecole des Sciences Sociales, Economiques, et Politiques of the University of Montreal was established in 1920; l'Ecole des Sciences Sociales of Laval University was begun in 1932; the first separate Department of Sociology was founded by Professor C. A. Dawson at McGill in 1923; and sociology became a semiautonomous section of the Department of Political Economy of the University of Toronto in 1929.[14]

Just as the development of political science was strongly influenced by notables such as R. M. Dawson, so sociology was influenced by scholars such as E. C. Hughes, whose intensive studies of the impact of industrialization on Quebec society attained the status of classics. Despite the attention his research and that of scholars such as Gerin, Clark,[15] Falardeau, Porter, and Elkin have attracted in the scholarly community, the institutionalization of sociology as a discipline languished in Canada until well into the 1960's. For example, during the period 1921–1940 there were two graduate Canadian M.A. programs and by 1969–1970 there still were only 23—ten of them in Ontario universities. No doctoral programs existed before 1940 and only twelve universities (five in Ontario) offered the Ph.D.

deau, The Rise of the Social Sciences in French Canada (Montreal, 1967); Jean-Charles Falardeau and Frank E. Jones, "La Sociologie au Canada," Transactions of the Third World Congress of Sociology [Amsterdam], VII (1958), 14–22; John Harp and James Curtis, "French and English-Speaking Sociologists in Canada: A Comparative Note," paper at the annual meetings of the Canadian Sociology and Anthropology Association, York University, Toronto, June, 1968; Mabel E. Timlin and Albert Faucher, The Social Sciences in Canada: Two Studies (Ottawa, 1968); Frank G. Vallee and Donald R. Whyte, "Canadian Society: Trends and Perspectives," in Bernard R. Blishen, et al. (eds.), Canadian Society: Sociological Perspectives, 3rd edition (Toronto), pp. 849–852; and Desmond M. Connor and James E. Curtis, Sociology and Anthropology in Canada: Some Characteristics of the Disciplines and Their Current University Programs (Montreal, 1970).

14. For a chronology of other major events in Canadian sociology, see Desmond Connor and James Curtis, op. cit., pp. 9–10.

15. As has been indicated, Professor Clark also has played a prominent role in Canadian political science.

by 1970. Consequently, only 406 M.A. degrees actually had been granted at the end of the academic year 1967–1968. And, until 1968, only 24 doctorates had been conferred, 15 by the University of Toronto. Nevertheless, although certainly underdeveloped by United States standards, Canadian sociology is growing, and, in fact, may soon outstrip political science—at least in number of faculty and in the number and variety of its course offerings. Thus, by 1969 fully forty-two Canadian universities offered an undergraduate major in sociology and thirty-three

Table 11. *Percentage Distribution by Region of Full Time Faculty and Number of Graduate and Undergraduate Courses in Socioloy in Canada, 1969–70*

	Full time faculty Ph.D.[a] (N = 219)	Other (N = 143)	Total faculty (N = 362)	Number of graduate courses (N = 425)	Number of undergraduate courses (N = 979)
Western provinces universities	37.0%	30.0%	34.3%	39.2%	34.6%
Ontario universities	40.6	37.1	39.2	36.7	32.2
Quebec universities [a]	15.0	15.4	15.1	16.3	22.7
Maritime universities	7.3	17.5	11.3	7.8	10.5

[a] These figures are somewhat lower than Vallee and Whyte's estimate that the number of English-speaking Ph.D. faculty alone was 275 in 1968.
Source: Connor and Curtis, *Sociology and Anthropology in Canada,* Tables 7, 3, and 4; pp. 78–80, 84–85.

offered an honors degree. Further, as is indicated in Table 11, by 1969 there were approximately 219 Ph.D.'s in the several sociology departments of Canadian universities, approximately 10 percent of these on the faculty of York University in Toronto. Table 11 also shows that 425 graduate and 979 undergraduate courses in sociology were regularly offered in Canadian universities with approximately one-third of these offerings being in the several departments of Ontario universities. And, although the Maritime universities continue to lag behind Ontario, Quebec and Western provincial institutions, the latter literally have created their sociology departments, *de novo,* since 1965. The principal and most prestigious outlet for research among sociologists and anthropologists in Canada has been the *Cana-*

dian Review of Sociology and Anthropology, begun in 1964. An examination of the articles published from 1964–1970 indicates that the great majority, 86 percent to be specific, are on sociological rather than anthropological topics. Among sociological articles, the largest proportion deal with "social organizations" (see Table 12), a finding that is consonant with the report by Connor and Curtis that social organizations and institutions was the area most frequently (42 percent) ranked first among the "top three professional interests" [16] of sociologists in Canada.

Table 12. *Distribution of Articles in* Canadian Journal of Sociology and Anthropology, *1964–1970, by Major Subfields*

Subfields	Percent (N = 87)
Social organization	35
Social problems	24
Theory	15
Population and urban-rural	10
Social psychology	8
Methodology	6
Social change	2

Interestingly, although only 12 percent of those responding to the Connor and Curtis survey rated "social disorganization" and "social problems" as their first professional interest, we were able to classify approximately one-fourth of the *Review* articles under this rubric. We also found, in comparison to the 5 percent who cited the area as their major professional interest, that "theory" was over-represented as a subfield. This suggests that there may be some validity to the claims of Davis,[17] who argues that Canadian sociology outside of Quebec has been overly concerned with what he terms the "arid and conservative" structural-functional theoretical formulations of Parsons, and to the claims of Vallee and Whyte,[18] who assert that there has not been

16. Desmond Connor and James Curtis, *op. cit.,* p. 14.
17. Arthur K. Davis, "Some Failings of Anglophone Academic Sociology in Canada," in Jan J. Loubser (ed.), *The Future of Sociology in Canada* (Montreal, 1970), pp. 31–35.
18. Frank Vallee and Donald Whyte, *op. cit.*

as much concern with theoretical and ideological issues on the part of Canadian sociologists as there has been in the United States. Concern over the relative paucity of theory, then, would appear to depend upon the perspective of the viewer— on "whose baby has the measles."

Table 13. *Rank Order and Distribution of Sociology Departments in Terms of Institutional Affiliations of Authors in* Canadian Review of Sociology *and* Anthropology, *1964–1970*

Institution	Rank order	Percent
Toronto	1	10
McMaster	2	8
McGill	3	6
Montreal	3	6
Alberta	3	6
York	3	6
Memorial	4	5
Carleton	4	5
Western Ontario	5	3
Calgary	5	3
Queen's	6	2
Trent	6	2
Simon Fraser	7	1
Waterloo	7	1
Manitoba	7	1
Sir George Williams	7	1
Dalhousie	7	1
University of British Columbia	7	1
Canadians not affiliated with university departments		2
U.S. departments		24
Departments other than in U.S. and Canadian universities		5

Insofar as the institutional affiliations of contributors to the *Review* are concerned, as is the case in political science, Toronto ranks first (see Table 13). Unlike the situation in political science, however, the difference in the rate at which the contributions of Toronto-affiliated faculty and of scholars affiliated with other universities have been published is relatively trivial. Also in contrast to the situation in political science, contributors out-side of the Toronto-McGill-Queen's axis are well represented in the *Review*. Whether this reflects a more egalitarian tendency in sociology, or whether the representation of authors from other universities simply derives from the fact that unlike political science, the majority of sociology departments were established at approximately the same time so that the "available talent" is more evenly distributed, is not clear.

The composition of the several editorial boards of the *Review* suggests that the former may be the case (i.e., that Canadian sociology has from its beginning been more of an "open" dis-cipline than has political science). Thus, although Professor Jean Burnet (Toronto and York) served as editor from 1964–1968, Professor Harry Zentner of the University of Calgary acted as managing editor during the same period. When Pro-fessor Frank Jones of McMaster became editor in 1969, Profes-sor M. A. Tremblay of Laval became associate editor.

The several editorial boards of the *Review* have been charac-terized by greater "turnover" in membership than the editorial boards of the *Canadian Journal of Economics and Political Sci-ence* during the first ten years of the latter journal's existence. There also has been greater representation of Western universi-ties and of universities outside the "big three" on the editorial boards of the *Review*. In fact, four sociologists from the Univer-sity of British Columbia and the University of Alberta respec-tively have served as editorial board members whereas only three members of the Toronto department have been on the board. Other universities that have been represented on the board are McGill (4); Montreal (3); Memorial (2); Laval (2); Guelph (1); Carleton (1); McMaster (1); Ottawa (1); and the Univer-sity of New Brunswick (1).

One other difference between sociology and political science that is worth observing with regard to contributions to their respective major journals is that the *Review* has published more articles by authors associated with United States sociology de-partments. Again, whether this reflects the relative newness of sociology in Canada and the necessity of relying on United States contributors for publishable research, or whether the editorial boards of the *Review* have been more closely tied to sociologists in the United States than were the editorial boards of the *Canadian Journal of Economics and Political Science* to political scientists in the United States, and therefore also have been more receptive to contributions from United States scholars, is difficult to ascertain.

Since there has been a relative paucity of completed doctoral dissertations and because the majority of dissertations have been written at the University of Toronto, we have not been able to employ these data to illustrate the development of sociology as a discipline. Unfortunately, data on doctoral dissertations in preparation in sociology were unavailable for this purpose at the time this paper was being prepared. Consequently, we will now examine the results of our mailed questionnaires to the several departments of sociology and political science in an attempt to throw more light on the United States impact on sociology and political science in Canada.

The American Impact

As was indicated, questionnaires were sent to 42 Canadian political science and sociology departments. We tried to obtain information on national origins of faculty, countries in which highest degrees were received, orientations of departments and individual faculty, and the distribution of faculty with respect to age and rank. The intention was to utilize these data to test the assumptions that, because of the influx of United States nationals and of Canadians trained in United States universities, Canadian departments of political science and sociology were: (a) neglecting the study of Canadian institutions and social and political processes in favor of other areas of social and political inquiry, and (b) becoming more quantitative and empirical as opposed to normative and traditional in their conceptual and methodological orientations.

An inspection of the data makes four matters clear: First, the study of Canadian political institutions and processes has not been neglected because of the influx of United States born and United States trained scholars into political science departments. Second, there are substantially more United States nationals in the several departments of sociology than there are in the several departments of political science. Third, sociology in Canada appears to be much more of a quantitative and empirically oriented discipline than is political science. Fourth, the orientations of United States nationals and of scholars trained in the United States appear to have no discernible effect on the orientations of Canadian political science departments. In fact, if a relationship does exist, it is in the opposite direction. It is more difficult to assess the effect of the influx of United States nationals on the orientations of Canadian sociology departments, chiefly because the great majority of sociology departments describe themselves as "essentially quantitative-empirical."

With respect to the first point, approximately one-half (i.e., thirteen) of the twenty-seven political science departments responding to our questionnaire listed "Canadian politics" as their strongest major subfield. When this datum is combined with the fact that Canadian politics is the area in which the greatest amount of dissertation research has been and still is carried on and also is the area in which the majority of articles appearing in the principal Canadian political science journal still are written, it is difficult to accept the validity of the "neglect of Canadian institutions" charge. It is true that only three of the sixteen responding sociology departments listed "Canadian studies," "Canadian minorities" and "Canadian society" as their strongest subfield. However, since subfields and research specializations in sociology normally are not structured in terms of geographic areas, but rather are described in more general and universal categories such as "social stratification" and "social theory," the fact that three departments did list some aspect of the study of Canadian society as the subfield in which they were strongest is worth noting. It also is worth noting that seven of the sixteen responding sociology departments list their strongest subfield as "social organizations" and "social institutions." [19] Some of the social institutions and organizations in which teaching and research are being carried on, it is safe to assume, are Canadian. Insofar as the number of United States nationals in Canadian universities is concerned, we find that approximately 35 percent of the members of responding sociology departments are United States nationals, but only 26 percent of the faculty of political science departments [20] are made up of United States nationals. Similarly, although 45 percent of the members of sociology departments are Canadian nationals, 55 percent received their highest degree (M.A. or Ph.D.) in United States universities. The corresponding figures for political science departments are 58 percent and 41 percent (see Table 14). We may infer from these figures that a substantially greater number of Canadian nationals who are sociologists, especially those who hold the Ph.D degree, were trained in United States universities. Connor and Curtis estimate that in 1967–1968 only 6 percent of 216 Ph.D.'s in sociology departments had received them from a Canadian university, whereas 72 percent held degrees from United States universities.[21] In contrast, a paper by March and Jack-

19. In this respect, our data are consonant both with the findings of Connor and Curtis, and with published research in the *Canadian Review of Sociology and Anthropology*. See Desmond Connor and James Curtis, *op. cit.*, and Table 12 above.

20. A comparison of our political science figures with data generated by W. H. N. Hull in his survey undertaken for the Canadian Political Science Association indicates that our "sample" is reasonably representative of the Canadian political science universe of which it is a part. Thus, for example, Hull estimated that 62 percent of political scientists in Canada were Canadian citizens, 19 percent were United States nationals, and approximately 19 percent were nationals of other countries. Table 14 indicates that the equivalent proportions in our data are 58, 26, and 16 percent. There are somewhat greater differences with regard to countries in which first degree and higher degrees were taken, although none were of a magnitude that would invalidate our general findings. With respect to first degree, Hull estimates that 57 percent were taken in Canada, 24 percent in the United States, and 19 percent in other countries. Again, Table 14 indicates the equivalent percentages in our data are 49, 29, and 22 percent. Finally, with regard to higher degrees, Hull estimates that slightly over 27 percent were taken in Canadian universities, 45 percent in the United States schools, and approximately 28 percent in higher institutions in other countries, principally Great Britain. Equivalent figures in the data we have generated are 37, 41, and 22 percent. We are grateful to Professor Hull for acquainting us with these data, which subsequently were published in a paper titled "Political Science in Canada: A Profile," delivered at the Annual Meetings of the Canadian Political Science Association, St. John, June 10, 1971.

21. Desmond Connor and James Curtis, *op. cit.*, p. 24.

son [22] points out that in 1966, 16 percent of Canadian political scientists holding the Ph.D. degree had acquired it in a Canadian university; 51 percent held American Ph.D's. More important, in terms of their potential influence within departments, is the fact that in political science 61 percent of the associate and full professorships are held by Canadian nationals and only 23 percent are held by United States nationals. In reporting sociology departments, 39 percent of the associate

Table 14. *National Origins and Educational Backgrounds of Political Science and Sociology Department Members*

	Political science (N = 291)	Sociology (N = 280)
National origins		
Canadian citizens	58%	45%
United States	26	35
Other countries	16	19
Educational level		
B.A. taken in Canada	49	36
B.A. taken in United States	29	39
B.A. taken in other countries	22	21
Higher degree taken in Canada	37	23
Higher degree taken in United States	41	55
Higher degree taken in other countries	22	22

and full professorships are held by Canadian nationals and 34 percent are held by United States nationals. In other words, in political science departments, Canadian nationals tend to be in the majority in the two ranks that at least in the past have made the majority of major departmental policy decisions, whereas in sociology departments, the distribution of Canadian and United States nationals in the two senior ranks is not appreciably different (see Table 15).

If these figures are approximately representative of actual distributions, we may assume that the charge of Americanization of Canadian universities is more accurate when applied to

22. Roman March and R. J. Jackson, "Aspects of the State of Political Science in Canada," *Midwest Journal of Political Science*, XI (1967), 433–450.

Table 15. Distribution of Political Scientists and Sociologists by Rank and National Origins

	Political Science				Sociology			
	Canadian nationals (N = 168)	U.S. nationals (N = 75)	Other countries nationals (N = 48)	Total (N = 291)	Canadian nationals (N = 108)	U.S. nationals (N = 96)	Other countries nationals (N = 53)	Total (N = 257)
Rank								
Lecturer	15%	9%	19%	14%	17%	9%	6%	12%
Assistant professor	40	53	40	43	54	61	53	56
Associate professor	21	24	27	23	12	20	26	18
Professor	24	13	15	20	18	9	15	14
Proportion of lecturers and assistant professorships who are:	55	28	17	100	43	39	18	100
Proportion of associate and full professorships who are:	61	23	16	100	39	34	27	100

sociology departments than when it is made for political science. The greater visibility of American nationals in sociology departments, we assume, generates complaints such as that made by David Coburn in a recent paper. According to Coburn, "Many or most immigrants [sociologists] lack any knowledge of the Canadian scene, formal or informal. For some foreign scholars their residence in Canada is temporary and it seems likely that many of these are merely physically present and remain intellectually oriented to events in the United States or elsewhere."[23]

Coburn feels that United States nationals have affected Canadian sociology generally, but Connor and Curtis claim that a distinction must be made between the impact that Americans have made on sociology within and outside the province of Quebec. They point out that the great majority of sociologists who are United States nationals, as well as the majority of Canadians trained in United States universities, take positions in English-speaking sociology departments. Consequently, universities in Quebec have had to depend on European and European-trained scholars to staff their sociology departments. Thus they argue, "English-Canadian sociology seems more like United States sociology, while French-Canadian sociology resembles the 'European' type."[24] They also point out that part of the seeming lack of concern on the part of English-Canadian sociology with social theory, with the sociology of knowledge and with ideologies[25] is a consequence of this American influence. It may well be, therefore, that the charge that Canadian society and the study of Canadian institutions is being neglected by sociologists in Canada merely reflects a more general lack of emphasis on holistic social theories by sociologists generally. In effect, Canadian society and its institutions are not the only ones being slighted, if indeed they are.

Although Coburn in his paper asks that Canada begin

23. David Coburn, "Sociology and Sociologists in Canada: Problems and Prospects," in Jan J. Loubser (ed.), *The Future of Sociology in Canada* (Montreal, 1970), p. 44.
24. Desmond Connor and James Curtis, *op. cit.*, p. 42.
25. See, however, the data in Table 12.

producing her own qualified sociologists, and also calls for the establishment of more courses in Canadian society and greater use of Canadian data in general courses, Arthur K. Davis's recent paper, "Some Failings of Anglophone Academic Sociology in Canada," [26] asserts that these remedial measures are not likely to have much effect—at least not so far as vitiating the American impact on Canadian sociology. Davis claims that anglophone sociologists in Canadian universities "have presented an abstract, bland and static picture of Canadian society. They see the world through a middle-class lens. . . . They abstract their variables from time and place—thus the images they present are largely timeless and placeless. . . . For the average person who pays most of the shot for academic sociology, it is more relevant to read Anne Landers." [27]

According to Davis, there are two reasons for the aridity of anglophone sociology in Canada. The first, he argues, is the preoccupation of English-speaking sociologists with structural-functionalism. Structural functionalism, he feels, is a culture-bound apology for continued middle-class domination of society. The second reason is the general identification of sociologists "with the Anglo-Canadian bourgeois Establishment" and with the latter's "country-cousin status as a branch plant of the American capitalist empire." [28] He feels that French-Canadian sociologists also have been affected by structural-functionalism but not as much as their English colleagues. These two tendencies are manifested in what he terms an array of rather useless "Mickey Mouse" textbooks imported from the United States or produced by Canadian branch plants of American publishers. He concludes that the attacks on the Americanization of Canadian universities are justified. However, the conventional solution—more Canadians, educated in Canada, teaching in Canadian universities—is inadequate. "What difference does it make so long as Canadian sociologists continue to be trained in such obfuscating as micro-empiricism, structural-functionalism and symbolic interaction? They will still remain docile junior lieu-

26. Arthur K. Davis, *op. cit.*, pp. 31–35.
27. *Ibid.*, p. 32.   28. *Ibid.*

tenants in the intellectual empire of the American Establishment." [29]

With respect to the third point made previously, an examination of the content during the past 25 years of major journals in political science and sociology makes clear the latter is more of an empirically oriented discipline than the former and that quantitative analytic techniques also have been accepted and regularly employed in research for a longer time in sociology. Our data also reflect these disciplinary differences; only three of the sixteen responding sociology department chairmen (19 percent) placed their departments on the normative end of a nine point scale ranging from "essentially normative" (0) to "essentially quantitative-empirical" (9), whereas over half (56 percent) of the twenty-seven responding political science department chairmen described their collegues as "essentially normative" in their orientations. Thus, the claim that the continued recruitment of American social scientists and Canadians trained in United States graduate schools is changing the orientations of political science and sociology departments from normative to quantitative-empirical in a sense is irrelevant insofar as the latter discipline is concerned. The majority of sociologists, regardless of the countries in which they are professionally employed, probably have thought of themselves as empiricists and of their discipline as empirical (and quantitative) for at least a decade. Nevertheless, we did cross-tabulate orientations of sociology departments with a number of variables, including the proportion of United States nationals in a department, and found that not one of the three "normative" sociology departments had a roster that was over 50 percent American. Conversely, in all three normative departments, Canadian nationals were in a majority (over 50 percent).

Since only three of the sociology departments labeled themselves "normative," it was felt that we might be better able to delineate an "American impact" by dividing the sociology departments into two groups: departments that included one-third or more United States nationals and departments in which

29. *Ibid.*, p. 34.

United States nationals made up less than one-third. We then placed these two groups of departments into a multiple discriminant function analysis.[30] This analysis allows for the combination of multiple variables into a linear function that will best discriminate between groups that have been defined a priori. As predictor variables we employed measures such as "orientations of Canadian faculty," "percentage B.A. from Canadian universities," "percentage higher degree from United States universities," and "orientations of United States nationals."

Table 16. *Multiple Discriminant Function Analysis for Sociology Departments with Respect to the Proportion United States Nationals Therein* [a]

Variable entered	F at entry	Stepwise multiple F	Percent correctly grouped
1. Percent B.A. United States	16.49 [b]	16.49	87.5
2. Orientation of strongest and major subfield	10.97 [b]	19.61	93.7
3. Orientation of "other" faculty	6.92 [c]	21.33	100.0

[a] The variables are listed for each sample in the order in which they appeared in the stepwise discriminant function. "F at entry" refers to the F value for the variable at its entry into the function; "Stepwise multiple F" refers to the multiple F, given each of the variables included; "Percent correctly grouped" indicates the percentage of cases correctly placed, given the number of variables involved at each step.
[b] Significant at .01 level
[c] Significant at .05 level

Table 16 displays the results of this analysis. As expected, the best predictor of differences between sociology departments containing a substantial and a relatively small proportion of United States nationals is "percent B.A. from United States." Although there is not a perfect relationship between the possession of a United States undergraduate degree and United States citizenship, the former can be considered a surrogate for citizenship. Thus, this variable correctly groups fourteen of the sixteen departments (87.5 percent). The variable "orientations of major

30. For a detailed description of this analytic technique see W. W. Cooley and P. R. Lohnes, *Multivariate Procedures for the Behavioral Sciences* (New York, 1962).

subfield" increased the proportion of correctly grouped departments to 93.7 percent, and "orientations of other (neither
United States nor Canadian nationals) faculty" completed the
correct grouping of the departments.

Interestingly, although the latter variable also was a significant predictor of differences between political science departments containing relatively large and relatively small proportions
of Americans, the variable "percent B.A. from United States"
was not a discriminating factor (see Table 17). Instead, "per-

Table 17. *Multiple Discriminant Function Analysis for Canadian Political Science Departments with Respect to Proportion of United States Nationals Therein* [a]

Variable entered	F at entry	Stepwise multiple F	Percent correctly grouped
1. Percent higher degree United States	36.71 [b]	36.71	81.5
2. Orientation of "other faculty"	12.22 [c]	32.71	92.6
3. Orientation of strongest subfield	3.89	25.72	96.2
4. Age of faculty	2.82	21.53	100.0

[a] The variables are listed for each sample in the order in which they appeared in the
stepwise discriminant function. "F at entry" refers to the F value for the variable at its
entry into the function; "Stepwise multiple F" refers to the multiple F, given each of the
variables included; "Percent correctly grouped" indicates the percentage of cases
correctly placed, given the number of variables involved at each step.
[b] Significant at .001 level
[c] Significant at .01 level

cent higher degree from United States" was the most powerful
predictor, accounting for the correct classification of 81.5 percent of political science departments. And, although "orientations of major subfield" and "age of faculty" correctly grouped
additional departments, their importance was not statistically
significant. A reasonable inference to be drawn from these
analyses with respect to the presence of United States nationals
in political science departments is that, rather than Americans
recruiting more Americans when new positions are to be filled
in a department, it is the Canadian nationals and other country
nationals who have been educated at the M.A. and Ph.D. level in
American universities who tend to suggest colleagues and friends

from these institutions as potential candidates for positions. Since the great majority of individuals attending United States graduate schools are, quite naturally, United States nationals, it follows that a substantial proportion of the recommendees will also be United States nationals and their number within a particular department will rise.

Another assumption is that the more nationals of other countries there are in departments of political science or sociology, the less likely there are to be significant numbers of Americans therein. Whether the orientations of "other" faculty (a variable that significantly discriminates between departments of political science and sociology with relatively large and relatively small numbers of Americans) induce certain departments not to recruit United States nationals, or whether United States nationals who are offered positions in such departments refuse them because they perceive their own orientations and the orientations of "other" scholars to be incompatible, or whether they simply regard such departments as uncongenial, is a matter that cannot be ascertained from the data. One may speculate, however, that all three conditions may hold. That is, departments with relatively large numbers of faculty who are neither Canadian nor United States nationals are not particularly receptive to the notion of having United States nationals as colleagues and the latter are not especially motivated to join such departments because they regard them as inhospitable.

It will be remembered that approximately one-half (i.e., fifteen) of the twenty-seven Canadian political science departments who responded to our questionnaire placed themselves on the normative end of a normative-empirical-quantitative continuum. The application of multiple discriminant function analysis to data on variations in orientations of political science departments indicates that the best predictor of departmental orientations are the orientations of its Canadian faculty members (see Table 18). The only other statistically significant predictor of orientations is the age of departmental faculty. As might be assumed, the younger the average age of a department's faculty, the greater the tendency to describe the department as essentially quantitative-empirical. However, other variables such as the orientations of United States faculty members, the proportion of individuals holding higher degrees from United States universities, and the orientations of other faculty are not significant predictors.

Our conclusions, based on these analyses, are that neither national origins nor even the locus of professional training directly affects the conceptual and methodological orientations

Table 18. Multiple Discriminant Function Analysis for Canadian Political Science Departments with Respect to Orientation of the Department [a]

Variable entered	F at entry	Stepwise multiple F	Percent correctly grouped
1. Orientation of Canadian faculty members	10.61 [b]	10.61	81.5
2. Age of faculty	7.48 [b]	10.41	88.8
3. Percent higher degree from "other" countries	2.96	8.50	85.2
4. Percent B.A. from the United States	4.11	8.26	88.8

[a] The variables are listed for each sample in the order in which they appeared in the stepwise discriminant function. "F at entry" refers to the F value for the variable at its entry into the function; "Stepwise multiple F" refers to the multiple F, given each of the variables included; "Percent correctly grouped" indicates the percentage of cases correctly placed, given the number of variables involved at each step.

[b] Significant at .01 level

of political science departments. Although sociology as a discipline is much more of a data-based enterprise than is political science, there is at least a hint in the data on the sociology departments that United States national origins and professional training may have some effect on the orientations of departments. They may even have some effect on the emphasis given to major subfields within a department. Overall, however, United States origins and professional training are not especially powerful predictors in these regards—certainly they are not as important as a reading of critics of the American presence in Canadian universities would suggest. Why then, we must ask, has there been so much concern voiced over the influx of United

States scholars into Canadian universities? And what factors explain that influx?

Let us initially consider the latter question, for the responses to the former derive largely from it. It seems clear that the concern voiced over the Americanization of Canadian universities has its origins in the enormous growth that higher education in Canada has experienced in the post World War II period. Although graduate training and research in the "hard sciences" (and in medicine) were fairly well developed and for sometime had enjoyed a reasonably adequate level of funding, this was not the case with the social sciences. However, graduate programs in political science and sociology have expanded rapidly during the past decade. Moreover, funding for basic research in the two disciplines also has increased, especially since 1965 when the Canada Council began receiving funds through annual parliamentary appropriations.[31] Despite this rapid programmatic expansion and the increase in the level of research funds that became available, the number of doctorates produced in political science, and particularly in Canadian sociology departments, could not begin to keep pace with the tremendous expansion in faculty that was required because of increased student enrollments. For example, David Coburn estimates that academic departments of sociology increased by 784 percent during the years 1956–1967, whereas only nine doctorates in sociology were awarded by Canadian universities during the same period.[32] Quite naturally, then, departmental chairmen and their administrative superiors looked to United States institutions with their seemingly inexhaustible supply of Ph.D.'s to staff new and/or expanded departments in the two disciplines. Readers should note the last sentence for an obvious reason: the development and expansion of graduate programs in political science and sociology required that the academic credentials of new faculty be upgraded and that the traditional external source for recruiting new faculty, Great Britain, virtually be abandoned. It

31. This is not to suggest that the Canada Council did not support social science research before 1965. It did.
32. David Coburn, *op. cit.*, p. 44.

was, after all, rather awkward for faculty who possessed only a B.A. or an M.A. (even if these were prestigious "Oxbridge" degrees) to sit on "prelim" committees and to evaluate the dissertations of those who shortly would hold "better" credentials than their own. Thus, two of the reasons for the concern expressed over the influx of United States scholars undoubtedly are: (1) heightened visibility and awareness of their presence that are consequences of an increase in their sheer numbers; and (2) a concomitant heightening of the insecurities of some already-established faculty because the academic credentials of newly arrived colleagues seemed better.

In political science these insecurities may have been increased by the fact that the professional training of recent recruits from United States graduate schools generally has been more congruent with the direction in which political science, as a discipline, appears to be moving. Taken together, the recruitment of large numbers of highly educated individuals trained to utilize the most sophisticated research techniques available constitutes a distinct economic threat to some already established faculty. Professor Harry G. Johnson, in a Convocation address at Carleton University, took note of the economic dimension underlying some of the protests of over-Americanization when he stated:

. . . some Canadian intellectuals, more gifted in elementary statistics than in economic and social understanding, have decried the results of Canada's ability to hire foreign scholars at short notice to teach its rapidly-expanding student body as "a takeover of the mind." It is true that foreign competition prevents third-rate Canadian academics from earning first-rate salaries, and also prevents them from managing second-rate departments in a fourth-rate way; but it is not clear that Canadian students would benefit from having their instruction monopolized by whatever intellectual rag-tag-and-bobtail can qualify itself as genuine Canadian.[33]

Professor Johnson's remarks may be excessively harsh but the complaints over Americanization of Canadian universities do appear, at least in part, to be not too different from the cry for

33. Harry G. Johnson, "Canada and Contemporary Society," Convocation Address given at Carleton University, Ottawa, 1970, mimeo, pp. 3–4.

"protection" against "unfair" external competition that spokesmen for vocal and economically threatened interest groups in
any country traditionally have directed toward their respective
publics and public authorities. In the present case, the perception of an economic threat appears to be grounded in reality;
the recent action of the Ontario government in curtailing funds
for the support of graduate programs in Ontario universities
may be regarded as an unpleasant omen of things to come
elsewhere in Canada. It seems safe to assume, if the expansion
of Canadian universities generally and their graduate programs
in particular slows, and the heavy recruitment of United States
nationals continues, that the professional opportunities initially
available to the products of Canadian graduate programs eventually will be considerably restricted. Ultimately, the tenure of
current incumbents of professorial positions also could be threatened.

It should be noted, although the large scale external recruitment of academicians has relatively recent origins, that the tactic
itself has a long history in Canada. Sociologist John Porter and
others have noted that whenever substantial technical and
professional skills have been required to meet expanded Canadian needs, the tendency has been to recruit the necessary
personnel from outside of Canada rather than to develop the
necessary Canadian resources to meet the need internally.[34]
It is understandable that some of those most immediately
affected by the utilization of this tactic should feel professionally
and economically threatened, but the latter reasons alone cannot explain either the volume and variety of complaints of
Americanization of Canadian universities or the relative sympathy with which the charges have been received. In our view,
an additional and more important explanation is that the complaints are symbolic of and a reaction to two basic changes that
have occurred in Canadian society during the past decade.
The first change is in the attitudes of some Canadian acade-

34. What is less known or, perhaps, less publicized—at least currently—is
that the United States for years has been the recipient of and benefited from
scientists and scholars trained in Canada.

micians toward new conditions within their respective disciplines. Very simply put, as a group, highly visible and relatively recently arrived United States nationals have been associated with and held responsible by some of their Canadian colleagues for substantive and procedural changes in the conduct of teaching, research and interpersonal relations that really are functions of the rapid growth and expansion of certain disciplines. Professorial incumbents in older, more "established" disciplines, have been most affected by these changes. As we have observed above, political science, for example, was dominated for approximately twenty-five years by a handful of men at elite Eastern universities such as Toronto, McGill, and Queen's. They carried out most of the research that was undertaken during this period; they read most of the papers presented at small, informal, and relaxed annual professional meetings; they and their friends tended virtually to monopolize positions on the editorial board of the *Canadian Journal of Economics and Political Science;* and, not unnaturally, their articles, notes, and reviews also appeared most frequently in the *Journal.* In addition, most of the available positions in the miniscule departments of political science of other universities were filled by their students. The most notable of the latter, after a period of "farming out," sometimes were offered appointments in the departments in which they had been trained.

Political science, then, had some of the qualities of a first-rate men's club. Gentlemen members, deriving from similar social and educational backgrounds, enjoying and feeling comfortable in one another's presence, structured the rules under which the club operated and also determined the conditions under which new members would be admitted. After 1965, however, Canadian political science became less of a club-like enterprise. So many new appointments were made so quickly that one no longer knew who was who in which department. Annual professional meetings grew large; the number of papers presented by authors whose names generally were unfamiliar increased; and each year the meetings of the Learned Society appeared to be attended more and more by strangers and by the importuning representatives of commercial publishers and less and less by old friends and colleagues.

Moreover, many of the recent additions to the several departments of political science, regardless of their national origins, often either were not sufficiently impressed with the eminence of great Canadian universities, or appreciative of the opportunity to be employed therein. Because of factors such as higher initial salaries, lower teaching loads, the availability of financial support for research, and better computing facilities, York was as likely to be preferred as Toronto by new faculty, Laval as McGill, Carleton as Ottawa, and Waterloo as Western. And, despite invocations such as the one by Butler and Shugarman quoted at the beginning of the paper, the scholarly models taken by many newly recruited political scientists (again, regardless of national origins) were more often Lasswell and Easton than Macpherson; Deutsch and Russet than Eayrs; and Almond, and Verba than Smiley. The availability of substantial research funds from the Canada Council also affected a basic change in interpersonal relations within departments in that they freed new faculty from almost total dependence upon departmental and/or university research grants and hence also made them less dependent on the goodwill of their senior colleagues. Finally, the establishment in 1968 of a journal devoted exclusively to the publication of political science research with an editor who had pioneered in the use of quantitative research techniques provided them with a major scholarly outlet for the research they were able to generate. At the same time commercial publishers, eager to encourage the collation and synthesizing of new and not-so-new research products into texts and "books of readings" for a burgeoning market, offered them an opportunity to enhance not only their professional prestige but also their annual incomes.

In our view then, some of the protests against Americanization are as much a response to the consequence of rapid disciplinary changes as they are to the values and orientations that American professors, as Americans, hold, or to the behavior in which they engage. In so far as values are concerned, the criticisms that have been leveled by some Canadian academicians against the conservative, status quo, establishment-serving and dehumanizing tendencies that presumably are manifest in American political science and sociology have been made far more trenchantly and effectively by American scholars themselves. Indeed, the so-called "caucuses" of various kinds in political science and sociology have been notably successful in making these tendencies matters of central concern not only to their disciplinary colleagues, but also (with a strong assist from the media) to a substantial segment of the informed public.

With regard to the specific impact of Americans on political science and sociology, our analysis indicates that within Canadian political science departments, the study of Canadian political institutions has (and still is) not being neglected; the bulk of research and teaching in Canadian politics is being carried out and will continue to be carried out by Canadians trained in the graduate programs of Canadian universities. It has been more difficult to determine whether Canadian social institutions and processes are being neglected by Canadian sociology because of the influx of United States nationals, or, whether Americans who are sociologists are either more or less ignorant of Canadian institutions and Canadian society than are their countrymen who are political scientists. All that we have been able to determine is that there appear to be more United States nationals in Canadian sociology than in political science departments and that the former are better represented in the associate and full professor ranks (and thus presumably wield more influence within their respective departments) than their countrymen who are political scientists. But if Canadian social institutions and processes are being neglected it can be reasonably argued that the neglect is more a consequence of the general paucity of empirical research than of the presence of American nationals in sociology departments. One also can speculate that this neglect is a function, in part, of the way some Canadian elites have tended to view their country—as a poor thing that is somehow not really worthy of serious study.[35]

35. Characteristic, in our view, is a recent series of eight articles by Vern Fowlie in the *Winnipeg Free Press* on the state of higher education in Manitoba.

In light of this historic view, the current outcry against the neglect of Canadian institutions is especially ironic. With respect to the claim that because of the influence of United States nationals, departments are becoming more quantitative and empirical, we have pointed out that sociology has been an empirically-oriented discipline for at least a decade. Examination of the data on the distribution of published articles and of dissertation research indicated there has been a definite trend toward empiricism and quantification in Canadian political science. But this trend reflects a disciplinary-wide process that is certainly not confined to Canada. It is, for example, also occurring in Europe where there are very few American nationals in professorial positions. As for the abandonment of so-called "traditionally Canadian" methods of scholarly inquiry, the latter also are not indigenous to Canada. The tendency to describe phenomena rather than to explain them, to ground theoretical formulations in speculation rather than in empirical tests, and to organize data in a chronological fashion are methods and approaches to scholarly investigation that probably still are employed by a majority of political scientists, albeit not sociologists, both within and outside of Canada.

Again, consider the charge that because so many American quantifiers and empiricists now are members of Canadian political science and sociology departments, research priorities in the two disciplines are being distorted. It seems clear from the paucity of published materials in political science and sociology (even of textbooks and books of readings) and from the virtual absence before 1965 of financial support for basic research in the two fields that there was neither much research nor few priorities to distort. It also is interesting (and somewhat ironic) to note in this regard that, in the "good old days" when there were far fewer Americans and presumably research priorities were not being distorted, the principal source of financial sup-

---

The lead article in the series, published June 28, 1971, is devoted to charges by unnamed high echelon educators in the Manitoba government that research by university professors in general, and by University of Manitoba professors in particular, "is a waste of time and money."

port for social science research in Canada was the Social Science Research Council. The latter, as is well known, secured the bulk of its funds from three giant U.S. foundations—Rockefeller, Ford, and Carnegie.

Not only have U.S. nationals in Canadian universities come to symbolize and to be held responsible for the consequences of some of the rapid changes that have occurred in Canadian higher education, they also have become symbols of conditions in American society that have affected profound change in Canadian attitudes toward the United States. That the presence of a gigantic adjacent society exercising powerful and relatively continuous influence on politics, the economy, the media and the arts should have inspired a degree of historically rooted anti-Americanism in Canada is to be expected. The point need not be labored. What is unexpected, are the quantitative and qualitative changes in anti-American feelings that seemingly have occurred during the last decade. Obviously, it is difficult to cite a specific event or date as the agent that precipitated these changes. A reasonable assumption, however, is that the Cuban missile crisis of 1962 made clear to Canadians of every stripe that their individual existence and their continued existence as a nation were in the hands of a small group of United States decisionmakers over whom they exercised neither control nor influence. Succeeding events which the American mass-media spotlighted, distorted, and transmitted to the rest of the world strongly suggested that the American public, even the Congress, also exercised only limited influence on or control of this small cadre of decisionmakers. Certainly, this realization must have further depressed, frightened and angered Canadians.

An ensuing series of events and conditions, principally incidents of mindless racism, rigid, uncompromising anti-Communism, urban blight, and environmental despoilation exacerbated these feelings. More recently, the application of vast military force against the civilian population of a small Asian country, coupled with the seeming insensitivity of successive Administrations to massive social protests against conditions within the United States and American actions abroad, have added disgust and a kind of xenophobic resentment of the United States to the already existing fears and frustrations of Canadians. In our view, it is this disgust and xenophobia that have added a new dimension to the anti-Americanism of Canadians. And, it is against the conditions symbolized by the term "Amerika" that many Canadian academicians really are protesting when they charge that Canadian universities are being Americanized, or that the study of Canadian institutions is being neglected, or that traditionally Canadian methods of scholarly inquiry are being abandoned. Regardless of the overt form these protests take, the underlying objection is to the United States as a society! Accordingly, if we were to rank the reasons for the protest against the Americanization of Canadian universities in order of their importance, we would rate first this qualitatively new hostility to the United States as a society.

It is precisely because United States nationals in Canadian universities have come to be symbols of the malaise within their society (despite the fact that many of them initially took employment in Canadian universities because of despair over current conditions in their country) that protests against their presence on Canadian campuses are likely to continue unabated, regardless of any changes they make in their values, their personal attitudes, and their methodological orientations. As long as the United States continues to be perceived by Canadians, especially Canadian academicians, as "Amerika," it will matter little if United States nationals teaching in Canada become thoroughly knowledgeable about Canadian society, if they stop making invidious comparisons between Canada and the United States during their lectures, if they never carry out another survey, or even if they denounce Talcott Parsons as a shameless apologist for the status quo and abjure structural-functionalism forever; their presence on Canadian faculties will continue to be resented.

It is ironic that the first systematic attempt to develop Canadian universities to meet the long-range need for highly trained academic social scientists internally should have required the relatively large scale external recruitment of the latter individuals from the United States. It is an even greater irony that the recruitees should come to symbolize to their Canadian colleagues precisely the conditions that led many of them to leave the United States. Of course, they can take comfort in the fact that as highly visible and convenient objects against whom Canadian colleagues can vent their hostility, they are performing a very useful and valuable cathartic function for them. So valuable, in fact, that one can speculate that if U.S. nationals did not exist in Canadian universities, they might have to be invented, or perhaps, manufactured under license—from an American parent firm, of course.

3

American Influences on the Conduct of Canadian Politics

Mildred A. Schwartz

No student of Canadian politics can ignore the impact of the United States on issues faced and policies adopted in Canada. But if there is one area of political life that stands almost immune to American influence, it is the style in which politics is conducted. The reasons for this are as numerous as they are obvious. At the most basic level, the reasons lie in the origins of the two countries. The United States began by breaking with the mother country and its monarchical institutions. Canada was a conscious rebuff to the American experience and a deliberate continuation of the British connection and its political traditions. Facing recurring common and unique political problems, each country developed its own political institutions. In the United States this included a presidential system, and a division of powers among legislative, executive, and judicial branches of government. In Canada, it was the British model of a parliamentary system that was adopted, and with it, united powers in the three principal functions of government. Such systematic differences have meant, for example, that there has been only minor adoption of American practices in the procedures of the House of Commons. Dawson tells us that this is confined to such things as desks for members, page boys for running errands, and roll call votes.[1]

In some respects the two countries are similar because of the

1. William F. Dawson, *Procedure in the Canadian House of Commons* (Toronto, 1962), p. 14.

diversity of their populations, but there is a crucial difference in both the extent and origin of this diversity. The United States too is made up of many peoples, but no single one successfully challenged the ascendancy of the white, Protestant, northern-European and basically Anglo-Saxon leadership classes. In Canada there has always been a challenger, whether or not a successful one. Here I mean of course those of French origin, incorporated into British North America as a conquered people, but also becoming one of the founding peoples of the Canadian nation. From the outset, Canada had to face the challenge of developing political mechanisms for dealing with the fact of French existence. For the French themselves, the best way to maintain their identity lay in continued union with British North America, and not with the republican institutions of the United States. In joining that country, efforts to retain a separate language, religion, and culture would soon be swamped by the pervading Yankee spirit. This was a view especially strong among the clergy,[2] and the political elite.[3]

The prevailing views of political leaders, from colonial times onward, were suspicious of the governmental practices of their American neighbors. Devoid of respect for authority, corrupted by the spoils system, infected with a missionary zeal that made them dangerously aggressive, there was little to admire in the way they conducted their political affairs.[4] With the advent of the Civil War, the worst features of their political system stood revealed.[5]

For such reasons, one would expect Canadian political forms to be successfully immunized against the American example. To the extent that this is true, it means that some of the most apparent differences between the two countries lie in this area.

2. Mason Wade, *The French Canadians 1760–1967* (Toronto, 1968), pp. 99–101.
3. S. F. Wise, "Colonial Attitudes from the Era of the War of 1812 to the Rebellions of 1837," in S. F. Wise and Robert Craig Brown (eds.), *Canada Views the United States: Nineteenth-Century Political Attitudes* (Seattle, 1967), p. 26.
4. Robert Craig Brown, "Canadian Opinion after Confederation, 1867–1914," in *ibid.*, pp. 98–120.
5. Robin W. Winks, *Canada and the United States: The Civil War Years* (Baltimore, 1960), pp. 238–240.

Yet there are also links in the practice and style of politics. To understand how they come about requires a different perspective on the nature of influence. If we understand influence to be confined to those situations where A is able to alter the behavior of B, whether or not B wishes to follow this course of action, then we have a notion of influence analogous to what is often labeled power.[6] Using this definition, it is clear that the United States has not had much influence in this particular area. One of the few exceptions was a result of incursions into Canada during the American War of Independence. Mason Wade writes that when elections were ordered in those Quebec parishes under American control, "This measure introduced into Quebec the new idea of the people's right to choose its own chiefs, and the innovation was exceedingly well received throughout the province."[7]

For the most part, such power-directed forms of influence are unusual. But to grant that influence can be used in a number of other ways does not carry us much further. What is more crucial is whether "influence" is the most appropriate way of conceptualizing affinities between American and Canadian political styles. James March's writing on power is instructive in this regard, when he asks, "To what extent is one specific concept of power useful in the empirical analysis of mechanisms of social choice?"[8] It is social choice itself which is constant, while in the forms it takes, the presence or absence of power factors is problematic. The situation of Canada exemplifies what March terms process models of choice, where power is at best a negligible factor. Two types of processes best account for Canadian choices of political conduct, those related to communication-diffusion and those related to problem-solving.[9] In the communication-diffusion model, choices are made as a result of the spread of information through elaborated communication networks,

6. For example, Robert A. Dahl, *Who Governs?* (New Haven, Conn., 1961); Talcott Parsons, *Sociological Theory and Modern Society* (New York, 1967), pp. 297–382.
7. Wade, *The French Canadians*, pp. 70–71.
8. James G. March, "The Power of Power," in David Easton (ed.), *Varieties of Political Theory* (Englewood Cliffs, N.J., 1966), p. 39.
9. *Ibid.*, pp. 65–68.

whether formal or informal. Here the United States acts as an analogue to an "opinion leader"; [10] it is, for whatever reasons, the pace-setter, the exemplar for action.

In the problem-solving model, March postulates "some kind of processes by which the system calls forth and organizes the information and skills so as systematically to reduce the difference between its present position and a solution." [11] I am suggesting that the information and skills at issue are similar in the two countries, as are the problems. I do not mean that this is necessarily always true, but only that there are many situations where both countries face common problems, and given a relatively restricted range of alternatives, come up with similar solutions. What may appear to be influence then is the result of a common fate. [12]

While it is difficult to find examples of conventional forms of influence qua power, we can more easily illustrate both models of choice behavior. For example, communication-diffusion processes operated in the framing of the Canadian constitution. Despite many overt criticisms of the United States and its system of government, opinions from the closest and best-informed of neighbors were often quite selective, sifting the admirable from the reprehensible. To completely ignore the United States would have been impossible, and to only find fault would have represented a meanness of spirit that Canadians have not normally displayed. Some positive assessment was inevitable, given the intellectual force of the early American leaders, men whose writings marked them as political sages not only for their time and country. Washington, Adams, Jefferson, Hamilton,

10. For example, Elihu Katz and Paul F. Lazarsfeld, *Personal Influence* (New York, 1955).
11. March, "The Power of Power," p. 66.
12. Campbell uses the concept of common fate as an indicator of a single social system. That is, to the extent that separate units share a common fate they can be presumed to be part of the same system. To a limited degree, I have a similar notion when I speak of the shared political problems that arise from the North American context. I am not in any sense, however, suggesting that the two countries are part of the same political system. Donald T. Campbell, "Common Fate, Similarity and Other Indices of the Status of Aggregates of Persons as Social Entities," in Dorothy Willner (ed.), *Decisions, Values and Groups,* I, *Reports from the First Interdisciplinary Conference in the Behavioral Science Division* (Oxford, 1960), 185–201.

Madison—such men could not simply be dismissed as apologists for a weak and ill-formed state, one with little prospect for survival. Whether they wanted to or not, Canadian political leaders had to take note of them. Common fate was also an important element in this attention. The United States had earlier developed a federal system of government to deal with the special interests of the separate colonies. Canada had also to face such contending interests, augmented by the even more insistent claims of what would become the Province of Quebec. American precedents and experiences were a major standard against which to judge the alternatives open to Canada.

We know that John A. Macdonald was a careful reader of Madison and Hamilton,[13] and that Hamilton's draft constitution provided him with several critical precedents in framing the Confederation agreements.[14] According to Macdonald, "It is the fashion now to enlarge on the defects of the Constitution of the United States, but I am not one of those who look upon it as a failure. I think and believe that it is one of the most skillful works which human intelligence ever created; [it] is one of the most perfect organizations that ever governed a free people. To say that it has some defects is but to say that it is not the work of Omniscience, but of human intellect." [15] To speak of Hamilton as the grandfather of Confederation,[16] or Macdonald's party as a Hamiltonian party,[17] may be exaggeration. But it is obvious that, in some ways, Hamilton's writings were an important influence in early Canadian politics.

This particular contact between the two countries, paradoxical as it may first appear, gives further insight into Canadian objections to American political style. It was Hamilton, after all, that provided some inspiration to Canadian politicians. Anti-

13. Donald C. Creighton, *John A. Macdonald*, I, *The Young Politician.* (Toronto, 1952), 308.
14. William Bennett Munro, *American Influences on Canadian Government* (Toronto, 1929), p. 18.
15. *Confederation Debates* (1865), p. 32, cited in R. MacGregor Dawson, *The Government of Canada*, 4th edition, revised by Norman Ward (Toronto, 1964), p. 40.
16. Munro, *American Influences*, p. 20.
17. Frank H. Underhill, *In Search of Canadian Liberalism* (Toronto, 1960), p. 33.

Americanism can then be understood as another manifestation of Canadian conservatism, a conservatism steeped in conceptions of elitism and limited democracy.[18] This is, of course, the familiar interpretation given to the counter-revolutionary origins of Canada, abetted by the influx of Loyalists—or is "Tories" in reality the more appropriate label?[19] The impact of this immigration may not have been totally of this ideological character. As McRae points out, "The American Loyalist undoubtedly never understood his own basic liberalism until the circumstances of his exile thrust it upon his consciousness with unmistakable clarity. Those who went to Upper Canada made the discovery most dramatically, for here they found their new townships still part of the old province of Quebec, administered according to the Quebec Act."[20] But regardless of how we wish to interpret the political ideology of the Loyalists, there were others at least who were unequivocal in their appreciation of American political institutions. These were the radicals, the Clear Grits in Canada West and les Rouges in Canada East, who saw in Jacksonian Democracy the model of effective democratic institutions.[21] If later, with the coming of responsible government, they were to lose much of their admiration for the United States, especially with the outbreak of the Civil War, the American experience at least prior to this was an important source of inspiration to the reformers.

The significance of common fates is even more apparent as we consider other developments in the political life of Canada. It has been the North American experience that set the stage for common practices, even as the United States was the originator of many of them. Canada followed, not as a blind borrower, but as a country beset with similar problems, having

18. Brown, "Canadian Opinion," pp. 111–113.
19. Wise, "Colonial Attitudes," p. 22.
20. Kenneth D. McRae, "The Structure of Canadian History," in Louis Hartz (ed.), *The Founding of New Societies* (New York, 1964), p. 237.
21. Wise, "Colonial Attitudes," pp. 30–38; S. F. Wise, "The Annexation Movement and Its Effect on Canadian Opinion, 1837–67," in Wise and Brown (eds.), *Canada Views the United States*, pp. 53–55, 61–62, 64–65. Craig Brown, however, questions the extent to which les Rouges were fully committed to Jacksonian principles. He sees them more in the Jeffersonian tradition. Brown, "Canadian Opinion," p. 111.

available the precedent of its neighbor to suggest modes of adaptation.

Some of the affinities between the two countries may be obscured by the very considerations first emphasized in this paper. In other words, because of deliberate adherence to the British model and repudiation of the American, many practices sound British while in fact they are American. Take for example the origin of the two major Canadian parties. They begin, with some shifts in party labels over time, as Liberals and Conservatives. But to understand their character, Underhill reminds us that there is little point in asking what they proposed to either conserve or liberate. To Underhill it is more relevant to note "the fact that the British names for the parties were preserved and that the parties operated within a British constitutional framework made little difference to their essentially North American quality. The stage properties were imported from Britain, but the plot of the play and the characters on the stage were all native products." [22]

In both countries, parties had to contend with problems of regional diversity, incorporation of a heterogeneous population, the governing of vast territories, opening a western frontier, and of developing political and other organizations that would work in the New World. Out of these experiences they both developed parties in which principles were subordinated to electoral success, where the experience of governing was more important than the reasons for governing. This is not to say that parties in the two countries are ideologically identical. Experiences have been sufficiently unique to create critical differences. For example, the Liberal Party has been more of a true center party than either of the American ones. This is, in no small measure, the result of both a greater degree of Toryism and of socialism in Canada.[23] Yet the similarities that do exist come from common conditions, while the differences are not primarily attributable to the association with names borrowed from Britain.

22. Underhill, *In Search of Canadian Liberalism*, p. 22.
23. Gad Horowitz, "Conservatism, Liberalism, and Socialism in Canada: An Interpretation," *Canadian Journal of Economics and Political Science*, XXXII (May, 1966), 143–171.

Similar arguments can be used to account for developments in extraparliamentary party practices. Americans had some form of extragovernmental party organization beginning with the Democratic or Republican Societies of the 1790's. The Societies were opposed to the governing Federalists at a time when the legitimacy of opposition was still in question. They were not true adjuncts of anti-Administration forces in Congress, and hence might be considered more pressure groups than early versions of the Republican Party, but they were clearly important in achieving success for Republicans in several elections.[24] While most of the Societies disappeared, they were to be precursors of Republican Party organizations leading to Jefferson's election in 1800,[25] as well as to later organizational elaborations.[26]

While coming later in the development of Canadian parties, the emergence of extraparliamentary organizations appeared as well to serve the functions of mobilizing partisans for electoral victory, especially in the case of opposition forces. When the Clear Grits held their convention in Toronto in 1859, the Reformers had already had some experience in coalition government. Under the constitutional conditions of the time, with the need for "double majorities," the experience had hardly been successful and the party was ripped with dissension. Was the party to dissolve, or would this be the fate of existing union between the two provinces? The convention was a means for dealing with these issues, by encouraging broad party support for a set of principles that the party caucus in the legislature could not by itself articulate. If problems were not solved, they were at least presented in a forum that could resolve some issues of party unity, and this compatible with general feelings of the Clear Grits in support of open party conventions, and other Jacksonian innovations in cheap and efficient government.[27]

---

24. William Nisbet Chambers, *Political Parties in a New Nation: The American Experience, 1776–1809* (New York, 1963), pp. 61–63.
25. *Ibid.*, pp. 152–153.   26. *Ibid.*, pp. 162–165.
27. George W. Brown, "The Grit Party and the Great Reform Convention of 1859," in Ramsay Cook, Craig Brown, Carl Berger (eds.), *Upper Canadian Politics in the 1850's*, II, *Canadian Historical Readings* (Toronto, 1967), 17–37; Dale C. Thomson, *Alexander Mackenzie, Clear Grit* (Toronto, 1960), pp. 55–56; R. M. Dawson, *The Government of Canada*, pp. 457, 474.

Ranney and Kendall express some bemusement at such developments in the extragovernmental party organization of Canada:

For no readily apparent reason, it has patterned itself upon American rather than British models, so that, for example, we find the Canadians picking their party leaders at national representative party conventions. . . . The Liberal party, the first to adopt the present system, did so with the avowed purpose of "democratizing" the nominating procedure—that is, of turning it over to representatives of the party's provincial organizations, which presumably could have been done without imitating such other features of the typical American convention as the keynote speech, the written platform, and nominating and seconding speeches. But the first Liberal convention (1919) imitated these features also, and departed from American precedent only by using the secret rather than the open ballot in the nominating process. The Conservatives began holding similar conventions in 1927 . . .[28]

What these authors do not note, and which I feel is the telling point in the adoption of these practices, is the opposition role of both parties at the time that they held their first leadership conventions. When the Liberals held their convention to choose Mackenzie King as leader, they were not only in opposition, but were in fact devastated by wartime experiences that had torn apart both the party and the country over the conscription issue. The convention was a mechanism for generating large-scale support, for involving large numbers in the affairs of the Liberal Party to aid it in again becoming a national political movement, capable of governing.

The Conservatives were slower to adopt this procedure for choosing leaders, waiting until 1927 to do so:

The disastrous reverse which the Conservatives had just suffered in the election and the contrasting success of the Liberals (who had used the convention system in 1919) convinced the majority of the conference that some greater effort should be made to identify the Conservative party as a whole with the selection of a new national leader. The obvious way to achieve this end was to hold a national congress of the party. The call was accordingly issued, and the first Conservative national convention assembled at Winnipeg in 1927. R. B. Bennett

28. Austin Ranney and Willmoore Kendall, *Democracy and The American Party System* (New York, 1956), p. 106.

was chosen leader, and the next election returned the Conservatives to power. Once again, a convention had been followed by victory.[29]

Choosing their next leader by this fashion, but without electoral success, the Conservatives reverted to the old method of selection by party politicians. Since this proved no more successful, the convention has become the accustomed technique. For the two major parties, conventions have been viewed from the pragmatic perspective of their usefulness, and not primarily from an ideological commitment to their democratizing function. It is the former which dictates their frequency and scope. As Dawson observed, apparently unconvinced himself of the benefit of conventions for opening political parties to broader participation,[30]

Success at the polls and the control of a government . . . are usually taken as a sufficient justification and authorization for continued leadership, even although the convention from which the power has been derived and which has laid down a programme is many years removed. The continued success of Mackenzie King thus led the Liberals to ignore the national convention and its legendary prestige and authority for twenty-nine years; while the Conservatives, with little love for conventions but less luck in elections, had no less than three conventions during that period.[31]

We can, I believe, continue to use our related models of communication-diffusion and problem-solving to interpret even what appears to be the most blatant borrowing from the United States. In the presidential election of 1960, the two candidates, John F. Kennedy and Richard M. Nixon, engaged in a series of television debates. These were watched by anywhere from 85 to 120 million viewers,[32] including large numbers in Canada, where the CBC carried the first and fourth debates. Audience reaction in Canada was generally favorable, and a large majority of those interviewed after the fourth debate felt that "heads of

29. Dawson, *The Government of Canada*, p. 504.
30. *Ibid.*, pp. 494, 505.   31. *Ibid.*, p. 475.
32. Kurt Lang and Gladys Engel Lang, *Politics and Television* (Chicago, 1968), p. 213.

the Canadian political parties should debate on television."[33] It was only a matter of time before Canadians would share this experience. The first occasion was a debate between the Union Nationale leader, Daniel Johnson, and the Liberal leader, Jean Lesage, prior to the 1962 Quebec provincial election. This too was favorably received, and viewers in Montreal who were interviewed after the debate were almost unanimous in their interest and in their desire for similar events.[34] In 1968, the format, suitably adapted to the multiparty situation of Canada, was given a national forum.

The debates, and the use of television in political campaigning generally, have meant a transformation of the conduct of politics.[35] There is a new emphasis on the use of technical, nonpolitical experts; on candidate images, the selection of candidates "quick on the verbal draw," along with a downgrading of issues. To some, the manifestation of these processes in Canada appears as the most pernicious form of the Americanization of Canadian politics. This would be true if we regarded these practices simply as mindless adoptions of what is done in the United States. But I believe that in fact they represent something quite different. It is television, and not its national setting, that has greatest bearing on the way it is used as a political instrument. The affinity between television and politics is greatest where there is major emphasis on the personal appeal of the leading candidate. It will be prominent where the political message has an audience spread over vast territories, where the population is diverse in interests and outlook, where a counterappeal is needed to localistic viewpoints and concerns, and where political parties tend to be weakly organized.[36] With the

33. Canadian Broadcasting Corporation, Audience Research Division, "Canadian Reactions to the 4th Nixon-Kennedy Television Debate of 21st October 1960 and to Certain Other Features of the U.S. Presidential Campaign" (Ottawa, Dec., 1960).

34. Société Radio Canada, Services des Recherches, "Réactions du public de la région métropolitaine de Montréal au débat 'Johnson-Lesage' télédiffusé le 11 novembre 1962" (Montréal, Avril, 1963).

35. Lang and Lang, *Politics and Television*, p. 299.

36. Leon D. Epstein, *Political Parties in Western Democracies* (New York, 1967), pp. 233–242.

high degree of technical development of the mass media in the United States, it is natural that they should have their greatest scope in that country. But since the conditions to which they are best adapted are also part of Canadian political existence, we can expect that the mass media, and especially television, will continue to play a prominent part in political campaigning. There are dangers attached to their use, but the dangers lie in the nature of the media themselves, and the unthinking way the technology is used.[37] Whatever choice Canadian political leaders and advisors have exercised in the use of the mass media, this has primarily been based on the nature of the Canadian electorate and the existing political machinery. No doubt the American example has been important, but its importance has derived from the similar problems posed by the electorates and political organizations of the two countries.

Canadian political styles are strongly defended against the penetration of American practices, particularly if we regard penetration as a display of the greater power of the United States. But if there has been any element of surprise in this paper, it is in relation to the number of instances where Candian and American political practices coincide. The explanation for this was suggested by treating March's communication-diffusion and problem-solving models of choice as interrelated. Characteristically, information about the conduct of politics spreads from the United States to Canada. Of course, this could be interpreted as a manifestation of the greater power of the United States. But the initiating capacity of the United States must also simply be expected, given its longer history as an independent political entity. Once information is available, the responses of Canadian political leaders are dependent on its relevance to whatever are current political problems. These problems, in turn, emerge with some frequency out of the common fate of life on this continent.

These conclusions can be illustrated with a final example; the so-called move toward presidential politics encouraged by

37. F. C. Engelmann and M. A. Schwartz, *Political Parties and the Canadian Social Structure* (Scarborough, 1967), p. 75.

the current Prime Minister, Pierre Elliott Trudeau. Denis Smith has argued that this is a change in political style that has been going on for some time, although he too agrees that Mr. Trudeau has given it greater impetus and used the changes with greater skill than his predecessors.[38] Mr. Trudeau gives no indication of being an uncritical acceptor of American practices and policies. This is also a time of grave doubt about the functioning of the American political system, doubt expressed as much in the United States as elsewhere. In particular, the division of powers guaranteed by the American Constitution seem more unwieldy than ever. A Canadian Prime Minister would appear to have too many advantages already to seek the imposition of presidential-style politics. Yet one sign of this move has been seen in the great expansion and strengthening of the Prime Minister's personal staff.[39] This does not mean, of course, that the Prime Minister's Office has attained the influence of the White House Office.[40] One of the things that appears to be occurring in Canada is an effort to augment the efficiency of executive functioning, given the great increase in what modern governments actually do, and at the same time introduce more adequate controls over the federal civil service. These concerns are common ones, and not unique to Canada. It was Max Weber who observed many years ago, that as the areas of expert knowledge grow, control by nonexperts—the political heads of governmental bureaucracies—is difficult to maintain.[41] I am not prepared to evaluate the success of Mr. Trudeau's efforts, or the virtues of presidential-style politics, but we should recognize that the former are at least partly related to growing bureaucratization, one of the endemic problems of the modern world.

The American presence is a primary fact of Canadian existence. To many, that presence is undesirable, at least without

38. Denis Smith, "President and Parliament: The Transformation of Parliamentary Government in Canada," in Thomas A. Hockin (ed.), *Apex of Power* (Scarborough, 1971), pp. 224–241.
39. Walter Stewart, "The Thirty Men Trudeau Trusts," *Maclean's Magazine* (Oct., 1969), pp. 36–48.
40. Joseph Wearing, "President or Prime Minister," in Hocking (ed.), *Apex of Power*, p. 256.
41. A. M. Henderson and Talcott Parsons (trans. and eds.), Max Weber, *The Theory of Social and Economic Organization* (New York, 1957), p. 310.

some restraints. Perhaps ways will be found to at least control the amount and character of American influence on Canadian life. But paradoxically, the style of politics may be most difficult to insulate from American contacts. The paradox is that, despite the many genuine barriers to the adoption of American political styles, the flow of information about these cannot be eliminated. We know, for example, that many Canadians engage in a symbolic participation in United States presidential elections. These are, we should note, people with a strong interest in Canadian politics as well.[42] Even that committed Canadian, Frank Underhill, has not been immune to the temptation of casting an imaginary ballot without the responsibilities of actual citizenship: "As for me, while I've wobbled somewhat in my political affiliation in Canadian politics over the last generation, I shall be voting again for Mr. Trudeau. In American politics I have never wobbled; ever since 1936 I have been voting the straight Democratic ticket, and I expect to continue doing so."[43] This suggests that almost every time a problem arises in Canada that had previously been dealt with in the United States, the latter's experiences will likely have some bearing on the decision made in Canada. This does not deny that those experiences will often be rejected or at least modified to better conform to the Canadian situation. It is their existence that cannot be denied. And if they exist, there is at least some chance that they will have an impact.

42. J. A. Laponce, *People vs. Politics* (Toronto, 1969), pp. 164–167.
43. Frank Underhill, "The Nation / Will the West Escape from Yesterday?" *Toronto Daily Star*, Oct. 29, 1970.

· 4 ·

The Automotive Agreement of 1965:
A Case Study in Canadian-American
Economic Affairs

Carl E. Beigie

Introduction

The theme of this conference, "American Influence on Cana-dian Development," suggests a one-directional framework which is particularly inappropriate for a commentary on the 1965 Automotive Agreement. In fact, during the past decade the North American automotive industry has evolved in response to a series of policy moves in which Canada has played the role of initiator and the United States the role of reactor. The culmina-tion of Canada's policy initiatives in this area came with the signing of an agreement liberalizing bilateral trade in new motor vehicles as well as parts and accessories to be used as original equipment in vehicle production. This trade pact has resulted in a rationalization of North American motor vehicle production accompanied by a dramatic improvement in Canada's automotive and overall trade balances with the United States.

The Agreement has been a definite success in terms of bring-ing increased efficiency to North American automotive produc-tion, but this very success has also contributed to an environment in which Canada-U.S. economic relations currently are unusu-ally strained. The apparent cause of this friction is that each country has its own view of what constitutes conduct in good faith under the Agreement. More basically, however, the results of this pact have demonstrated how poor was the U.S. original understanding of its possible consequences and how haphazard are each country's trade policies toward the other.

This is a fairly critical period in Canadian-American economic affairs. A number of problems facing both countries—security of energy supplies and pollution control are prime examples—would be easier to resolve if a series of coordinated efforts were adopted. Also, actual and potential expansion of regional trading blocs have confronted the U.S. and Canada with new challenges in traditional export markets. But while these and other factors suggest the need for increased bilateral cooperation in policy formation, opposing forces are creating pressures to adopt more inward-looking policy measures. One step toward resisting these latter forces would be to encourage a more balanced appraisal of the 1965 Automotive Agreement than has been given by spokesmen of either country. This paper is an effort to assist in such an appraisal.

This discussion will be divided into four parts. First, a brief background section will describe developments leading up to the 1965 Agreement and list its main features. Second, the results of the Agreement in terms of the integration and distribution of North American automotive production will be analyzed. This review will introduce a number of issues arising from the implementation of this trade pact, and these issues will be explored in the third section of the paper. Special attention will be given to issues involved in the adjustments of the Canadian economy to the sharp boost in net exports to the United States following the Agreement. Fourth, a concluding section will comment on some alternatives for resolving the contentious aspects of the Agreement.

Background: History and Terms of the 1965 Automotive Agreement

One of the main reasons for the political difficulties which have arisen over the Automotive Agreement is that Canada's goals for the development of its motor vehicle industry appear to have changed markedly during the past ten years or so. We shall return to this point later, but for now it will be sufficient to note four key factors behind the original Canadian decision to push for a dramatic alteration in the structural determinants of this particular industry's performance.

First, rapid growth in Canadian exports of secondary products was felt to be essential if Canada was to maintain and possibly improve its standard of living relative to that of the United States. These exports, it was argued, were necessary to provide well-paying jobs for Canada's fast-growing labor force. Furthermore, the greater the improvement in export performance the broader would be the range in Canada's economic policy options in terms of an increased import potential and/or a reduced reliance upon net capital inflows from abroad. Recall too that we are talking now about the period of the late 1950's, a time when the degree of foreign ownership of Canadian industry was again becoming a significant policy issue, so any proposal for achieving a better merchandise trade performance had considerable political appeal in Canada.

Second, the automotive industry has existed in Canada for just about as long as in the United States, and the same major companies—General Motors, Ford, and Chrysler—dominate production in both countries. It was essentially a political necessity to maintain the viability of this long-established industry in Canada, and if amicable economic relations between the two countries were to be maintained the United States government had at least a part interest in this obligation. Also, the fact that a few U.S.-owned affiliates had a virtual lock on Canadian vehicle production made it feasible to contemplate strict adherence to the terms of what would have to be a fairly complex agreement to increase production efficiency in an industry of this sort.

Third, the automotive industry is characterized by significant scale economies. If Canada was to produce automotive products at prices which would be competitive in world markets, two conditions had to be met: certain components had to be imported from companies able to achieve large production runs in foreign markets; a significant proportion of any automotive products made in Canada would have to be exported to generate the volume necessary to achieve the full benefit of scale economies. Canada's commercial policies could be adjusted to encourage fulfillment of the first condition; but unilateral Canadian efforts to achieve a tariff environment which would help fulfill the second were more complicated.

Fourth, one American influence on Canada which was important with reference to this Agreement was that concerning Canadians' tastes for automotive products. This influence may be primarily a passive one due simply to the proximity of Canada to the United States market, or an active one involving continuous U.S. advertising reaching the Canadian consumer. Regardless of the precise reason, Canadians choose almost exactly the same bewildering array of styles and models in their vehicle purchases as do Americans. The proportion of total Canadian car purchases accounted for by North American models has ranged between 75 and 90 percent, only a little below the ratio in the United States in most years. What is significant about this similarity of tastes is that it would almost certainly have been impossible to restructure the Canadian automotive industry along the lines of the Swedish example, to cite another small economy with its own highly efficient motor vehicle industry. Canadians were most unlikely to support a drastic reduction in their choice of vehicles just to have a predominantly Canadian product.

Prior to 1960 the Canadian automotive industry owed its existence primarily to a high tariff wall which encouraged a duplication in miniature of the U.S. industry. A system for receiving remission of duties on certain parts imports encouraged assembly in Canada as opposed to importing completed vehicles. As a result, virtually all models other than luxury lines were produced by the Canadian affiliates of U.S. parent companies, using imported parts equal in value to about 40 percent of the factory cost of the vehicle. Instead of permitting market growth to bring increased efficiency in the production of a select group of models, the manufacturers appeared to have dissipated most of the potential for productivity gains in a proliferation of models assembled in Canada.

By the late 1950's prospects for the Canadian automotive industry were not at all encouraging. Cars coming from overseas, primarily duty-free from Britain, surged temporarily to almost 30 percent of Canadian new car registrations. In addition, net imports of parts from the United States totalled about $300 million and could be expected to increase by an amount equal to roughly 40 percent of the increase in the value of North American-type vehicles produced in Canada. To top it all off, the only markets to which Canada could deliver its automotive production more cheaply than could the United States were countries in the British Commonwealth where lower tariffs applied to Canadian exports, but in these countries, demand for this type of vehicle was falling away to European producers.

Against this background, the Canadian government in August, 1960, appointed Dean Vincent W. Bladen as a one-man royal commission to examine the prospects of the Canadian automotive industry. Less than a year later, Dean Bladen submitted his findings and recommendations, calling for a basic change in the character of the industry. Instead of relying almost exclusively upon production as a substitute for imports, he suggested that output be directed toward export markets via a plan which would make the payment of automotive import duties conditional upon automotive export performance.

The precise terms of the Bladen proposal were never adopted, but the basic concept of an increased export orientation through duty incentives was. On October 31, 1962, Canada introduced a program whereby duties could be recouped on imports of automatic transmissions and engine blocks, provided automotive exports from Canada were increased sufficiently. In October, 1963, this program was extended to provide duty remission on all new vehicles and original-market parts, again conditional upon export-growth performance.

Shortcomings in Canada's duty-remission plans were economic and legal in nature. In an economic sense, maximum efficiency in North American automotive production was impossible so long as United States tariffs on imports from Canada remained. The Canadian initiative could moderate the impact of the United States tariff, but neither country alone could eliminate completely the influence of the other's tariff policies so as to achieve a fully rationalized North American pattern of production. From a legal standpoint, the duty-remission concept threatened to run afoul of U.S. law. If such were found to be the case, countervailing duties to offset the impact of the duty-remission plan would have been applied automatically by the U.S. to imports from Canada. When in March, 1964, Modine Manufacturing Co. filed a petition for a ruling on this issue, a potentially serious threat to Canadian-American trade relations erupted and set the stage for the 1965 Automotive Agreement.

The Automotive Agreement, signed on January 16, 1965, is difficult to describe precisely. Essentially, it provides for duty-free trade for vehicle producers in Canada and the U.S., so long as certain minimum guarantees concerning the type and volume of production in Canada are met on an annual basis. Specifically, the Agreement itself calls for the total value of Canadian automotive output to be no less than that achieved in the 1964 model year, and the ratio between Canadian vehicle production to vehicle sales in Canada to match or exceed that achieved by each manufacturer and for each major vehicle class (cars, trucks, and buses) during the same 1964 model year.

The formal Agreement, though, contains only part of the story, and is the least controversial aspect of the total package. In separate side agreements negotiated between the Canadian government and the vehicle manufacturers, commitments were made which ensured that Canada's automotive output would expand by a minimum percentage of the growth in Canadian automotive consumption. Additionally, in one of the most puzzling features of this whole episode, these side agreements guaranteed a further $260 million increase in Canadian automotive output, over and above all other commitments, by the

1968 model year. This particular segment of the program has been the source of most of the controversy over the Agreement in Washington.

Results of the Agreement

The results of the Agreement to date should be discussed under two headings: integration and market shares. In terms of integration criteria, the Agreement has been a remarkable success. Whereas prior to the Agreement almost all but the most expensive lines were produced in relatively short runs in Canada, specialization in a limited range of models has now been accomplished by the Canadian manufacturers. Chrysler, for example, has phased out Polera and Monaco production in Canada, concentrating now upon Dart and Valiant models. Ford is specializing in Pintos and Mavericks in its Canadian operations, while General Motors Canada is concentrating upon low- and medium-price Chevrolet and Pontiac models.

The practical results of increased integration in the North American automotive industry can be seen by observing that in November, 1970, (a) of shipments in Canada, excluding those for export, 56.6 percent were of vehicles imported from the U.S. (this compares with a figure of 7 percent in 1960); (b) of shipments of made-in-Canada vehicles, 83.4 percent were exported (in 1960 the comparable figure was 5.8 percent).

There has been considerable debate on the question of whether or not Canadian automotive production is now as efficient as in the United States. Much of the debate has overtones of policy strategy on the part of the two governments, and no hard and fast test is available for determining the issue decisively. Still, it would be my contention that the huge margin by which the manufacturers have exceeded their production commitments in Canada is fairly conclusive proof that the bulk of this production costs no more to achieve in Canada than in the United States, and possibly somewhat less.

This last point brings us to the impact of the Agreement on the distribution of production shares in the industry. Canada is currently exporting to the United States about three times as many vehicles as it imports, while at the same time running a deficit of over a billion dollars in its parts trade with the United States. The best single measure for evaluating the Agreement's effects on production shares is the overall automotive trade balance between Canada and the U.S.: a surplus for one indicates that it is producing a greater amount of automotive output than it is consuming.

There are a number of difficult technical and statistical problems in trying to obtain an exact estimate of changes in Canada's automotive trade balance with the United States, but reasonable assumptions lead to the conclusion that there was a Canadian deficit of about $600 million in 1964, the year prior to the Agreement, and a Canadian surplus of about $200 million in 1970, or a change of $800 million in total. There is no more contentious issue concerning the Agreement than this very dramatic reversal of North American automotive trade patterns at a time when a number of other factors were placing severe pressure on the international value of the U.S. dollar.

Issues Raised by the Agreement

The Automotive Agreement has shown that under the appropriate circumstances Canada can manufacture secondary products at a cost which is competitive with United States production. There is no better illustration of the potential benefits of more efficient production in Canada or, conversely, the costs involved in maintaining a highly protective environment for Canadian industry.

To come to grips with the numerous issues which have arisen from this Agreement it is important to realize that one's perspective is critical in the assessment. Most economists would conclude that the Agreement was a sound one because it increased the total value of output which could be produced from a given level of labor and capital inputs in North America. But here the agreement ends, for the problems involved in distributing the fruits of these efficiency gains and then adjusting other economic activities in response to them raise exceptionally difficult theoretical and practical issues which transcend strictly economic interpretations.

Two issues are illustrative. The first is so-called wage "parity," which has been agreed to in principle by the vehicle manufacturers in their negotiations with the United Automobile Workers, although full parity was put off for another three years in the 1970 contract settlement. Wage parity, the payment of the same money wage in Canada as in the U.S., accomplishes the following:

1. It distributes more of the gains from the Agreement to Canadian automotive workers, and away from automotive producers and consumers.

2. It reduces the level of automotive output in Canada.

3. It causes pressures from other workers in Canada to achieve the same treatment or, alternatively, to gain entry into the Canadian automotive industry.

In other words, even though wage parity most certainly will increase Canada's share of the net gains from the Automotive Agreement, it creates strains upon wages and therefore prices in other Canadian industries which cannot match U.S. productivity levels in a protected environment.

The second issue is one which has remained almost unexplored. One of the reasons for Canada's exceptional success with the Agreement is that the industry was already strategically located from a North American standpoint. But what about regions in Canada other than the Windsor-Toronto area? These other regions have the benefit of a lower differential between Canadian and U.S. car prices, but their industries and their workers gained little more.

In fact, the strong trade performance in Canada's automotive industry has been a primary factor in the upward movement of the Canadian dollar following the decision in May, 1970, to unpeg. The greater the relative value of the Canadian dollar, of course, the more difficult it is for export industries in Canada to compete internationally. Thus, one view is that the Automotive Agreement has tended to exaggerate regional economic disparities in Canada and may contribute to an unfavorable environment for expanding Canada's nonautomotive secondary manufactures in the future.

Conclusions

The most basic objection that can be raised concerning the Automotive Agreement is that it was an ad hoc response to a specific policy problem which showed little appreciation for possible long-term complications. It is ironic indeed that something which has worked so well in terms of its original justification—increased efficiency—has caused so much political ill will and so many secondary economic adjustment problems.

In fact, however, the Agreement was fated to cause problems. The more successful it was by one criterion, increased production efficiency in Canada, the less successful by another, increased opportunities for Canadian employment in the automotive industry. The only way to avoid this conflict within a single industry context was for the U.S. automotive trade balance with Canada to deteriorate, or for growth in Canadian purchases of North American-type vehicles to continue at an exceptionally rapid rate.

One solution to the problems arising from the Automotive Agreement is to strive for an extension of the trade-liberalization principle to additional sectors. The rationale for Canada to seek such an extension is fairly obvious, but in the case of the United States the potential benefits are less apparent. To make such a proposal attractive to the United States, Canada would probably have to include the following elements in its strategy:

1. Certain industries would have to be put on the block in the sense that an absolute decline in Canadian employment would have to be expected and permitted.

2. An incentive in the form of a concrete settlement of the foreign investment issue in Canada and joint approaches to

resource, pollution, and other common interests would demonstrate how much advantage there is for the United States to maintain close economic ties with Canada, particularly at a time when division of the world into rival trading blocs seems to be accelerating.

3. Attempts by Canada to relieve its net demands on U.S. capital markets would reduce the importance of a deterioration in the U.S. merchandise trade account resulting from the Automotive Agreement.

In any event, time will help resolve many of the issues concerning this specific trade pact. Future growth in Canadian automotive consumption is likely to be supplied largely from net imports, reducing the importance of the main negative feature of the Agreement from a U.S. point of view. Those who are hopeful that the Automotive Agreement will be followed by other trade pacts in Canada's favor, however, are going to be very disappointed. Canada's best hope for increased production efficiency in other secondary manufacturing industries lies in pressing for a long-term, mutually-beneficial trade policy with the United States, but this is one economist's judgment and leaves many issues, both economic and noneconomic, unresolved.

· 5 ·

American Direct Investment and Canada's Two Nationalisms

Robert Gilpin

The unprecedented growth of American direct investment in Canada since World War II has accentuated both English-Canadian and French-Canadian nationalism, and intensified the competition between them. The growing desire of English-Canadian nationalists to limit American investment in Canada increasingly clashes with the desire of French Canadians to develop economically and "catch up" with English Canada through encouraging American investment in Quebec. As a consequence of these intricate interrelationships, a realistic treatment of American direct investment in Canada must give primary consideration to its influence upon both English-Canadian and French-Canadian nationalism.

The primary concern of this paper is the political implications of American direct investment in Canada. In particular, the focus is on the relationship of the increasing American penetration of the Canadian economy, the rise of English-Canadian nationalism, and the intensification of nationalist sentiment in Quebec. That these three developments can not be separated has been noted by numerous writers in observing that what Ottawa is to Quebec, America is to Ottawa. Whereas Québécois increasingly demand greater independence from Ottawa, English Canadians intensify their complaints against American domination. Thus, American investment in Canada is inadvertently a contributing factor to Canada's constitutional crisis.

As the following quotation from the *New York Times* observes, American investment and the Canadian constitutional crisis cannot be dissociated:

A curious and significant economic tug-of-war is taking place in Canada. While the Federal Government in Ottawa is trying to achieve a greater measure of economic independence from the United States, it is losing control over domestic economic policy to Canada's ten provincial administrations.

The upsurge of economic regionalism is more intense and serious than the stirrings of economic nationalism. To a considerable extent, nationalism is the response of Canadian federalists to provincialism. The Federal Government is asking Canadians to resist the lure of the United States and to work and invest in Canada.[1]

The Canadian fear of American domination and the French-Canadian desire for greater independence from English Canada have deep historical roots. Recent developments, however, have stimulated both nationalisms. In the case of English Canada, the recession of European and British influence in Canada and the increasing integration between the Canadian and American economies have brought Canada's "two goals of political independence of the United States and economic growth in rivalry with the United States into open conflict."[2] Similarly, Quebec is confronted by the two contradictory and popular goals of rapid economic development, which is impossible without substantial non-French-Canadian investment, and the desire for more French-Canadian control of the economy.[3]

Under these circumstances, the impact of increasing American investment in Canada has been to intensify English-Canadian and French-Canadian nationalism. At the same time that English Canadians stress the importance of unity against the threat of American domination, French Canadians seek to increase American investment and their independence from Ottawa. While this Québécois nationalism reflects Quebec's *révolution tranquille*, it also is a response to the impact on Canada of American investment. By increasing the economic

1. *New York Times*, June 13, 1966.
2. Harry Johnson, "Economic Nationalism in Canadian Policy," in Harry Johnson (ed.), *Economic Nationalism in Old and New States* (Chicago, 1965), p. 90.
3. William Griffith, "Quebec in Revolt," *Foreign Affairs* (Oct., 1964), p. 31.

gap among the provinces, especially between Ontario and Quebec, American investment has actually accentuated provincialism. As French Canadians point out, Ontario has captured the lion's share of American investment particularly in the more advanced industrial sectors such as durable consumer goods and high technology products. Reflecting an attitude prevalent in other provinces and lesser developed countries, Quebec would like to have its own steel, electronic and chemical industries.

In order to attract American investment and overcome their "backwardness," the provinces seek to decrease the control of Ottawa over their economic policies and developmental efforts. Seen from this perspective, American investment in Canada is a powerful centrifugal force which Canadian nationalists are seeking to counteract through appeals to anti-American, nationalist sentiments. As such there can be little doubt that the increasing vehemence of appeals to Canadian nationalism and anti-Americanism are, at least on the unconscious level, a response to the increasing economic attraction of Quebec and the other provinces toward the United States.

Similarly the debate in Quebec between those Québécois who favor continued federation with the rest of Canada and the Séparatistes as exemplified by the Parti Québécois is in part between two different approaches to American investment and its place in Quebec's effort to catch up with English Canada. On other specific issues (setting aside differences with respect to the desirability of preserving Canada)—the defense of French-Canadian culture, the québécoisization of the economy, and the need for greater freedom from Ottawa for provincial economic planning—the two sides do not appear at least to this foreign observer, to be in stark opposition. But on the implications of separatism for the economic development of Quebec, for the continuation of the Canadian common market, and for the future of American investment, the two sides are in fundamental disagreement.[4]

4. For an analysis of the two dominant schools of French Canadian thought on the future of Quebec, see Gerald Clark, *The United States and Canada* (Cambridge, Mass., 1968), pp. 285–296.

The basic position of the Séparatistes is that unified government is required for effective economic development and industrialization. In contrast to the existing situation where decision-making with respect to economic policy is divided between Ottawa and the provinces, authority should be centralized.[5] While theoretically the centralization of decision could take place in Ottawa rather than in Quebec, the price which French Canada would have to pay for this political unification, it is argued, would be eventual loss of its culture and complete absorption into English Canada. Therefore, the Séparatistes favor the unification of decision-making in an independent Quebec.[6]

In part, the Séparatistes argue, the unification of political decision is necessary in order to eliminate wasteful duplication between federal and provincial activities. More importantly, economic and social modernization in Quebec in the middle of the twentieth century necessitates a powerful role for the state. The state must not only refashion the institutional framework for economic activity, but in a complex, technological world, the economic role of the state as consumer, producer, and investor is crucial. If Quebec is to become a highly industrialized society then the state must use its powers to marshal scarce resources and rationalize Quebec's fragmented economy.

Furthermore, the Séparatistes argue, a sovereign and independent Quebec would be in a stronger bargaining position vis-à-vis American industry. Freed from control by Ottawa, it could pursue policies which would encourage American investment in Quebec especially in high technology industries and reduce the economic gap between Quebec and the richer provinces. In addition, an independent Quebec could use American investment as a counterweight to English-Canadian financial power and accelerate the redistribution of wealth and status in Quebec. Thus, in contrast to those who argue a sovereign Quebec

5. The division of authority between Ottawa and Quebec with respect to economic matters is treated by André Raynaud, *The Canadian Economic System* (Toronto, 1967).

6. The economic position of Le Parti Québécois is spelled out in *La Souveraineté et L'Économie*, Mars 1970; see, René Lévesque, *An Option for Quebec* (Toronto, 1968), and *La Solution, Le programme du Parti Québécois présenté par René Lévesque* (1970).

would come under the "*'diktats' de la finance américaine,*" the Séparatistes point out that the availability of American capital enabled Quebec to defy English-Canadian capital and gave Quebec the courage to nationalize the hydroelectric industry.[7]

While French-Canadian proponents of continued federation generally accept the principle of active state intervention in the economy, they do not agree that this necessitates a complete unification of economic decision-making in either Ottawa or Quebec. While the main burden for promoting and managing economic development should rest with the province, this does not require the dissolution of Canada. It does mean, however, the holders of this position tend to argue, a greater willingness on the part of Ottawa to assist the provinces in carrying out these economic responsibilities.

In the opinion of these French Canadians, separation would cause irreparable damage to the Quebec economy. The great risk of separation, these people argue, would be the loss of Quebec's greatest asset, membership in Canada's common market. An economically isolated Quebec could not attract sufficient American investment to carry out its ambitious plans for economic development. Furthermore, separation would drive English Canada—Quebec's first trading partner—toward the United States, and would cause the Quebec economy to stagnate completely. Surrounded by a more dynamic English North America composed of over 200 million people, an independent French Canada could not possibly survive economically, politically, or culturally.[8]

Although these political issues are central to any appraisal of the impact of American investment in Canada, one is struck by the absence of many frank discussions of this crucial American, English-Canadian and French-Canadian triangular relationship.[9]

7. Le Parti Québécois, *op. cit.*, pp. 147–148.
8. For a statement of the federalist position, see Pierre E. Trudeau, *Federalism and the French Canadians* (Toronto, 1968).
9. There is, on the other hand, an excellent professional literature on the economic aspects of American investment. Among the best examples are the following: Bernard Bonin, *L'Investissement Étranger à Long Terme au Canada* (Montreal, 1967); A. E. Safarian, *Foreign Ownership of Canadian Industry* (Toronto 1966); and A. E. Safarian, *The Performance of Foreign-Owned Firms in Canada* (1969).

By way of introduction, therefore, to the main points I would like to make in this paper, let us examine how the political issues generated by American investment have been handled by English-Canadian nationalists, French-Canadian nationalists, and the American investors.

The so-called Watkins Report is the best example of those Canadian writings which have strongly attacked the impact of American investment on Canada.[10] Though the Report contains much rhetoric about American domination and, as Watkins tells us in *Gordon to Watkins to You*,[11] he restrained himself from using the term "American empire," the sections dealing with the political relations among American corporations, Ottawa, and the provinces, especially Quebec, are very vague. There is an inadequate discussion, for example, of Canadian participation in American firms,[12] and the federal-provincial division of policy making responsibility with respect to foreign investment is dealt with in one brief and uninformative paragraph.[13] Instead the major emphasis of the report is on the extraterritorial application of American law (anti-trust, trading with the enemy, and balance of payments). While these issues are important, they are not the central political issues raised by American investment, issues which would really have to be resolved if the objectives of the Report were to be achieved.

This criticism is not meant to deny the value of the Report. The point is rather that it does not treat the basic political issues raised by the rapid growth of American investment in Canada and its impact on provincialism. If "Canadian participation" is, as it probably is, an euphemism for transferring control over American subsidiaries from Americans to Canadians, the basic issue is: To *which* Canadians? What precisely would be the respective roles of the federal government and the provinces, if Canada should engage in an active policy of reducing the power of American corporations over the Canadian economy? While

10. Task Force on the Structure of Canadian Industry, *Foreign Ownership and the Structure of Canadian Industry* (Ottawa, 1968).
11. Dave Godfrey and Mel Watkins, *Gordon to Watkins to You* (1970).
12. Task Force on the Structure of Canadian Industry, *op. cit.*, p. 411.
13. *Ibid.*, p. 303–304.

these are extremely sensitive issues, they would be at the heart of any program for the Canadianization of American corporations in Canada.

The Parti Québécois, on the other hand, in its publication, *La Souveraineté et L'Économie*, is quite frank that its primary objective is the redistribution of wealth and status from the English-speaking minority of Quebec to a French-speaking elite. To achieve this objective and to industrialize Quebec, their position is that Quebec must be independent of Ottawa, the seat of English-Canadian power. But what the Séparatistes do not discuss with equal frankness is the future of American investment in Quebec and the conditions under which it would be tolerated. While they acknowledge the importance of American finance for development and as a counter-weight to English-Canadian economic power, they are not clear how an independent Quebec would treat American investment. What, for example, would be the relative positions of Americans and Québécois in American subsidiaries? What would be the division of authority between Quebec and the United States government over American corporations? Again, these issues are highly sensitive ones, but their resolution would be of great practical consequence.

Turning to a discussion of American attitudes toward the political aspects of their investment in Canada, what one discovers, in the phrase of the late Jacob Viner, is "a vast unawareness." [14] There is very little appreciation in the United States of the impact on Canadian society of American investment. The problem is deeper, however, than traditional American neglect of its northern neighbor. It is due to very fundamental attitudes of Americans toward the relationship of economics and politics. Like important segments of Canadian society, American political and economic leaders see the world largely in terms of the British tradition of laissez-faire and the philosophy of the 19th-century liberal state. [15]

14. "The Outlook for the Relationship: An American View," in John S. Dickey, *The United States and Canada* (Englewood Cliffs, N.J., 1964), p. 145.
15. Though he is a Canadian teaching in an American university, I suspect most American investors and economists would be sympathetic to the views of Harry Johnson. See his *The Canadian Quandary* (New York, 1963).

At the core of this doctrine is the complete divorce between economics and politics. "The classical economists conceived a natural economic order with laws of its own, independent of politics and functioning to the greatest profit of all concerned when political authority interfered least in its automatic operation." [16] From this perspective, nationalism and the nation-state are impediments to the free development of economic forces and the maximization of the economic welfare of all.

The underlying faith of this laissez-faire philosophy is that the market rather than the state is the most efficient regulator of economic activity. The free play of economic forces maximizes the efficiency with which men exploit their resources and organize their economic life. Through the resulting expansion of the market, the increase in the division of labor, and the advance of technique, men increase their wealth. Through these market associated mechanisms, too, this generated wealth is distributed throughout the economic system so that all eventually benefit.

In this ideal system there is no room or need for politics because underneath the flux of economic activity the true interests of all are in harmony: capital-labor, creditor-borrower, American-Canadian, English Canadian–French Canadian. The intervention of political authority is not only misguided, but it destroys the efficiency of the system and eventually will lead to the impoverishment of all. If men really knew their true interests, political relations would be displaced by economic relations and organizations.

Perhaps the American who is most representative of this prevailing American ideology is former Under Secretary of State, George Ball. Presently a partner in Lehman Brothers, investment bankers, and an outspoken advocate of the multinational corporation, it was Ambassador Ball who startled a session of the Canadian House of Commons Committee on External Affairs and National Defence with his views on the inevitability of economic union between Canada and the United States.

Central to Ambassador Ball's prediction and the views of many American leaders and economists is the belief that the international economy is being, and should be, reorganized by the

16. E. H. Carr, *The Twenty Years' Crisis* (New York, 1951), p. 114.

large multinational corporations, most of which are American. These individuals share a conviction that these organizations are the most effective instruments for ensuring an efficient utilization of the world's resources. Unwarranted efforts by states to restrict the rational development of the multinational corporation can only result in detracting from the maximum exploitation of resources and production of wealth. As Ambassador Ball wrote in *Fortune* magazine, "The structure of the multinational corporation is a modern concept designed to meet the requirements of a modern age; the nation state is a very old fashioned idea and badly adapted to serve the needs of our present complex world." [17]

If one takes solely an economic perspective, then the logic of Ambassador Ball is probably irrefutable. As the Canadian economist Harry Johnson has argued, American investment has benefited Canada enormously, and, "there is no substantive evidence that American enterprises in Canada have acted contrary to the national interest. . . ." [18] In this judgment, he is on balance supported by A. E. Safarian in the latter's *The Performance of Foreign-Owned Firms in Canada*, which attributes shortcomings more to the Canadian economic environment than to the fact of foreign ownership. [19] Even the Watkins Report does not make the case that American investment has been economically detrimental and therefore should be prevented. It argues rather for continued American investment but under conditions less challenging to Canadian sovereignty.

The nub of the problem, however, is not economic but political. What distresses Canadians is the extraterritorial operation of American laws through which American corporations become instruments of United States policy and infringe upon Canadian sovereignty. Secondly, they are concerned over the possible loss of Canadian control of the "commanding heights" of their economy: communications, finance, and advanced technological industries. And, thirdly, the mere fact of American "domi-

17. "The Promise of the Multinational Corporation," *Fortune*, LXXV, No. 6 (June 1, 1967), 80.
18. Johnson, *The Canadian Quandary, op. cit.*, xi.   19. Safarian, *op. cit.*

nation" of such a large fraction of the Canadian economy creates resentments and gives rise to the counter-reaction of nationalism. In short, what distresses Canadians are the political implications of American investment.

Contrary to the laissez-faire philosophy of Americans, economics and politics can not be separated. As numerous critics have pointed out, classical liberalism is the ideology of the dominant economic power. While a free market may very well bring economic benefits to all, economic relations are in reality also political relations. As a consequence whereas the nation-state may be an anachronism to Ambassador Ball, to representatives of other societies the nation-state is a means to counter-balance the expanding economic power of American corporations and the United States.

Without doubt the economic expansion abroad of the United States since the end of the Second World War is one of the most prominent features of contemporary international relations. The scope and magnitude of American direct investment throughout the world and the penetration of foreign economies by large American corporations has caused allies as well as enemies of the United States to equate American economic expansion with Soviet military expansion and, in some cases, even to see the former as the greater evil.[20]

In response to this rather unprecedented phenomenon a great volume of literature on the American empire has arisen. Whether the motive ascribed to America is the desire for access to raw materials, for control of foreign markets, or simply for power, critics see America driven by an internal dynamic to reduce all other centers of power to a subservient position. The instruments of expansion of this new Rome are not its legions, but its large multinational corporations.

Although I share many of the apprehensions of others concerning the expansion of American economic power, I think that analogies to Rome, or to 19th-century British imperialism are misleading. A more appropriate analysis is that of the French

20. For the case of France see my *France in the Age of the Scientific State*, (Princeton, 1962).

economist Francois Perroux. As Perroux observes, "[t]he world economy did not develop as a result of the competition among equal parties, but through the emergence and influence of great national economies that successively became dominant." [21] Each dominant economy organizes world markets and the international divisions of labor, insofar as it is able, in terms of its own interests, thus giving shape to the world economy.

Since the end of the Second World War and with the decline of the European empires, the United States has clearly emerged as the dominant economy in the world. The effort to restructure the international economy at Bretton Woods in 1945, the attack on preference systems, and the achievement in 1958 of currency convertibility all reflect America's desire for a world system of multilateral trade. As Richard Gardner has written, America's effort to reform the international economy after 1945 reflected "the transformation of the United States into a major exporter of mass-produced industrial products . . . particularly vulnerable to the impact of tariff preferences and other forms of discrimination. The United States quickly recognized that its growing industrial efficiency might be progressively offset if American products were not guaranteed equal access to foreign markets." [22] Thus, through policies fashioned largely in its own self-interest and in the conviction that economic well-being is a key to world peace and stability, the United States became the center of an immense international economic system comprising Western Europe, Japan, and the rest of the non-Communist world.

In its own self-interest and, I believe, on balance in the interests of the world economy as a whole, the United States created a highly interdependent international economy. Hardly an empire by any traditional use of the term, it is nevertheless an economic system which does give American corporations and the United States government considerable leverage over other societies. As Albert Hirschman brought out in his analysis of

21. "Esquisse d'une théorie de l'économie dominante," *Economie appliquée,* I (1948), 243–300.
22. *Sterling-Dollar Diplomacy,* (New York, 1969), p. 17.

economic power, interdependencies among national economies do create political leverages which can be used to achieve political objectives.[23]

Although American corporations and the American government are the dominant participants in this international economy, they do not have the monopoly of power that the critics of American imperialism charge. Nor do the American government and American corporations necessarily work in concert, and in opposition to foreign governments and corporations. The system is indeed far more complex than that and involves constant bargaining situations among governments and corporations. Governments and corporations ally and conflict with one another across national boundaries depending upon interest and circumstance.

Under present international conditions multinational corporations behave more as independent actors than as instruments of an imperial or of national policies. There is a constant struggle between governments attempting to make corporations subservient to their policy aims and the desire of the corporations for autonomy. At one moment in time a corporation such as IBM in the case of not selling computers to Communist bloc countries may be carrying out American foreign policy objectives abroad; at another time, IBM in alliance with France may be seeking to change American policy to its own corporate advantage. In such a world where giant multinational corporations have become powerful actors and may pursue at times interests divergent from those of their home or host governments, countervailing power on the part of government is of enhanced importance.

As Richard Cooper has pointed out in another context, this open and interdependent international economy poses a new and significant challenge to all nation-states.[24] At the same time that they have undertaken new responsibilities for maintaining full employment and promoting industrial development, the openness of the contemporary economy and its increased sus-

23. *National Power and the Structure of Foreign Trade* (Berkeley, Calif., 1944).
24. *The Economics of Interdependence* (New York, 1968).

ceptibility to external influences including decisions of multinational corporations may distort or undermine these domestic goals. This combination of more ambitious goals for national economic policy and greater openness has produced an unprecedented challenge for all nations.

The paradox of this situation is that increasing interdependence among national economies is accompanied by increased intervention of governments in the domestic economy. In order to improve their competitive economic positions or to adjust their balance of payments, governments have developed new or refashioned old instruments of economic policy: interest rates, government procurement, export-promotion, tax incentives to domestic investment, and changes in domestic-tax structure. But as governments have only limited control over the instruments which influence trade balances or the balance of payments, and as success depends upon what other countries are doing, the result, as Cooper points out, is international competition in economic policy.

These neomercantilistic features of the contemporary world economy have considerable relevance for the debate in Canada over American investment. While they do not point necessarily to one solution or another for Canada's constitutional crisis, they at least help clarify the nature of the problem as the Canadians (both English and French) have defined it: Under what conditions is it possible for Canada to enjoy the benefits of American investment without sacrificing Canadian (or Quebec) individuality?

In an era where economic bargaining power vis-à-vis multinational corporations and other governments is of unprecedented importance, the Séparatiste argument for unification of decision over economic affairs is well taken. As Cooper argues, "successful economic policy requires an adequate number of policy instruments for the number of economic objectives, and it requires that these objectives be consistent with one another. If either of these conditions fails, policy-makers are bound to be frustrated in their efforts." [25] While this does not necessarily mean centrali-

25. *Ibid.*, p. 157.

zation of decision-making in Ottawa or Quebec, it does at least imply the need for close coordination between Ottawa and the provinces in determining policy objectives and policies.

In Canada, on the other hand, provincialism is leading to an increased division of authority between Ottawa and the provinces with respect to Canadian economic policy. As the aforementioned editorial from the *New York Times* stated, "[at] a time when every advanced industrialized nation is centralizing the weapons of economic policy to insure full employment, Canada is engaged in a decentralization—and a dissipation—of economic control." [26] Similarly, the struggle between Ottawa and the provinces with respect to foreign investment weakens the capacity of Canada to develop a coherent policy toward American corporations.

The importance of this issue of unified versus decentralized authority over foreign investment can be appreciated if one compares the situations of Japan and Western Europe. The experience of these two immense markets with respect to American investment has, I believe, great relevance for Canada.

Although American corporations covet both the Japanese and Western European markets, they have been able to establish hundreds of subsidiaries in the latter but only a few in the former. The reason for this difference is largely political. Whereas the former has one central government controlling access to Japan's internal market of 100 million population, six political centers control access to the European Common Market. By interposing itself between powerful American corporations and intensely competitive Japanese firms desiring American capital and technology, the Japanese government has been able to prevent the latter from making agreements undesired by the Japanese government. As a consequence, the Japanese home market has been protected as the almost exclusive domain of Japanese industry and American firms have had therefore a strong incentive to license their technology to the Japanese or to form corporate arrangements as a minor partner.

26. *New York Times, op. cit.*

In Western Europe, on the other hand, an American firm denied the right to establish a subsidiary in one Common Market country has the option of trying another and thereby still gaining access to the whole Market. Moreover, the strong desire of individual European countries for American investment enables American corporations to invest on very favorable terms and, in certain cases, to play a "divide and conquer" strategy. Thus it was several years ago that, denied permission by President de Gaulle to invest in France, General Motors established in Belgium one of the largest automobile assembly plants in the Common Market. The sequel to this story is that Ford was not only invited subsequently to invest in France but regional competition for that investment became a major issue in the French parliamentary elections.

While the Japanese and European examples support the argument for unified government, they cause one to raise a question with respect to the Séparatistes' resolution of this problem. In both the Japanese and the Common Market cases what is important is control or absence of control over access to the market. A solution of the Canadian constitutional crisis which maintained the Canadian Common Market, but divided even more than it is now the access of foreign goods and investment to the Canadian Common Market, might create a situation which the Europeans are trying to overcome in their efforts to establish a common external commercial policy, a uniform corporation law, and a unified monetary system. It was a similar situation as well that forced the United States in the earlier part of this century to nationalize corporation law and reduce the economic powers of the states. In short, while this analysis does not argue for one solution or another to Canada's constitutional problem, it does suggest that a solution to what Canadians see as the problem of American domination would require a resolution of the issues arising out of the division of authority between Ottawa and the provinces in three areas of economic policy: (1) control over foreign investment; (2) industrial policy; and (3) regional development.

As of this writing, the responsibilities of Ottawa in these three important areas are minimal. Control over foreign investment has remained largely a provincial responsibility, although Ottawa's exercise of a veto power has increased as Canadians have become more concerned over American penetration of their economy.[27] Consequently, in recent years, Ottawa has prevented American "take-over" in the "commanding heights" of the Canadian economy: finance, publishing, broadcasting, etc. These actions, however, are primarily negative and do not raise serious issues of a federal-provincial division of responsibility.

With respect to regional development and industrial policy, Ottawa's role has been modest, and has appeared mostly in the form of financial incentives or transfers to the provinces. Although new federal agencies for regional development have been established, regional development continues to be primarily the responsibility of the provinces. The result, according to one authority, has not been very successful due in part to the unwillingness or inability on the part of the federal government to define precisely overall policy objectives.[28]

A successful Canadian or Quebec response to the increasing penetration of the economy by American corporations would require greater exercise of leadership in these three areas. Again, setting aside the issue of who should exercise this leadership— Ottawa, an independent Quebec, or some combination of the two—important issues would have to be resolved with respect to industrial, investment, and regional policies.

With respect to industrial development there are essentially three industrial policies Canada could follow in response to the American challenge. The first is to support industrial development across the broadest front possible. A nation following this broad-front policy seeks to maintain a position especially in all those advanced fields considered to be of military, economic, and political importance: atomic energy, electronics, computers,

27. Present Canadian policy is treated in Task Force on the Structure of Canadian Industry, *op. cit.*, chapter 3.
28. T. N. Brewis, *Regional Economic Policies in Canada* (Toronto, 1969), p. 243. A contrasting view is expressed by Jacques Parizeau, "Prospects for Economic Policy in a Federal Canada," in P. A. Crepeau and C. B. Macpherson (eds.), *The Future of Canadian Federalism / L'Avenir du fédéralisme canadien* (Toronto and Montreal, 1965).

steel, chemicals, aerospace. This policy tending toward autarchy of course is the one followed by the two great powers—the United States and the Soviet Union. It is also the strategy which Great Britain attempted to follow until the early 1960's and which France pursued under the leadership of President Charles de Gaulle. This is the direction, for example, that proponents of an independent Canadian space program would have Canada take. But it raises immense problems of scale and the possible dispersion of resources into many programs many or most of which may yet remain below the critical mass of effectiveness. Canadians would pay, therefore, a high economic price for such a move in the direction of autarchy.

The second policy is that of industrial specialization. The essence of this strategy is to select for support specific areas of industry and technology of commercial utility and concentrate one's resources upon them. This means an innovative policy in these areas extending from basic research through technological development. Among the countries which have most successfully followed this policy are Sweden, the Netherlands, Switzerland, and increasingly Great Britain. While this is the course proposed by a number of Canadians, it requires a greater Canadian effort in scientific and technological research, and a radical rationalization of Canadian industry into more highly concentrated units.[29] This policy, moreover, assumes a high degree of integration between the American and Canadian economies, and a fairly high degree of coordination among industry, the provinces, and Ottawa.

In contrast to the first two policies, which depend upon a stronger scientific and technological effort in Canada, the third policy is to import technologies and industries. This importation policy places emphasis on the importation of foreign industrial technology, particularly American, through the purchasing of licenses or by means of direct investment. While this policy like the second implies specialization and a high degree of dependence on the world economy, it differs in that relatively little

29. See Craig, *op. cit.*, p. 272.

basic research or technological development is necessary. Either foreign technology is adopted without modification, or else indigenous scientific and technological resources are concentrated on improving imported technologies, especially for subsequent export.

Two countries which have followed this latter industrial policy are Japan and Canada. But whereas Japan has imported licenses and has perfected the art of improving imported technology, Canada has been dependent upon direct investment, and relatively little industrial research and development is conducted in Canadian firms. These policies reflect of course the differences in economic, technological, and political capabilities between the two countries. While this policy has paid off handsomely for both societies, each of them is becoming increasingly concerned over their technological dependence upon the United States.

Whether Canada retains this policy, or moves in the direction of other alternatives, has important implications for Canadian policy with respect to foreign investment. If Canada desires to develop "Canadian" industry independent of the United States, then it has to exercise much greater centralized control over American investment on the Canadian Common Market. Once it decides which industries to develop, it would undoubtedly have to protect those firms at least initially against more powerful American firms and favor them through government purchasing policies, research funds, and other forms of subsidy. The government would also have to play a strong role in rationalizing industry and creating Canadian corporations powerful enough to compete in world markets. This at any rate has been the experience of European countries in their own efforts to concentrate their industry and achieve the economies of scale required in high technology industries.

As economists like Harry Johnson point out, Canada would pay a very high economic price for such a policy of economic nationalism; [30] a policy against American domination would primarily benefit the Canadian middle and professional classes rather than the overall welfare of the Canadian people. It would

30. *The Canadian Quandary.*

also necessitate hard political choices with respect to which industries to develop and which regions to favor. The resolution of these issues would pose a delicate dilemma for Canada. As Western Europe has discovered in trying to develop a unified technological and industrial policy to meet the American challenge, a conflict may exist between the goal of industrial development and of regional development. Whereas the purpose of the former is to concentrate on one's strengths and to encourage specialization, the purpose of the latter is to spread resources and to diversify in order to lessen interregional differences. As a consequence the task of achieving these two goals simultaneously would be a difficult one and would at least require close inter-governmental coordination.[31]

In conclusion, the political challenge of American investment for Canada may be summarized in several short paragraphs:

(1) A highly interdependent world economy dominated by the United States and large multinational corporations has unleashed economic forces which are pulling Canada more and more toward the United States. Unfortunately for Canada the traditional counter-balancing power of Europe is subsiding with the growth of economic regionalism and as Commonwealth ties relax.[32] While some writers still see hope in using Japan and the European Common Market to balance American power,[33] these rising economic powers might actually accentuate Canada's problems by pulling the Canadian West toward the Pacific and the East, especially Quebec, toward Europe. Both of these huge economic concentrations, moreover, see Canada more as a source of raw materials in exchange for their manufactured goods than as an industrial trading partner.[34]

(2) The existence of large economic discrepancies among the provinces, the growing problem of unemployment, and the new emphasis on industrial development have stimulated the rise of provincialism and interprovincial competition for American

31. For the European situation see Gilpin, *op. cit.*, chapter 12, "Prospects for a European Solution to the Technology Gap."
32. Johnson, *The Canadian Quandary*, pp. 70–71.
33. Claude Julien, *Canada: Europe's Last Chance* (New York, 1968).
34. Johnson, *The Canadian Quandary*, chapter 6.

investment. As a consequence, in an economic era which necessitates increased coordination of economic policy to ensure
the achievement of domestic and international economic goals,
Canada is experiencing an accelerating fragmentation of decision-
making responsibility. Politically, this disunity weakens Canada's
bargaining position in dealing with the United States and American corporations.

(3) Unfortunately, the political problems caused by economic
discrepancies among the provinces are greatly reinforced by
ethnic differences. This combination of economic and ethnic
grievance has produced the present grave constitutional crisis.
Within Quebec itself, the choice between Canada and separatism
resolves itself largely as an economic issue: Which route will
solve Quebec's growing problem of unemployment and its increasing desire for industrialization, both of which depend in
large measure upon non-French-Canadian foreign and in particular, American investment?

(4) The internal challenge of French-Canadian nationalism
and the external challenge of American domination have produced in English Canada an intense and growing English-
Canadian nationalism, the theme of which is "Buy Canada
Back." [35] Although the economic consequences of this increasing
anti-Americanism could be, as numerous economists point out,
extremely costly for Canada, political pressures for action against
American corporations will increase. Thus, as economic forces
within Canada and the United States bring the two economies
closer together, political forces will further increase the conflict
within Canada and across the forty-ninth parallel.

35. A fascinating insight into English-Canadian nationalism is provided by
Gordon to Watkins to You, op. cit.

6

American Influences in the Development of Irrigation in British Columbia

Lawrence B. Lee

The role played by Americans in the systematic development of British Columbia irrigation institutions during the formative period running from 1900 to 1920 was relatively modest, however significant, and limited pretty largely to advice and example. American capital investment in provincial reclamation enterprise was practically nonexistent, offering a contrast to the mining industry at the same time. Furthermore, American influence in the shaping of a British Columbia water code, in the engineering of dams and canals and the perfecting of irrigation agriculture came at the invitation of the provincial government and agricultural interests. In this instance American imperialism was not at issue.

British Columbia's reclamation history also reenacted some of the features of Canadian irrigation development east of the Rockies after the Northwest Territories Irrigation Act of 1894 introduced reclamation to the Dry Belt of the future Alberta and Saskatchewan. Differences related to the fact that the Dominion government owned the natural resources in the Territories and reclamation on the prairies antedated the B.C. provincial effort by at least a decade. They had this in common that each Canadian irrigation "frontier" benefited from the advice and example of reclamationists south of the border.

What essentially was involved was a communication-diffusion process between the two nations in the matter of the dissemination of irrigation information.[1] The American states had priority in reclamation practice and the American civil engineering fraternity was one of the most important vehicles in the transmission of this American irrigation expertise. Thus John S. Dennis, architect of the Canadian Irrigation Act of 1894, wrote in that very same year asking for admission to the American Society of Irrigation Engineers. He intimated that his qualifications might not be acceptable since "irrigation . . . is a new subject in our country and I have had little opportunity as yet to gain much experience."[2] Of course, afterwards he was to become Canada's leading reclamationist and Commissioner of Irrigation for the Canadian Pacific Railway's vast irrigation projects in Alberta.[3] There was also William Pearce, Dominion land surveyor and pioneer promoter of irrigation for the Northwest Territories since 1884 who also belonged to the American engineers' association.[4] When it came time to frame a suitable water code for British Columbia after the turn of the century, Professor Louis G. Carpenter, founding father of the American Society of Irrigation

1. James G. March, "The Power of Power," in David Easton, (ed.), *Varieties of Political Theory* (Englewood Cliffs, N.J., 1966), p. 66.

2. Letter, John S. Dennis to Louis G. Carpenter, Feb. 21, 1894, L. G. Carpenter Papers, Denver Public Library.

3. John S. Dennis, (1856–1939) Canadian civil engineer, was born in Ontario in 1856, the son of Lieutenant Colonel John S. Dennis, deputy minister of the Interior, went west as a youth in 1872, subsequently became an employee of the Hudson's Bay Company, and later organized its Land Department. He was chief inspector of Dominion surveys from 1887 to 1894 and then administered surveys as the chief engineer of the Dominion Irrigation Department until 1902 when he became commissioner of irrigation for the Canadian Pacific Railway. After war service the then Colonel Dennis augmented his colonization work with the Canadian Pacific Railway through promotion of a Western Canada Colonization Association on the order of the Western Canada Irrigation Association. H. J. Morgan, *The Canadian Men and Women of the Time* (Toronto, 1912), p. 317; James B. Hedges, *Building the Canadian West: The Land and Colonization Policies of the Canadian Pacific Railway* (New York, 1939), pp. 367–386.

4. William Pearce, (1848–1930) a civil engineer born in Ontario in 1848, active in Western Canada as a land surveyor since 1873, was with the Canadian public service from 1882 as dominion lands' inspector, superintendent of mines and chief inspector of dominion surveys. He championed the cause of irrigation for the Northwest Territories from 1885 and together with John S. Dennis is considered responsible for passage of the Irrigation Act of 1894. He was active on behalf of the organized irrigation movement attending meetings of the Irrigation Congress in the United States (1894–1895) and as an officer of the Western Canada Irrigation Association. Morgan, *Canadian Men and Women*, p. 892; W. S. Wallace, (ed.), *The Macmillan Dictionary of Canadian Biography* (New York, 1963), p. 586.

Engineers, served as a member of the Royal Commission that made recommendations incorporated into the British Columbia Water Act of 1909.[5]

British Columbia reclamation efforts seemed particularly subject to American influence. A profusion of water claims antedated by fifty years the provincial codification of water law and so the British Columbia situation resembled that of such states as Wyoming, Colorado or California instead of the Northwest Territories where the Act of 1894 was in effect in advance of water claims. Also the government of British Columbia owned all land and water resources (except within the Canadian Pacific Railway Belt) and was thus especially suited for applying the model of irrigation institutions developed among the members of the American Society of Irrigation Engineers under the leadership of the state engineer of Wyoming, Elwood Mead.[6] American influence was exercised most effectively, if not exclusively, through the services of American engineers who were asked to make recommendations for institutional reform. Their recommendations were also voiced at the numerous meetings of the Western Canada Irrigation Association, 1907–1924, an organization which in itself was a Canadian imitation of the respected and sometime prestigious [American] National Irrigation Congress.[7]

The modern application of engineering knowledge to recla-

5. Louis G. Carpenter, (1861–1935) civil engineer, was born at Orion, Michigan in 1861, graduated with a B.S. degree in 1879 and M.S. degree in 1883 from Michigan Agricultural College. Graduate work in engineering followed at the University of Michigan and Johns Hopkins University. He was a professor of engineering at Michigan Agricultural College from 1881 to 1888 and at Colorado Agricultural College from 1888 to 1911. Carpenter organized at Colorado the first course in irrigation engineering and investigation in an American university in 1888. He was an engineer with the State Experiment Station, was Colorado State Engineer from 1903–1905 and was employed by the U.S. Department of Agriculture Irrigation Institutions. Then he became consultant for irrigation projects in Colorado and for the British Columbia Ministry of Lands (1907) also an expert on important water rights litigation. *Irrigation Age,* III (June, 1892), 74–75; *Denver Post,* Sept. 12, 1935; J. W. Leonard, *Who's Who in Engineering: A Biographical Dictionary of Contemporaries,* 1922–23 (New York, 1922), p. 238.
6. U.S. Cong., Senate, *Cession of the Public Lands,* S. Doc. 130, 55th Cong., 1st Sess., 1897, pp. 1–73.
7. Lawrence B. Lee, "Dominion Ditches and British Columbia Canals: A History of the Western Canada Irrigation Association," *Journal of the West,* VII (January, 1968), 31–40.

mation projects through the instrumentality of irrigation began with British Indian engineers, trained by the East India Company at Addiscombe School in England and elsewhere, who subsequently saw service in Piedmont, India and Egypt.[8] Later this Indian engineering experience was transferred to Australia. Here under the influence of Sir Arthur T. Cotton and others the state of Victoria adopted Indian legal forms innovative for Anglo-Saxon law in the Irrigation Act of 1886.[9] When Canada sought information upon which to design its irrigation law for the Northwest Territories it sent John S. Dennis, its chief of Dominion land surveys to witness Australian practice as well as American.[10] In effect the Canadian Irrigation Law (1894) adopted the innovations that came from India via Australia wherein the common law doctrine of riparian rights was rejected and ownership of land and water was vested in the government. When it came to obtaining the services of engineers Canadian projects found few British engineers at hand. Furthermore conditions in southern Alberta and Saskatchewan, as well as the Dry Belt of British Columbia, were different from those in India, Egypt or Australia. American engineers were available and eager to be hired as consultants on all Canadian projects. Another consideration was important. Imperial engineers had been accustomed to working huge governmental projects without budgetary limitations whereas Canadian projects were private undertakings and in British Columbia, particularly, they were on a small scale. American engineers had learned to work efficiently with the critical cost factors that beset these smaller capitalistic undertakings.[11]

The American Society of Irrigation Engineers had an especial relevance for the Canadian irrigation effort since it encompassed the activities of the principal American civil engineers engaged

8. C. S. Burchill, "The Origins of Canadian Irrigation Law," *Canadian Historical Review*, XXIX (Dec., 1948), 353–362; Robert L. Tignor, "British Agricultural and Hydraulic Policy in Egypt, 1882–1892," *Agricultural History*, XXXVII (April, 1963), 63–74; W. H. G. Armytage, *A Social History of Engineering* (Cambridge, Mass., 1961), pp. 162–163.

9. Burchill, p. 362.

10. Canada, Parliament, "General Report of Irrigation," *Sessional Papers*, X, No. 13, Pt. III (1895), 5–7.

11. *Irrigation Age*, I (Oct., 1891), 213–214.

on irrigation projects. They were caught up in the promotional efforts of the [American] National Irrigation Congress movement starting in 1891 and were dedicated to private irrigation ventures under state engineering supervision. There were probably as many irrigation engineers as there were mining engineers in the American West in the early 1890's.[12] The engineers who attended the first Irrigation Congress at Salt Lake in September, 1891, formed the nucleus of the irrigation engineering association inaugurated there.[13] The fundamental purpose of the organization was to upgrade the qualifications of engineers working on reclamation projects so that only professionally trained practitioners would be employed. Investment capital would thus be encouraged by the high standards of workmanship applied on each project. Equally important was the exchange of professional information of a practical on-the-job character through annual meetings with the reading of papers and the publication of a journal.[14]

This association held several important meetings and maintained respectable professional standards until its untimely demise early in the new century.[15] Canada's John S. Dennis, who had moved his base of operation to Calgary and was about to begin the implementation of the 1894 Act, attended the Denver meeting of the engineers in conjunction with the fourth annual Irrigation Congress.[16] He was elected vice president in 1896. The organization included all prominent irrigation engineers in the

12. *Ibid.*, III (June, 1892), 75.   13. *Ibid.*, I (Oct., 1891), 217–218.
14. George G. Anderson, "Irrigation Engineering," *Irrigation Age*, II (Feb., 1892), 484.
15. The Society of Irrigation Engineers held at least six annual meetings, often in conjunction with the National Irrigation Congress though Denver was its headquarters. Papers were read by practicing irrigation engineers including one titled, "Canadian Irrigation Survey," by John S. Dennis in 1896. At least one quarterly of the Society was published. Correspondence between the founder, L. G. Carpenter, and Elwood Mead and George G. Anderson, the last president, describe the financial plight of the organization and anticipate its imminent demise. Louis Carpenter ultimately transmitted its records to the Secretary of National Irrigation Congress. Letter, A. D. Foote [first president] to L. G. Carpenter, March 8, 1892; Carpenter to Mead, Oct. 14, 1895; Carpenter to J. S. Titcomb [secretary], Jan. 13, 1896; George G. Anderson to Carpenter, Feb. 24, 1898; Mead to Carpenter, March 29, 1898; Carpenter to Arthur Hooker, Feb. 14, 1912; *Denver Daily News*, Dec. 12, 1896; L. G. Carpenter Papers, Denver Public Library.
16. *Denver Republican*, Sept. 5, 1894.

United States and several from abroad.[17] Charter members who sought to make irrigation engineering a recognized branch of civil engineering and contributed substantially to the advancement of irrigation institutions in Canada included the Americans Louis G. Carpenter, George G. Anderson, Samuel Fortier and Elwood Mead. Carpenter and Fortier would be linked with Mead in state experiment-station projects when Elwood Mead assumed the position of Expert in charge of the Irrigation Investigations of the United States Department of Agriculture's Office of Experiment Stations.

It was Elwood Mead's irrigation investigations program that was drawn upon by British Columbia authorities when the provincial water law was codified in 1909 and significantly amended in 1914 so as to encourage the full development of irrigation.[18]

17. The Society's membership list looked like a Who's Who in irrigation engineering at one time, with N. S. Nettleton, R. J. Hinton, Hiram Chittenden, Morris Bien, Frederick Newell, Arthur P. Davis, J. B. Lippincott and James Schuyler who had or would see service with the federal government Agriculture Inquiry or Geological Survey. Others who had distinguished themselves in private practice or as state engineers included William Hammond Hall, C. L. Stevenson, A. D. Foote, James Maxwell. Dennis and Pearce represented the Canadian engineers. *Ibid.*

18. Elwood Mead (1858–1936) civil engineer was born in Indiana in 1858 and received his B.S. degree at Purdue University in 1882, his C.E. degree at Iowa State (1883) and M.S. at Purdue (1884). He was professor of irrigation engineering at Colorado State College and then in 1888 became first territorial and in 1890 state engineer of Wyoming. Mead had worked under the Colorado water code (laws of 1879 and 1881) with its system of dividing the state into water districts with water commissioners supervised by a state engineer. Mead also drew upon the water law of Victoria which dispensed with riparian rights when he drafted the provisions in Wyoming's constitution (1890) and statutes which provided a model water code copied by other states. His efforts to secure the cession of U.S. public domain lands to western states and territories failed though the National Irrigation Congress initially organized to promote cession, continued as a movement which contributed to passage of the Newlands Act (1902). In 1899, Mead was appointed Chief of the U.S. Department of Agriculture Irrigation Investigations Office and sought the adoption of uniform water rights laws in western states so as to curb deleterious litigation. His agency in cooperation with state experiment stations carried on studies of "duty of water," irrigation agriculture, agricultural engineering. He set up the University of California department of irrigation institutions, lectured there and at Harvard, wrote prodigiously for popular and technical journals and in government reports. In 1907 he became Chairman of Victoria (Australia) State Rivers and Water Commission. On his return in 1915 Mead became professor of rural institutions at the University of California and became director of the California land settlement board which supervised two land colonies. From 1915 he advised the Secretary of the Interior on Reclamation Projects on a planned Soldiers' Settlement program which Congress neglected to approve. In 1924 his work on the Fact Finders Committee led to his appointment as Commissioner of the Reclamation Bureau. His experience proved invaluable in supervising the construction of the Hoover and Grand Coulee

This Wyoming system as it was called was championed in America's Arid Domain as an alternative to national construction and ownership of reclamation dams and projects which became the pattern in the United States with passage of the Newlands bill through the American Congress in 1902.[19]

Irrigation agriculture in British Columbia long antedated similar practices in the Northwest Territories. Significantly, in 1858, only a few months after the Crown Colony was established, the first water right for agriculture was granted by the authorities.[20] Although most claims related to placer mining, by 1865 agricultural use of water was generally accepted and it was customary to impose "beneficial use" restrictions on the grants. Travellers crossing the interior valleys in the 1860's and 1870's noted the widespread use of "artificial irrigation in growing garden truck for the predominately mining population." [21] In 1888 the province underwrote a survey of artesian sources of water for agriculture and experimental well boring in the Yale district.[22]

During the 1890's the advertising program of the province and the Canadian Pacific Railway attracted farmers to take up residence in the Okanagan Valley.[23] This was the famous British Columbia Dry Belt which was (along with the Kamloops district) the first physiographic region in the province to make extensive use of irrigation. It constituted the semi-humid plateau and valley lands stretching some 160 miles from the American

---

Dams before his death in 1936. Letter, Elwood Mead to Sen. William Stewart, May 9, 1889; Mead to Fred Bond, June 26, 1901, State Engineer Correspondence 1888–1901, Wyoming State Archives, Cheyenne; Francis Warren to Pres. Theodore Roosevelt, Oct., 29, 1901, Warren Letterbooks, Western History Research Center, University of Wyoming, Laramie; *Dictionary of American Biography*, XI, Supp. 2, 443–444; "Elwood Mead, Commissioner of Reclamation, Dies," *The Reclamation Era*, XXVI (Feb., 1936), 33–39; R. G. Dunbar, "The Significance of the Colorado Agricultural Frontier," *Agricultural History*, XXXIV (July, 1960), 119–125; Elwood Mead, *Irrigation Institutions* (New York, 1903).

19. Paul W. Gates, *History of Public Land Law Development* (Washington, D.C., 1968), pp. 652–698.

20. E. Davis, "The Development of Irrigation in British Columbia," *Irrigation Review*, V (July, 1924), 241–245.

21. H. Spencer Palmer, "Remarks upon the Geography and Natural Capabilities of British Columbia. . . ," *Journal of the Royal Geographical Society*, XXXIV (1864), 171–195; H. L. Langevin, *Report of the Hon. H. L. Langevin, Minister of Public Works* (Ottawa, Canada, 1872), p. 2.

22. British Columbia, *Report of the Chief Commissioner of Lands and Works* [1890] (Victoria, 1891), p. 273.

23. Margaret Ormsby, *British Columbia: A History* (Toronto, 1958), p. 314.

border in the north-south rift between the Selkirk Range on the east and the Cascade Mountains on the west featuring Okanagan Lake and its many tributary lakes and streams.[24] Here it was, starting in 1891, that the first commercial orchards were set out adjacent to and on the Coldstream Ranch lands of Lord Aberdeen, Governor General of Canada. Thereafter ranches were subdivided according to demand and by 1910 orchard districts were situated up and down the Okanagan Valley near the future towns of Penticton, Summerland, Peachland, Kelowna, Vernon, Armstrong and Enderby, then serving as supply and packing centers.[25]

As the 20th century opened there were increasing signs that both private interests and the British Columbia government wished to foster agriculture in the Dry Belt of the interior with the two-fold purpose of promoting immigration and freeing the province from dependence upon American farms in Washington and Montana.[26] The shift already under way in the Okanagan from grazing to the more intensive horticultural form of agriculture was accomplishing these purposes but would require special assistance from the government. An up-to-date system of irrigation institutions must be created for the province in order to facilitate the agricultural transformation of the Dry Belt. As early as 1895 agents of the provincial department of agriculture advocated the appointment of a commission to investigate irrigation needs for the interior valleys.[27] The Water Clauses Consolidation Act of 1897 provided a statutory foundation for change when it vested ownership of unappropriated water in the provincial government.[28] Not many years later one of the leading provincial newspapers suggested that legislation was overdue.[29] First, information was necessary concerning the engineering

24. Margaret Ormsby, "Fruit Marketing in the Okanagan Valley of British Columbia," *Agricultural History*, IX (April, 1935), 80–97.
25. F. W. Andrew, "The Summerland Experimental Station," *Twelfth Report of the Okanagan Historical Society* (1948), pp. 172–179; *Irrigation Review*, II (June, 1921), 6.
26. Frances MacNab, *British Columbia for Settlers: Its Mines, Trade and Agriculture* (London, 1898), pp. 10–11.
27. British Columbia, *Sessional Papers, 1897*, p. 1017.
28. British Columbia, *Sessional Papers, 1913*, p. D119.
29. *Victoria Daily Colonist*, March 28, 1901.

problems of conserving water, the best system for disposing of the lands and raising money to construct irrigation works. Also an important decision would have to be reached whether the government or private enterprise should undertake the project. Answers to these questions could best be secured in the United States where large scale irrigation had long been practiced.

Insistent demands for an irrigation inquiry encouraged two members of the provincial parliament, Fred J. Fulton of Kamloops and Price Ellison of the Okanagan, to introduce a resolution which would put the government on record for this investigation. As the irrigation boom in the Okanagan Valley gathered force after 1904 with from fifteen to twenty companies promising to supply irrigated acreage to purchasers of their lands, concern mounted over the lack of legal procedures for registering new water claims, or providing arbitration of disputed claims thus posing the specter of litigation.[30] The time was ripe for water law reform. In light of this background the movement for a permanent Canadian irrigation promotion organization which had its genesis at Calgary, Alberta in March, 1907, seemed most opportune to the Okanagan irrigation interests. They anticipated this organization might serve their purposes to generate enthusiasm for legal reform and promotion of British Columbia irrigation.

The Western Canada Irrigation Association (W.C.I.A.) truly represented the irrigation interests of Western Canada, those of British Columbia equally with the concerns of the prairie provinces, the small farmer as well as the capitalist entrepreneur and governmental agent.[31] The organization promoted the cause of irrigation from its inception in 1907 until its last meeting in 1926. Not only did the Association meet alternately on each side of the Rockies, but the two different systems of irrigation agriculture were given equal consideration in terms of programming and attention. The [American] National Irrigation Congress was

30. *Ibid.*, April 18, 1901; British Columbia, *Sessional Papers, 1904*, p. A13.
31. Lee, "Dominion Ditches and British Columbia Canals." The official journal of the W.C.I.A., the *Irrigation Review*, published between 1920 and 1926, was a valuable source of Canadian reclamation news and scientific information as it was the vehicle for publishing the papers read at annual meetings.

the model for the W.C.I.A. and close ties were maintained between the two associations, including a joint meeting held at Calgary in October, 1914.[32] In addition to the promotional aspects and the exchange of technical engineering and agricultural information at the sessions, the Association very definitely influenced governmental policy on the provincial and Dominion level.[33] The forty members from British Columbia in attendance at the Calgary meeting in 1907 won approval for a resolution asking the provincial government to amend the 1897 Water Act so that existing water records could be revised and nonusers claims cancelled.[34]

A royal commission on irrigation was constituted in British Columbia in 1907 in response to the prolonged campaign for such an inquiry. The Minister of Lands, Fred J. Fulton, and Professor Louis G. Carpenter were members of the commission. Carpenter's qualifications were well known to such Canadian irrigationists as John S. Dennis and William Pearce, associates of his in the Society of Irrigation Engineers. His expert knowledge of every aspect of irrigation development in Colorado recommended him to the local authorities. Colorado was believed to offer the closest parallel to conditions in British Columbia. The American spent a month in the province devoting most of his time to the irrigation works in the Dry Belt.[35] Fulton then accompanied Carpenter on his return to Colorado and visited projects and interviewed leading experts in that state.[36] Carpenter's portion of the commission report offered a lengthy description of practices in Colorado. He congratulated the Canadian province on their natural resources, the notable beginnings in reclamation launched by private enterprise in the Okanagan and the advantage given them in legal matters when they dispensed with riparian rights.

First among Carpenter's recommendations was the suggestion

---

32. *Official Proceedings of the Twenty-first International Irrigation Congress held at Calgary, Alberta, Canada, October 5–9, 1914* (Ottawa, 1915).
33. *Report of the Proceedings of the Third Annual Convention of the Western Canada Irrigation Association . . . Lethbridge . . .* (Ottawa, 1910), p. 10.
34. *Vernon News,* July 25, 1907.   35. *Ibid.,* Aug. 22, 29, 1907.
36. *Colorado Springs Gazette,* Sept. 30, 1907.

that the province's water law make provision for storage of water. The problem of excess recording of claims must be eliminated by the establishment of a commission to handle disputed claims. A water administration with one officer at the head should be instituted to provide for the surveys of streams and the grant of licenses for new recordings. Perhaps because Carpenter was an American guest, his report did not carry the sense of urgency and demand for immediate and arbitrary denial of unused water claims that permeated John Dennis's recommendations for reform.[37] Dennis's advice was also requested by Minister Fulton. The government's measure was submitted to farmers' institutes and the second annual Western Canada Irrigation Association meeting at Vernon, in August, 1908, for suggested revision before ultimate passage as the Water Act of 1909.

The Vernon assembly of the W.C.I.A. was notable for the debate about government ownership precipitated by Price Ellison, one of the first spokesmen for reclamation in the Dry Belt and later Minister of Lands succeeding Fred Fulton. He spoke for provincial government ownership as opposed to mere government control of irrigation works.[38] He was impressed with the millions of dollars that were being spent by the Bureau of Reclamation in the United States and was convinced that the provincial government had the assets to operate on a larger scale than private enterprise. He believed it could build the necessary reservoirs and provide water for all at a cheaper cost. Mr. Fulton countered in favor of the current system of government control with the view that their government was a "business government" and could not afford to spend four or five millions in projects all over the Dry Belt. The Commissioner of Irrigation for the Canadian Pacific Railway, John S. Dennis, then spoke on behalf of the system of government control in Alberta where it had been their experience that the Dominion government had merely to provide the necessary surveys, location of reservoir sites and the licensing and inspection of private irrigation works, and capital was

37. British Columbia, *Sessional Papers, 1908*, pp. D1–D13.
38. *Report of the Proceedings of the Second Annual Convention of the Western Canada Irrigation Association . . . Vernon . . .* (Ottawa, 1909), pp. 24–26.

forthcoming to meet their needs. Nevertheless the example of the Wenatchee project of the U.S. Bureau of Reclamation across the border presented a tempting argument for government ownership.[39]

The British Columbia Water Act of 1909 reflected the contributions of both John Dennis and Louis Carpenter, the American engineer, whose recommendations influenced Minister of Lands Fulton who bore the chief responsibility for drafting this complicated measure regulating the disposal of all water in the province for all purposes: domestic, irrigation, power, industrial, etc. From one point of view the legislation resembled most closely the epochal Wyoming statute of 1890 in providing machinery for an administrative adjudication of prior water rights. An agency called the Board of Investigations reviewed all prior existing water records, some dating back to the Gold Fields Act of 1859, and a license was then granted when each record was validated. All new water rights were to be awarded by a member of the Board called the Comptroller of Water Rights. The Minister of Lands was empowered to carry on extensive hydrographic surveys to provide the information requisite to the granting of licenses. The Water Rights Branch of the Department of Lands administered this act through irrigation subdistricts approximating drainage basins.[40] The Colorado and Wyoming models were implicit in this design. The framers of the California water code of 1912 imitated several provisions of the B.C. Statute.[41] The Western Canada Irrigation Association and the British Columbia farmers' institutes had played their part in the measure's enactment.[42]

The W.C.I.A. recognized that American agricultural engineering might offer Canada's irrigationists practical information derived from years of American experience and scientific inquiry. Mr. John S. Dennis made reference at the Lethbridge meeting

39. *Vernon News,* April 18, 1907.
40. British Columbia, *Sessional Papers, 1913,* p. D120.
41. *Report of the Proceedings of the Sixth Annual Convention of the Western Canada Irrigation Association . . . Kelowna . . .* (Ottawa, 1913), p. 109.
42. *Vernon News,* Aug. 12, 1909; British Columbia, *Sessional Papers, 1909,* pp. M38–M39.

in 1909 to the bulletins published by Elwood Mead and his U.S. Irrigation Investigations office containing information on the laws of different territories and jurisdictions "with the ultimate object of trying to present an ideal law which they hope the different states will adopt." [43] A resolution was adopted by the W.C.I.A. in 1909 requesting the provinces and the Dominion Department of Agriculture to inaugurate a similar series of publications which would cover all aspects of irrigation engineering and farming modelled after those of the American Department of Agriculture.[44]

Mr. W. H. Fairfield, also in attendance at Lethbridge, advocated a program whereby the farmers' institutes would secure lecturers in irrigation agriculture.[45] Fairfield was assistant director of the Lethbridge, Alberta, experiment station and had been a student of Professor Carpenter's and an associate of Elwood Mead in Wyoming before coming to Canada. Fred Fulton commended the work of the Lethbridge station and suggested British Columbia must have a branch of its federal experiment station in the dry lands region.[46] The Dominion experiment station program had been adopted by the Canadian government in conscious imitation of the American model and Canada's two great irrigation regions looked for continuing advice from the cooperative programs of the American states and federal office of Irrigation Investigations.

One of the American agricultural engineers who was employed by the British Columbia Department of Agriculture was Bernard A. Etcheverry, a professor in the University of California Irrigation Institutions Department.[47] He was a consultant for several irrigation companies in the Kamloops district and was employed by the province during the period 1912–1914. His

43. *Proceedings*, W.C.I.A., Lethbridge, 1909, pp. 23–24.   44. *Ibid.*
45. *Ibid.*, p. 26.   46. *Ibid.*, p. 24.
47. Bernard A. Etcheverry, a civil engineer, was born in California in 1881. He received his B.S. and C.E. degrees in 1902 from the University of California. He was a professor of civil engineering at the Universities of Nevada and California, 1903–1910, and then professor of irrigation engineering from 1910. He held a joint appointment in the U.S.D.A.'s Office of Irrigation Investigations from 1910 to 1913. During the years, 1912–1914 he was employed by the British Columbia Department of Agriculture to make a systematic survey of irrigation systems in the province. *Who's Who in Engineering*, 1922–23, pp. 600–601.

booklet titled *Practical Information on Irrigation for British Columbia Fruit Growers* was distributed throughout the province in 1912 and in a handsomely bound edition became the gift of members of the Western Canada Irrigation Association meeting at Kelowna, British Columbia in 1912.[48]

Ranchers were appreciative of the provincial government's efforts to instruct them in the proper application of irrigation farming techniques. By 1910, however, a sense of dissatisfaction began to pervade the whole Dry Belt concerning the administration of the Water Act of 1909. Imperfections in the statute were the subject of yearly amendment. In fact these annual amendments became something of a joke to the legislators at Victoria as it seemed a complete water code might never be designed. The chief complaint with administration was the slowness with which the Board of Irrigation Investigations was hearing cases. The result was a growing bitterness towards the holders of prior records who were not using their rights or were wasting water. At the Kamloops convention of the W.C.I.A. in 1910 this problem was fully aired with reference to ranchers taking the law into their own hands.[49] One speaker demonstrated an acquaintance with the Wyoming practice of the 1890's where water commissioners went right down into the district and settled disputes in rapid fashion. Another wished that British Columbia might have a counterpart of Commissioner John Dennis to help them straighten out their mess.[50]

Against this background of small results under the system of government regulation, it was inevitable that the question of government ownership should come up again. Price Ellison's arguments were revived to demonstrate that the government of the province could spend two million out of its anticipated revenue of eight million dollars to finance the large-scale system of reclamation the province demanded.[51] The proponents of the status quo were afraid that private investment would be fright-

48. B. A. Etcheverry, *Practical Information on Irrigation for British Columbia Fruit Growers* (Victoria, 1912).
49. *Proceedings, W.C.I.A.*, Kamloops, 1910, pp. 91–99.
50. *Vernon News*, July 28, 1910.
51. *Proceedings, W.C.I.A.*, Kamloops, 1910, pp. 91–99.

ened away if the government were involved. What was essential was to have the Water Act of 1909 administered efficiently so that conflicts over water rights were eliminated. Then private enterprise would achieve all the needed reclamation.

Sentiment definitely began to shift the next year in support of some means of government ownership to supplement the existing system of government regulation. It was reported at the farmers' institutes that private companies in the Okanagan formerly opposed to government ownership were working to bring it to pass. The B.C. Water Commissioner, Mr. Drewry, spoke in favor of a limited form of government ownership that might be attempted by means of a water municipality charter since none of the projects in the province were very large.[52] The new view was confirmed at the 1914 meeting of the W.C.I.A. at Penticton in the Okanagan. Minister of Agriculture Price Ellison thought the Water Act of 1909 had not gone far enough, as there was no use in making rules and regulations if there was not enough water to go around. He believed that private enterprise unassisted was not able to develop the water resources on the scale that was needed. Now it was too late, however, for the government to take over all irrigation projects in British Columbia—too many millions had been invested already.[53]

In 1912 the deteriorating state of affairs with respect to British Columbia irrigation water rights controversies and threatened litigation brought a halt in opening new projects and forced the government of the province to call in American experts again to study the situation and make recommendations for change. They summoned a leading authority on irrigation agriculture in the United States. Samuel Fortier, a native-born Canadian who had taken his engineering training at McGill University, had joined the staff of Elwood Mead's Irrigation Institutions agency in 1900. He headed the University of California Irrigations Institutions Department when he was chosen to succeed Mead as chief of the irrigation branch of the Department of Agriculture

52. British Columbia, *Sessional Papers, 1911,* pp. L53–L54.
53. *Proceedings, W.C.I.A.,* Penticton, 1914, pp. 26–27.

at Washington.[54] The Minister of Lands in British Columbia, H. M. Ross sought Fortier's knowledge in the summer of 1912 for specific recommendations on reorganizing the Water Rights Branch. Mr. Fortier spent sixty days travelling in the province and acquiring the data for several reports to the government. Some of the conclusions of Fortier's studies were delivered to the sixth annual convention of the W.C.I.A. at Kelowna in August, 1912.[55] His role as he saw it was to tell his fellow Canadian irrigationists how to avoid the mistakes that had been made in American reclamation. The Act of 1909 incorporated a great number of the beneficent features of the Wyoming law whose chief purpose had been to limit litigation. The Water Act was fine on its face but the fact that there were still some five thousand claims to be adjudicated meant that it must be strengthened in respect to supervision and control. In connection with the granting of rights, experience with the "duty of water" studies by the Department of Agriculture had disclosed that water was always granted too liberally. The B.C. water code limited recordings to "beneficial use" in accordance with "duty of water" findings so the actual amount needed would be limited for a given crop under certain soil and climatic conditions. Furthermore, in order to preserve the waters of the province a long range water resource survey must be carried on indefinitely. Fortier assured his audience that every fact that the U.S. Department of Agriculture had obtained from its continuing investigations would be put at their disposal. A postal card to the Irrigation Investigations office would bring them any of the

---

54. Samuel Fortier, a civil engineer, was born in Ontario in 1855, and acquired his B.S., Master's and Doctor's degrees at McGill University. He was an engineer with the Denver Water Works and Ogden Water Works and chief engineer for private irrigation companies like the Bear River Canal Company. He became professor of civil and hydraulic engineering at the Utah Agricultural College. He served as hydrographer for the U.S. Geological Survey in Montana and Idaho. In 1900 he joined the U.S.D.A. Irrigation Investigation's staff and by 1904 was professor of irrigation institutions at the University of Calfornia. He succeeded Elwood Mead as chief of the Office of Irrigation Institutions in Washington, D.C. He was called in as consultant for irrigation by the British Columbia Ministry of Lands in 1912 and the Canadian Pacific Railway in 1915. *Who's Who in Engineering*, 1922–23, p. 456.
55. *Proceedings*, W.C.I.A., Kelowna, 1912, pp. 108–116.

bulletins they wished. "In this subject of irrigation we know no north or south. We are all working for the cause of humanity."[56]

The American expert sensed the growing demand in the province for local control of irrigation works. While the province primarily depended upon individual enterprise and canal companies, the practice in the United States was for cooperative enterprise of the water users to take over. He was all for this and recommended such institutional organization of water users as mutual water companies and irrigation districts.[57] There was no need for the government of the province to embark upon construction of projects or the lending of its credit to other projects. There was every probability, despite the current depression in agriculture, that British Columbia would follow the example of Colorado and California and develop irrigation agriculture whose productivity would surpass that of the mining industry.[58]

Another American who also worked for the Irrigation Investigations office of the U.S. Department of Agriculture was called to British Columbia at Mr. Fortier's suggestion to investigate the water law of the province. He was Mr. H. W. Grunsky, who was in charge of the irrigation investigations work in Oregon in 1912 and then became an employee of the British Columbia Water Rights Branch.[59] His training was in law and his recommendations were followed in reforming the internal administration of the Water Rights Branch, with regard to amending the Water Act of 1909 and in his proposal for the Irrigation Corporations Act that was adopted in 1914.[60] Mr. Grunsky's inquiries revealed the need for new legislation in the province authorizing mutual water companies and irrigation districts. Extended experience as with the highly successful Modesto and Turlock districts in California were cited as authority for the adoption of this type of local government district body.[61]

The popular clamor in the Dry Belt for governmental action

56. *Ibid.*, p. 114.   57. *Ibid.*, pp. 115–116.
58. British Columbia, *Sessional Papers, 1913*, pp. DD112–DD116.
59. U.S. Department of Agriculture, Office of Experiment Stations, *Annual Report, 1912*; British Columbia, *Sessional Papers, 1915*, p. H5.
60. British Columbia, *Sessional Papers, 1913*, pp. D117–D125.
61. British Columbia, *Sessional Papers, 1914*, pp. L1–L42; *Proceedings*, W.C.I.A., Kelowna, 1912, p. 102.

was given direction by the reports of the American experts, Fortier and Grunsky, but the resulting institutional change did not save the Okanagan horticultural belt from financial disaster. The specific demand for the creation of irrigation districts in the affected area was advanced by the recommendations of the Western Canada Irrigation Association at Kelowna in 1912 and by a Royal Commission of Agriculture in 1913. The Water Act of 1914 provided one means by which canal companies could be taken over by the water users who had bought the land of these companies. Unfortunately this act could not accommodate itself to the financial paralysis that ensued. Supplementary legislation had to be adopted in 1918 whereby a Conservation Fund with $3,000,000 in assets shored up the distressed companies and enabled the water users to buy out vested interests and organize themselves into improvement districts under a 1920 statute.[62]

The problems that perplexed the British Columbia irrigation companies during the period 1914 to 1920 grew out of the slowing down of the irrigation and realty boom period. From 1904 to 1914 companies in the Okanagan Valley had been formed to sell land on consideration that water would be provided for the land. The land parcels were bought by fruit ranchers who pioneered today's flourishing horticultural industry in Okanagan. Land prices remained high during the boom and the land and canal companies made fortunes from the increase in land values. The water works, however, were cheaply constructed of wood and lasted without deterioration for only a few years. Immigration started to slacken in 1912 and with the onset of World War I the companies began to lose money and many went into bankruptcy. The water users saw the water works on which they were dependent for irrigating their orchards decay before their eyes and demanded that the government rescue them and provide institutions whereby the water users could control their source of water. This was where the advice of Fortier, Grunsky and others was so valuable. Amelioration came too late. After

---

62. *Irrigation Review*, V (Sept., 1923), 36–40; J. C. MacDonald and J. W. Clark, "Economic Survey of . . . Irrigation Districts," typescript report to Minister of Lands, T. D. Pattullo, Feb. 18, 1927, British Columbia Archives, Victoria.

1920 the money that was advanced by the government's Conservation Fund to buy out the former companies—some $2,300,000 taken up as debt by the irrigation districts—was never paid off completely. The fruit industry, however, flourished until the onset of the Depression, and the irrigation works had been modernized.[63]

While it can be stated that the pioneer period in British Columbia irrigation organization had been passed by 1920, the full extent of American influence in that development has not been plumbed. Members of the Western Canada Irrigation Association periodically attended the annual meetings of the [American] National Irrigation Congress and other irrigation associations in Washington, Oregon and Montana.[64] The exchange of information was beneficial on both sides. British Columbia had followed the advice of the editorial writer in the *Victoria Colonist* back in 1901 in looking to the United States as the great source for irrigation ideas.

The focus of the above study has been on the activities of the engineers who since the days of the American Society of Irrigation Engineers had helped Canadian leaders shape their irrigation institutions. They talked to Canadian civil engineers as well as government leaders and ranchers and always the spirit underlying these exchanges was one of cooperation, for they all believed as with Samuel Fortier in obliterating differences between north and south with respect to irrigation. They were all working for humanity. In this spirit the esteemed British engineer of Egypt's Aswan Dam, Sir William Willcocks shared his memorable experiences with members of the W.C.I.A. In this same spirit the American engineers who were associated with and inspired by the Elwood Mead vision of model irrigation institutions came to British Columbia to help this province during its pioneering irrigation period.[65]

63. British Columbia, *Sessional Papers, 1930*, pp. AA1–AA23.
64. *Irrigation Review*, V (Dec., 1923), 86; *Proceedings of the Second Annual Meeting of the Washington Irrigation Association* (North Yakima, 1915).
65. The Elwood Mead influence persisted in British Columbia irrigation. When Mead returned from Australia it was his plan that prompted the state of California to establish its land colonies at Durham and Delhi. The American example in colonization influenced the British Columbia government when it embarked

upon its soldiers colony at Oliver in the Okanagan Valley near the border in 1918. At the same time Mead was an advisor to Secretary Lane of the U.S. Interior Department and suggested the British Columbia colony as a possible model for American soldiers colonies. Congress, however, opposed the colonization program for veterans. In 1930, the Sanford Evans Royal Commission investigating the fruit industry in British Columbia adopted the formula for servicing the debt of the B.C. irrigation districts that had been followed on U.S. reclamation projects at the recommendation of the so-called Fact Finders Commission (1924). Each project should pay what it was able to as the total debt was scaled down to manageable proportions. Elwood Mead was the architect of the Fact Finders report and in the same year became Commissioner of the U.S. Reclamation Bureau. R. O. Hall, "Early Days of Fruit Growing in the South Okanagan," *Twenty-fifth Report of the Okanagan Historical Society* (1961), p. 110; Walter Packard, "Some Factors to be Considered by the Beginner in Irrigation Farming," *Irrigation Review* (July, 1924), pp. 246–250; British Columbia, *Sessional Papers, 1930,* pp. AA1–AA23.

7

Contributions of Its Southern Neighbors to the Underdevelopment of the Maritime Provinces Area, 1710–1867

Andrew Hill Clark

John Fiske, the 19th-century New England savant, lawyer, historian of science and one of the more sprightly writers (if not scholars) of the history of the United States, once told an anecdote about a group of expatriate Americans having dinner in Paris in the mid-19th century. The loyal toasts developed into a contest for the best description of the boundaries of their homeland. Overcome by the sense of manifest destiny—and no doubt by the wine—one proposed: the United States, bounded on the east by the rising and on the west by the setting sun, on the south by the South Pole, and on the north by the North Pole. But that was immediately capped by a Californian who proposed: my country, bounded on the east by primeval chaos, on the south by the precession of the equinoxes, on the west by the Day of Judgment and on the north by the Aurora Borealis.[1] It is the eastern part of that Aurora, Atlantic Canada, that has been my prime concern, as an historical geographer, for many years.

Atlantic Canada is a northeastward extension of that somewhat vaguely defined region of difficult terrain conditions and pervasive socio-economic problems, widely known to political scientists and sociologists—and, for that matter to newspaper readers, and television viewers—as "Appalachia." The land-

1. John Fiske, *American Political Ideas* (New York, 1885), pp. 101–102.

form region includes Quebec's Shickshock Mountains and Gaspé peninsula, and Newfoundland, but at its heart are the three provinces, lineal territorial descendants of most of ancient Acadia or Nova Scotia, long known popularly simply as "The Maritimes."[2] The rough hill and mountain area on the west made contact by land with the St. Lawrence valley difficult, except by way of territory now part of the United States, until well after 1867. The navigation of the St. Lawrence had its problems even in summer and it was completely closed by ice in the winter. In contrast, easy year-round contact with New England and New York was available. The "north-south grain" of the continent is a hackneyed phrase but unusually apposite here except that the directions are a bit more northeast-southwest. There is no doubt that the barrier function of the Appalachian roughlands has been exaggerated in the interpretation of the history of the United States, but I would suggest that it was a major factor in the evolution of New France and its post–1783 successor, British North America. In a somewhat equivocal comment on the matter R. G. Trotter[3] averred that the region of the Maritimes was always more important to the power in control of the St. Lawrence than to that centered on Massachusetts Bay, that it controlled the former's access to the world before the railroad era and, afterwards, provided it, belatedly, with winter port facilities. Yet in the very year before Confederation a writer in the *Acadian Recorder*[4] said, of the relations between the Maritimes and Canada, "we are shut off from each other by a wilderness geographically, commercially, politically and socially. We always cross the United States to shake hands." Certainly, as we shall see, trade between the Maritimes and the United States in the middle 19th century was heavy whereas Maritimes-

2. I.e., New Brunswick, Nova Scotia and Prince Edward Island. The writer has described the situation of the area and its physical and biotic characteristics in two books: *Three Centuries and the Island: A Historical Geography of Settlement and Agriculture in Prince Edward Island, Canada* (Toronto, 1959), and *Acadia: The Geography of Early Nova Scotia to 1760* (Madison, 1968).

3. "The Appalachian Barrier in Canadian History," *Annual Report of the Canadian Historical Association, with Historical Papers* [hereafter, *Historical Papers*] (1939), pp. 5–21.

4. July 27, 1866, p. 60, as quoted in J. S. Martell, "Intercolonial Communications, 1840–1867," *Historical Papers* (1936), pp. 41–61.

Canada trade was light, although this was by no means solely a matter of terrain and access. Whatever the advantages or disadvantages of location it is a hard land in terms of resources. Maritimers have a living standard at least a fifth below the national Canadian level and about half that of Ontario. This is not so apparent in the Halifax metropolitan area where conditions are relatively much better,[5] but circumstances are far worse in the smaller cities, towns, villages and dispersed rural homes. One of the most banal truisms about the human condition, surely, is that we judge our own well-being chiefly in terms of our nearest neighbors. Almost since the beginning of permanent settlement in the 17th century, the lot of the Maritimers has seemed even less attractive than it otherwise might have by comparison with the settled Atlantic areas to the south. But beyond the question of perception it is clear that in comparison with urban Quebec or southern Ontario, but particularly with the well settled lowland areas of nearby New England, New York, Pennsylvania and central New Jersey, with which cultural ties of Maritimers long have been close, there is no doubt that the Maritimes are, in economic terms, relatively backward or underdeveloped.

The venerable Canadian sport of blaming their problems on the United States [6] has had very good backing in interpretation of the history of the Maritimes' area for the 17th century and for the last hundred odd years since Canadian Confederation. In the former period the scattered, almost forgotten, settlement legacies of the local French fur trade were chronically harassed (if sometimes also economically supported) by New England. In the latter period the great hemorrhage of Maritime youth, as it drained west and south (mostly to the United States), is a

5. Halifax has had some boom years in the past thirty which helped to boost Nova Scotia's per capita income in 1968 to $1917 as compared with a national average of $2460. There's no doubt that most of Newfoundland and Prince Edward Island are less well off than New Brunswick and Nova Scotia but each of the latter has extensive patches of rural poverty deserving the rubric "rural slums." However the new statistical entity "Atlantic Canada" has made the Maritimes look worse than they really are by the addition of the depressed figures from Newfoundland and Labrador.

6. Or, before the Revolution, the difficulties of present Canadian territories in relation to the English-speaking colonies to the south.

conspicuous platitude of our regional historiography. But the case for a malign influence from the south in the period from 1710 to 1867 is by no means as clear, and it is to that period that I should like to direct my comments in this paper. For the first third of that sesquicentury I have published my views and will summarize only briefly here.[7] Much of what follows will reflect a long recent bout with some of the standard documentary series[8] although each of the individual conclusions may have been anticipated many times in the secondary literature and every effort has been made so to recognize and acknowledge where known.

The most significant geographical characteristics of the Maritimes are their location and the nature of their resources. Both matters are of great moment in connection with influences from the southward, benign or otherwise, and they have been important in the entire human history of the area. The appreciation of the endowment of nature may be on the upswing as Americans, in particular, in search of beautiful scenery, uncrowded countrysides and relatively unpolluted air and water, may exploit their recreation potential; but the soil, mineral and biotic resources of the region (except for fish, and while they lasted, pine forests) have always been modest.

Atlantic Canada's location, nearest of settled North America to western Europe, has often seemed deceptively advantageous.

---

7. Particularly in *Acadia, op. cit.,* footnote 2, and in "New England's Role in the Underdevelopment of Cape Breton Island during the French Regime, 1713–1758," *Canadian Geographer,* IX (1965), 1–12.

8. The Public Archives of Canada (hereafter, PAC), Manuscript Division, has an inventory, under the title "Manuscript Group 11," of the Colonial Office Papers in the Public Record Office (hereafter, PRO), London, of which it has manuscript or microfilm copies. The writer has worked chiefly with material relating to Nova Scotia including Cape Breton Island, Prince Edward Island and, to a lesser degree, New Brunswick as a separate unit after 1784. PAC holdings include manuscript copies of a great deal of the correspondence, entry books, legislation, etc. (much of it done in the 19th century), and microfilm copies of the originals. The most useful single collection is of official correspondence between London and (chiefly) Halifax (with all of its miscellany of addenda), which is designated "Nova Scotia A" and "Cape Breton A" for the transcripts and "C.O. 217" for the whole series as it is available on microfilm. The writer has read some of this in the original in London but most of it in transcript or microfilm in Ottawa. In the past year he has been particularly deeply immersed in it and a great many of the conclusions of this paper otherwise undocumented, are attributable to that experience.

In fact, Europe's first great push to the northwest ran out there a thousand years ago when the Vikings found nothing beyond Greenland worth staying for. Pre-Columbian cultural diffusion from Middle America to the northeast also ended there; even the minimal trappings of agriculture barely reached the St. John River valley.[9] Although in the 16th and 17th centuries it became the westernmost frontier of Europe, first for the fishery and then the fur trade, it quickly was converted to "in between" country: its eastern and southern coasts were the western margin of the fishery while the fur trade pushed rapidly inland and left it behind. At the same time, militarily, it became a tension zone between the power of France (anchored at Quebec and irregularly, at Louisburg) and that of Britain and her Atlantic seaboard colonies.

After the undisputed award of all of peninsular Nova Scotia to Britain in 1713, this location made it desirable for France to develop its two islands, St-Jean and Royale,[10] for the support of its fortress of Louisburg. Yet when Captain Samuel Holland surveyed the islands after their final British conquest in the later 1760's, the marks of a half-century of French occupation, except around the razed remnants of the fortress, were light indeed.[11] Instead of the effective settlement and exploitation of their soils and forests, it had proved simpler for the French to have Louisburg and the fishery supplied (however clandestinely or illegally) from the Acadian Fundy farmlands and even more from New England. Canada was able to make only relatively negligible contributions to its support; and the merchants of Old France were much more interested in more direct investments in the fishery.[12]

9. The various southeastward probings of various Eskimoid cultures appear to have stopped on the shores of the Strait of Belle Isle. This theme has been explored recently by the writer and D. Q. Innis in "The Roots of Canada's Geography," in J. Warkentin (ed.), *Canada: A Geographical Interpretation* (Toronto, 1968) pp. 13–56.

10. I.e., Prince Edward and Cape Breton of today.

11. D. C. Harvey, *The French Regime in Prince Edward Island* (New Haven, 1926) and D. C. Harvey (ed.), *Holland's Description of Cape Breton Island and other Documents*, Public Archives of Nova Scotia Publications, No. 2 (Halifax, 1935).

12. Much of the primary documentation is cited in *Acadia*; the bulk of it is from the Archives Nationales, Archives des Colonies Series C11B, "Correspon-

Between 1710 and 1755 it is true that the Acadians, under only nominal British control (chiefly based on Boston) had prospered, had increased in numbers many fold, and had solidly established themselves on their dyked marshlands. But vital to their economy, for so many of the essentials of life they could not raise, trap, shoot or gather, was trade with New England— and, ironically, the chief medium of exchange, beyond barter, appears to have been specie proceeds from smuggling to Cape Breton. In that half-century the Acadians consolidated their earlier dependence on New England for tools, implements, and hardware of all kinds—and scores of other things—that can only have inhibited even elementary industrial development. Indeed the very presence of the Acadians clearly discouraged what otherwise well might have been a substantial earlier anticipation of New England's "down east" migration of the 1760's. The official colonial correspondence is rich with reference to plans by Shirley and many other New Englanders for colonization of Nova Scotia after 1710; and one of the reasons for New England's enthusiasm for the Acadian diaspora of the later 1750's was an anticipation of such plans. Whether New Englanders feared more the possible infection of popery or of scalping by Micmac friends of the Acadians—or whatever—is moot, but the key point was the actual presence there of the Acadians. In one way or another it seems to me that a strong case can be made to show that the primary and secondary influence of nearby New England contributed strongly to the area's underdevelopment before 1755. With regard to Cape Breton, the irony is particularly sharp that while the English equivalent, for Louisburg, of "Delenda est Carthago" kept thundering in Catonian cadence from New England's ports and, indeed, while much New England blood was spilled in the 1740's both on Isle Royale and the

---

dance generale, Île Royale, 1712–1762" which has been copied by PAC and is listed as Series 5 of their Manuscript Group 7. Particularly useful as secondary sources with leads to a wide variety of primary materials are H. A. Innis "Cape Breton and the French Regime," *Proceedings and Transactions of the Royal Society of Canada*, XXIX, series 3, sec. 2 (1935), 51–87; Charles de La Morandière, *Historie de la pêche française de la morue dans l'Amérique septentrionale*, 2 Vols. (Paris, 1962); and A. G. Reid "Intercolonial trade during the French Regime," *Canadian Historical Review*, XXXII (1951), 236–251.

present Nova Scotia mainland, it was New England's abundant exports which made possible the continued French maintenance of the fortress.[13]

A gross and oversimplified view of Nova Scotia's patterns of cultural/national origins at the time of Confederation showed an English west (very roughly, of the meridian of Halifax) and a Scottish east (with apologies to the Lunenburgers, a few groups of Irish, many pockets of Acadians, and some unfortunate blacks).[14] The "English" west was, outside of Halifax, over-whelmingly of colonial origin, being made up of pre-Revolutionary New Englanders (Brebner's "Neutral Yankees")[15] and Loyalists, mostly of the 1780's, and mostly from New York, New Jersey and Pennsylvania. Thus, it would seem that the lack of English settlement earlier in the century was substantially re-dressed. But neither group spread to the east and indeed, al-though most of the descendants of the New Englanders stayed and consolidated themselves during the succeeding century, many Loyalists, or their children, filtered back to their original homelands.

The east was left largely for the socioeconomically deprived Highlanders whose settlement there resulted from the con-vergence of several locational factors.[16] Generally there was little competition for the land by the English of colonial ancestry to the west. Furthermore, new migrants from the better off regions

13. See footnote 7. To the general studies cited in *Acadia, op. cit.*, footnote 2, dealing with New England involvement with Nova Scotia I would now add, in particular G. A. Rawlyk's *Yankees at Louisbourg* (Orono, Me., 1967), which consolidates some of his earlier studies.

14. Maps of the regional predominance of origin groups bear out this gen-eralization but show more complicated patterns at a large scale. See A. H. Clark, "Old World Origins and Religious Adherence in Nova Scotia," *Geographical Review*, L (1960), 317–344.

15. J. B. Brebner, *The Neutral Yankees of Nova Scotia* (New York, 1937) is the standard work on the period of the American Revolution.

16. The PRO C.O. 217 series is laced with details of this immigration. In a dispatch from Maitland to Goderich, Nov. 14, 1831, he reported that no emigrant ship had sailed to Nova Scotia from England in many years. In a somewhat incomplete record of 1831 of immigration to peninsular Nova Scotia since 1810, and to Cape Breton Island since 1821, a total of 19,845 people was recorded, of whom 13,001 were from Scotland, 5,826 from Ireland and only 1,018 from England (many of whom may have been Irish, in fact). The correspondence makes clear, however, that very large numbers of Scottish immigrants were unloaded unceremoniously, and without record, on outlying areas of Cape Breton Island in particular (C.O. 217/152, pp. 149–150, 207, 254–256).

of the British Isles (south and east of the "Celtic Fringe") usually preferred to go to areas of more fertile land and higher wages, partly in Canada, but mostly in the United States. The unfortunate Gaels, whether from Scotland or Southern Ireland, had had little choice about leaving their homeland: the alternatives were often as grim as starvation itself. The nature of the fishery and the lumber trade meant that passenger space going out to Newfoundland and the Maritimes was available for a pittance. It may have been worth even less than that; but it brought them in their tens of thousands to just those nearest parts of the New World in which employment could be had in the pineries or fishery, or where land for farming (of a kind) was available for purchase or rental at minimum levels of expense. Indeed a large number of the "farmers" simply squatted.[17]

The point here about the negative effect of the United States on Maritimes' development is that relative location and comparative disadvantage in resources exercised a distinct "sorting" influence in terms of immigration, with the Maritimes getting the poorest and the least skilled. Since six of my eight great-grandparents were of this Maritimes' Scottish migration of which I speak, I hope no chauvinistic hackles will be raised.[18] When they first came, and often for a generation or two or three afterward, they contributed to the disparity between the Maritimes' development and that of the republic in general. The higher socioeconomic levels of immigration from the British Isles flowed north and (chiefly) south of Nova Scotia. Its ancient position as an eddy or backwater on the margins of major currents of movements of peoples or trade thus was strongly reaffirmed and the relative location and character of the provinces (soon to become states) to the south did little to ameliorate, and much to exacerbate it.

17. In one of dozens of similar official complaints, Kempt reported to Horton from Halifax, Sept. 14, 1826, that so many poor settlers "simply sit down upon vacant lands with no authority whatsoever" (C.O. 217/146, p. 269).
18. I readily (perhaps even proudly) concede the leading role of Canada's Scottish population in government, religion, education and engineering. At one time, when W. L. Mackenzie King was federal Prime Minister, the premiers of all the provinces but Quebec were of recognizably Scottish derivation. But experienced and progressive farmers most of them were not.

Because, except for Louisburg, France did so little to develop the area, its complete cession to Britain in 1763 can be viewed as opening rich opportunities for development; and it certainly was so perceived by Boston residents in particular. A Yankee population largely replaced an Acadian one. Other major events of the period involving influences from the south and west on the Maritimes included the American Revolution, the French wars culminating in the War of 1812–15, the Maine border dispute and its resolution, the literally endless controversies over the fisheries, the nature and amounts of commercial exchange highlighted by the Reciprocity period from 1854 to 1866, and the side effects of the American Civil War. The impacts on the Maritimes were of varying degrees and both positive and negative, but the net effect was disadvantageous. Clearly, there is space for only a few selected comments to support this view.

That the regional impact of the Revolution generally was negative during its course and in its results is by no means an historiographic consensus. The Loyalists are very much a case in point. In all, something on the order of 30,000 people, well acclimatized and acculturated to North American conditions, and probably somewhat above the socioeconomic average, came into an area the development of which, I have argued, had been hindered earlier by New England's economic and military interests. They brought some capital of their own and induced the British government to provide much more, in terms of tools, implements and seed. Whatever the degree to which this group and its descendants tended to melt away and seep back to the south, and however irritating it became in its demands and pretensions to the pre-Revolutionary inhabitants and British officials alike, the effect of this immigration had to be favorable on balance. In the long run, its most negative aspects were the legacies of a pensioner attitude toward Britain, which undermined self-reliance and often made intercolonial cooperation within British North America difficult, and a nearly perpetual petulance toward the United States. Economically, in terms of the fishery, trade with the West Indies, and the net balance of privateering activity, it seems probable that Halifax was a modest gainer, and the outports generally losers by the Revolution. Of course, as in all British-French or British-U.S. crises of relationship after its founding, Halifax also benefited directly and largely from expenditures for military and naval pay, construction, repair and maintenance. Some of this seeped out through the rest of the region. But one item in the balance sheet of the results of the Revolution, the re-erection of a national boundary on the south (which had marched north in 1713 and been eliminated in 1763), became a major long-term liability to the area, particularly as it inhibited trade, nourished the threat of war, left festering disputes as to boundary location, and probably hindered the northward movement of commercial and industrial personnel and capital.[19]

Perhaps the most negative political effects of the Revolution on the Maritimes were, first, the slowing down of processes of political reform and increased democratization, and second, largely as a direct result of the Loyalist invasion, the splitting of greater Nova Scotia into four distinct elements, the colonial provinces of New Brunswick, Nova Scotia, Cape Breton and St. John. The last, present Prince Edward Island, was in fact given a separate government in 1769, but it had little settlement before the Revolution and fewer than 5,000 people by the end of the century.[20] The cutting off of Cape Breton during the period 1784–1820 with its manifold and almost insoluble problems, can be judged to have been a blessing.[21] But the separation of the two major elements of present New Brunswick and penin-

---

19. It seemed at the time, and generally has continued so to be considered since, that majority sentiment in the United States never really wanted to incorporate the Maritimes. The Articles of Confederation specifically provided for the inclusion of Canada, but not Nova Scotia or Newfoundland. It is true that some elements in the several continental congresses had considered the acquisition of Nova Scotia essential and it is also true that New England always wanted maximum degrees of freedom in the coastal fisheries of Nova Scotia. But annexationist sentiments on both sides of the border, from the Revolution to Confederation, were focused on the interior, Canadian, areas of British North America, not on the Maritimes. See, especially, R. W. Van Alstyne, "New Viewpoints in the Relations of Canada and the United States," *Canadian Historical Review*, XXV (1944), 109–131.
20. See the writer's *Three Centuries* . . . , *op. cit.*, footnote 2, chapter 4.
21. See W. S. Macnutt, *The Atlantic Provinces* . . . (Toronto, 1965), especially pp. 98, 113–114, 117–118, 181–182, for some sharply drawn vignettes of Cape Breton's problems during this period.

sular Nova Scotia seriously weakened the region in its confrontation and negotiations with the Canadas, united or divided.[22] It
certainly can be argued that a united Maritimes province either
might have stayed out of Confederation, to its possible advantage, or might have secured better terms from Canada when it
did enter. Although this sounds like a passage from the century-
old Maritimer's litany of complaint, I believe the ultimate federal health of present Canada has suffered as much from its
political fragmentation on the east as from the unhappy creation
of three separate provinces between the Great Lakes and the
Rockies.[23] It has been far too easy for the dominant provinces of
Ontario and Quebec (and more recently British Columbia) to
play off the poorer provinces against one another. And I cannot
believe that without the very special circumstances of the Loyalist influx such a division of Nova Scotia ever would have occurred.

The boundary dispute with Maine, often mentioned as a contributing factor to the slowing of Maritimes' development, was, I
judge, far less significant than the creation of the boundary itself, as an international barrier.[24] In fact, the Treaty of Paris
of 1783, ending the American Revolution, was locally a territorial standoff. The boundary between Nova Scotia and the
Maine district of Massachusetts had been in doubt beforehand
and remained so afterwards. The ultimate settlement in the
Webster-Ashburton Treaty of 1842 is seen by latter-day Canadians as only one of many instances in the history of the

22. Even as late as the mid-19th century, when the population of the Maritimes approached a half-million people, the limited size and population of any of
the units was a grave disability. As D. G. G. Kerr has observed, ". . . this
smallness was not only a physical characteristic but pervaded its whole political,
social and economic outlook as well" ("Head and Responsible Government in
New Brunswick," *Historical Papers* [1938], pp. 62–70).

23. See especially D. K. Elton (ed.), *One Prairie Province Conference and
Selected Papers* (Lethbridge, Alta. 1971).

24. It is probably of much significance that, in the hot debates in New
Brunswick over entry into Confederation, the matter of military defense against
the United States (despite the excitement of the last years of the Civil War and
the Fenian raids) never seemed to carry as much weight as dollars-and-cents
concerns. The boundary was less a political-military line than a political-economic
boundary. See A. G. Bailey, "The basis and persistence of opposition to Confederation in New Brunswick," *Canadian Historical Review*, XXIII (1942), 374–
397.

resolution of the whole border between British North America and the United States in which the home government curried diplomatic and commercial favor with the Republic at the expense of her own colonies.[25] That, of course is not very indirect negative American influence.

Perhaps the single most vexed and long-lived politico-economic problem arising between the Maritimes and the United States was that of the perennial disputes over rights and/or privileges of republican fishermen in British North American coastal waters. The documentation and secondary literature on the matter is extraordinarily voluminous and one thing is clear: legally or illegally, U.S. (chiefly New England) vessels continued to haunt the coasts of British North America through most of the period.[26] The sometimes legal excuses of drying fish on "uninhabited" coasts, or of seeking shelter, food or water in emergencies, made smuggling so simple as to be commonplace. Most fishing vessels heading north to the banks or British coastal waters were underladen and, except in actual wartime when naval vessels and privateers often raised the risks to unacceptable levels, the hazarding of a few hundredweight of contraband seemed a small gamble indeed. Moreover, they bought or obtained by barter substantial quantities of local fish.[27] The results were, of course, as suggested above, not only the loss of customs' revenue but the inhibition of various lines of local

25. There is a summary of the border problems in A. H. Clark and D. Q. Innis, "The Roots of Canada's Geography," *op. cit.*, footnote 9, with a brief bibliography (p. 53n). It is interesting that as early as the negotiations for the Peace Treaty of 1763, when Nova Scotia's claims to the country between the St. Croix and Penobscot were strong, the Board of Trade apportioned it to Massachusetts to mollify the latter's resentment at the broad extent of Quebec. (Board of Trade to the King, Oct. 5, 1763, C.O. 218/6).

26. Perhaps the most succinct and pertinent comments can be found scattered throughout H. A. Innis, *The Cod Fisheries* (Toronto, 1940 and 1954), but see especially pp. 331–356. The C.O. 217 series and the journals of the Nova Scotia Legislative Council and Assembly have literally hundreds of relevant items.

27. Again one example among scores of complaints may be cited. General Ainsley (then governor of Cape Breton), in writing to Bathurst from Sydney, Cape Breton, May 12, 1817, pointed out that ships of that colony often were fitted out in the spring by local merchants on credit, but that at sea (or, presumably, in one of the innumerable coves or harbors) many traded their fish to American vessels for much wanted American supplies. Thus they not only imported American supplies illegally—and presumably at much lower prices than those asked by local merchants—but often did not bring in enough fish to pay their "just" debts. C.O. 217/135, pp. 66–67R.

industry. When the intruders trespassed on immediate coastal waters, as unquestionably they did chronically, they produced fish more efficiently, with better capital and equipment, to compete seriously with the Maritimes' own exports in world markets.[28]

After the Revolution came the well-advertised, initially well-promoted, but in the end rather half-hearted attempts to have the Maritimes replace New England and the Middle Colonies in the supply of food, animals and forest products to the British West Indies (and Newfoundland) in an attempt to preserve for the second British Empire the closed mercantilist system of the first. For a variety of reasons the attempts very largely ultimately failed. It would be my contention that had the British been willing and able to exclude the Republic from the trade, the Maritimes well might have been given a tremendous boost at a critical time in their history. The demands for crops, animals, forest products, fish, vessels and commercial facilities and services of all kinds, with their possible multiplier effects, should have shown results paralleling developments in New England a century earlier. But the immediacy of the needs of the sugar islands, their effective London lobbies, the problems of agricultural development in the Maritimes, the quantity, quality and price of American goods available, and the prime and inescapable geographical realities of relative location, all were negative. In particular, American abundance, efficiency and aggressiveness continually undermined what periodically looked to be platforms of a Maritimes take-off.[29]

It is, of course, true that areas of active immigration may have very low surpluses, or even deficits, of food despite abundant production. This was a notable feature of transappalachian ex-

28. Innis, *Cod Fisheries*, pp. 333–335.
29. In 1790 it was noted that Nova Scotia imported 80,000 bushels of grain, 40,000 barrels of bread and meal, 54,000 staves and headings, 16,000 hoops, 285,000 shingles and nearly 1,000,000 feet of boards. David Macpherson, *Annals of Commerce*, IV (London, 1805), 12. Writing to Sydney, July 15, 1791, Carleton noted, "The lumber which has been sent to the West Indies Islands in vessels belonging to this province has been mostly taken from the American States, but no part of that lumber could be legally imported for the supply of the inhabitants, and hence the price here became an inducement to hazard an illicit importation. Which in our situation is next to impossible to prevent." (PAC, British North America, V, 30–31.)

pansion in the United States. Such regions, even when subjected to vast and long-continued inflows of people, developed their agriculture fast enough, in most cases, to feed and sustain the newcomers. This large on-the-spot market made almost all American frontier farming highly commercial from the very beginning, even when no regional export occurred. The "self-sufficient," or even highly subsistent, pioneer was ephemeral—and very largely mythical. But the point here is that this commercial farming did expand to meet the needs of the inflow and soon created steadily increasing surpluses.[30] It is my view that in the transappalachian American movement the rate of inflow of people was very directly controlled by the amount of food available; the families of the reconnoitering menfolk usually did not follow until food was there for them.

Now, in the Maritimes, heavy surges of immigration did occur as of the Loyalists, the Scots to Prince Edward Island and eastern Nova Scotia, and of the Irish to the New Brunswick pineries. These inflows indeed did have a very damping effect on the creation of food surpluses for shipment to Newfoundland or the West Indies, so far as local production was concerned. But they appear to have done more to encourage imports from the United States than to stimulate local production, a combined result of deficiency of local resources and American adjacency.

Much, if not most, of the trade between the Republic and the Maritimes was clandestine for decades after the Revolution. Some Maritimes imports were invited or encouraged by local governors to avert critical shortages but much of it was always illegal (and therefore not officially recorded) as New England ships and schooners constantly cruising up to Maritimes' waters to fish, with excess cargo capacity, found smuggling along that intricately serrated, island-studded and often fog-bound, coast extremely easy.[31] Indeed, it is a somewhat celebrated fact of the War of 1812 that throughout most of it, by one device or

30. This point is rather fully discussed in my "Some Suggestions for the Geographical Study of Agricultural Change in the United States, 1790–1840," *Agricultural History,* XLVI, No. 1 (Jan., 1972).
31. The loophole was the provision of Article I, of the Convention of 1818, that despite severe and specific restrictions on U.S. fishermen, they could be admitted to territorial waters, coves and ports "for the purpose of shelter and of repairing damages therein, of purchasing wood and of obtaining water."

another, American food continued to flow into the Maritimes, often paid for by British manufactured goods flowing in the opposite direction.[32] Of course one must bear in mind that much food, wood products, even fish, for long made its way legally or illegally to Maritime ports to sail in British bottoms to markets that were closed to American ships, and it is often hard to assess just how much of the imports were needed and used locally. But there is no doubt that their presence in Halifax, St. John, or wherever, had a chilling effect on the development of Maritimes' agriculture.[33]

There were a number of cases (perhaps including the Reciprocity Period—although this is a matter for debate) when actions of the United States, or exigencies of British-U.S relations, led to unusual opportunities for the Maritimes and to unusually rapid spurts of economic activity there. In the normal case these didn't last and the long-run effect of hot-house stimulation

32. The PRO C.O. 217 series is especially rich in detail of the two-way trade during the war. There are dozens of inventories, one of the longer (Sherbrooke to Bathurst, Nov. 8, 1813, C.O. 217/92, pp. 26–29) of which is given here for illustration:

October 1813

Exports to U.S.	*Imports from U.S.*
(16 vessels, 83 men, 1119 tons)	(18 vessels, 97
Sugar 344 hogsheads, 209 barrels	men, 1518 tons)
Molasses 55 hh.	Flour, 9723 bbl.
Merchandise (27 bales, 104 cases, 4 bbl. 68 pkgs.	Bread, 773 bbl. and 339
43 casks, 3 trunks) including: 1881 yds. cloth,	bags
885 yds. Kersey ware, 133,956 yds. cottons, 200	Indian corn,
pieces and 1532 yds. muslin, 2199 shawls, 12	1800 bus. Tar,
gross shoemaker's awls, 12 gross penknives, 100	49 bbl. Onions,
pieces crapes, 270 doz. pr. stockings, 2077 yds.	8650 bunches and
velveteens, 250 lbs. pins, 203 yds. checks, 531	5 bags
yds. coating, 153 pr. blankets, 100 lbs. thread,	
430 yds. carpeting.	

The trade in British manufactures under export licenses to the United States was estimated to be worth £1,000,000 (C.O. 217/96, pp. 3–5).

33. The variety of the American goods flowing to the northeast is well illustrated by a British proposal, during the fifth conference of U.S. and British negotiators for a convention, for reciprocal trading privileges for U.S. and British ships trading between the United States and New Brunswick and Nova Scotia, in which the British enumerated the following articles of American origin (suggesting that they were among the principal wanted imports): "scantling, planks, staves, heading boards, shingles, hoops, horses, neat cattle, sheep, hogs, poultry, or livestock of any sort, bread, biscuit, flour, peas, beans, potatoes, wheat, rice, oats, barley, or grain of any sort, pitch, tar, turpentine, fruits, seeds, and tobacco." The only items specifically mentioned for the reverse trade were "gypsum and grindstones." *Diplomatic Correspondence of the United States: Canadian Relations, 1784–1860, I, 1784–1820* (Washington, D.C., 1940), 868–871.

of production, with subsequent rapid collapse of demand, often was negative. In the decade following 1795 Atlantic trade had become a bonanza for U.S. vessels. Then suddenly embargo, nonintercourse and war greatly inhibited American trading activities. J. B. Brebner described these events as "a mighty fillip of almost monopolistic prosperity in the fisheries . . . to Newfoundland and Nova Scotia." From 1808 to 1815 the Maritimes' economic expansion was very rapid. After 1815, however, came the rather unequal see-saw struggle that lasted for seven years at least until 1822 when Britain, in effect, surrendered most of the comparative advantages that Maritimers had had over New England and other Americans in the West Indies trade in particular. By 1830, American shipping had complete freedom of access to the British section of the latter trade.

Somewhat similar circumstances had built up the New Brunswick timber trade unusually rapidly;[34] then came the critical step in the 19th-century process of dismantling British tariffs and colonial preferences that removed the advantages of the Maritimes in the transatlantic trade in wood and wood products. Between 1842, when the preference was 30 shillings a load, and 1860, the duties were cut five times, the last act being their elimination. Exports of New Brunswick pine fell from 100,000 tons in 1856 to 27,174 tons in 1865 (although exhaustion of local resources also was involved). Without such artificial defenses the disadvantages of less capital, poorer equipment, more limited markets, smaller scale of operation, and many more, created difficult local competitive conditions.

Counterfactual historical speculation is one of the easiest and often least rewarding of scholarly exercises, but although one can argue that even the problems of supply of a wide variety of manufactured goods from Britain might not have led to the development of a compensatory industrial enterprise in the Maritimes, it is difficult for me to believe that the agricultural development that took place slowly through the 19th century

34. Shipping tonnage employed in the North American timber trade (of course including areas outside of the Maritimes) rose from 21,782 in 1802 to 110,759 in 1814 and 340,537 in 1819. W. T. Easterbrook and H. G. Aitken, *Canadian Economic History* (Toronto, 1958), p. 145.

might not have been much more rapidly accelerated if American supplies had not been so near, so cheap, and (despite periodic very serious legal restrictions or outright official proscriptions or embargoes) so easily available.[35]

Among the rather lengthy catalogue of contemporary Canadian complaints about negative American influences on present or future Canadian developments is that of massive American consumption of Canadian mineral resources which otherwise might have served Canada's future. Thus, it can be argued that the very large shipments of gypsum and coal, in particular, in the period from the Revolutionary to Civil Wars in the United States, deprived Nova Scotia of subsequent opportunities for development.[36] But they also provided much needed exchange and, in their raising and handling, jobs to sustain the greatest prosperity (or least depression) the Maritimes' area was to know since it came within the European political and economic ambit. Indeed, could one accept only half of the claims of the General Mining Association, which raised and exported so much coal to the United States in the period from the 1820's to the 1860's, its unrequited expenditures for construction and wages were one of the major stimulants to the economy of the Sydney region of Cape Breton Island and the Pictou region of the Nova Scotia mainland.[37]

35. It is possible to argue that had not American supplies been available, and had prices risen enough to stimulate Nova Scotia's laggard and handicapped agriculture, the higher living costs (and presumably labor costs) well might have inhibited the fishery, lumbering, mining or other activities such as shipbuilding. From this vantage point, American supplies were helpful. Which, if nothing else, perhaps should discourage counterfactual speculation!

36. Cape Breton's coal was described by Nicolas Denys in 1672 in *Description géographique et historique des costes de l'Amérique septentrionale*, 2 Vols. (Paris), and had been known since the 16th century at least. Much use of it was made by both French and English in the early 18th century, but its use and shipment to the thirteen-colony area had been greatly restricted in the 1760's and 1770's both to conserve it for the use of the Royal Navy and on the mercantilist principle that coal might aid colonial manufacturing. See Macnutt, *Atlantic Provinces*, pp. 66–67, and especially R. Brown, *The Coal Fields and Coal Trade of the Island of Cape Breton* (London, 1871).

37. Because the people of Nova Scotia bitterly resented the near-monopoly on mining long held by the General Mining Association, and because it was constantly petitioning for relief from the terms of its royalty payments to the government, the PRO C.O. 217 series is thoroughly peppered with relevant material from the 1820's onward. To help the Duke of York pay his debts George III had granted him extensive (if vaguely defined) mineral rights in Nova Scotia (most clearly in Cape Breton). The creditors, to whom the rights were transferred,

Despite problems of competition with British coal (the export duty on which was drastically cut in the 1830's), including that brought as ballast in timber ships returning to British North America, American tariffs, freighting costs and the completion of American railroads eastward from the anthracite mines, a very substantial part of Nova Scotia's coal production moved south —mainly for the production of domestic gas in the Boston area.[38] The lethal blows came when large numbers of furnaces were converted to use anthracite, and could not use Nova Scotia's bituminous coal at any price; and when the end of reciprocity reestablished a crippling tariff. Despite the inflow of money and jobs to Nova Scotia, the years of the American market may have inhibited greater efforts to make more effective local industrial use of it in the halcyon days of steam.

Another case of forced-draft growth followed by rapid collapse was that of wooden shipbuilding, which was the most spectacular and successful industrial activity in the Maritimes in the 19th century.[39] Its use as an example here is admittedly somewhat strained, because the industry maintained itself very well through the 1860's, but the decline thereafter was sharp. Earnings from the sale and operation of the vessels from all three provinces amounted to millions of dollars a year, with New Brunswick usually in the lead, but with activity taking place in literally dozens of scattered coves and harbors. Some of the

---

formed the General Mining Association in the hope of making substantial profits. It did succeed in raising a lot of coal and selling it in New England despite structural problems of mining, costs of shipping, and certain problems of utilization because of chemical composition. Details of the G.M.A. claims of expenditures in Nova Scotia are given in many places, notably C.O. 217/154, *passim*, and, especially, pp. 623 and 672.

38. In one not atypical year, 1839, roughly 100,000 chaldrons (Winchester measure and not greatly different from "long" tons of 2240 lbs.) of coal were raised in Nova Scotia of which 68 to 70 percent (there is some conflict in the figures) was shipped to the United States, and in that same year, British exports of coal to the United States exceeded those of Nova Scotia by about 10 percent. See C.O. 217/174, p. 85, and C.O. 217/178, p. 186 in particular. Other years of the 1830's and 1840's indicate variable but comparable proportions. In the 1834–1836 period, for example, about two-thirds of the coal went to the U.S. (C.O. 217/163, pp. 350–353).

39. Among many useful secondary sources, F. W. Wallace, *Wooden Ships and Iron Men* (1924) is particularly good. The Public Archives of Nova Scotia has a large collection of records of individual shipbuilding firms and widely varied collateral information.

largest wooden vessels ever built were launched in waters tributary to the Bay of Fundy. Much of the external market was
British but the demands from the United States increased in
importance and reached a peak during the Civil War. Moreover many vessels operating out of local ports, with local masters
and crews, were American owned. The late, specifically American stimulus helped to prevent the decline that the shift from
sail to steam (and, following in its wake, from wooden to iron
hulls) which began in Britain was inevitably to bring; and the
sudden elimination of that stimulus emphasized the abruptness
of the decrease in activity. With that fall, New England in
particular was waiting like a Venus Fly-trap to attract and ab-
sorb technologically surplus population in its mills and factories
(or widely scattered laboring and service occupations) before
alternatives developed in the Maritimes. In New England, fortunes made in shipbuilding and shipping in a somewhat earlier
but overlapping period very often were reinvested there and
skilled workmen, if they became technologically surplus in
one craft, had many others to turn to. But the sharp decline of
wooden shipbuilding in the later 19th century in the Maritimes
too often, unhappily, was followed by emigration of both men
and accumulated capital. The relative location, prosperity, and
often century-long family connections with New England left
little doubt where most of it would go.

I have left a general discussion of the Reciprocity experience of the years 1854 to 1866, to the end, and there have
been many strongly expressed differences of opinion as to its
effects, both long-term and short, and both on the United States
and different parts of British North America. I would judge that
the colony of Canada gained more from the Treaty, and lost
less by its abrogation, than did the Maritimes, but this proposi-
tion is most difficult to test.[40] The Maritimes indeed were com-

40. It well may be true that despite this circumstance (if the conclusion is
correct) Maritimers have had less of a negative reaction to the United States in
the last century than most other Canadians. Despite the fisheries dispute, British-
U.S. confrontations centered mainly on central Canada. One of the more interesting essays on the latter problem is Robin W. Winks's "A Nineteenth-century
Cold War," *Dalhousie Review*, XXXIX (1960), 464–470.

paratively prosperous in the 1850's and 1860's but in the 1870's they seemed to hit the skids and they haven't had as good a relative position since. Because certain American interests worked very hard to draw the Maritimes into Reciprocity [41] which, it can be argued, overstimulated many sectors of the local economy, and, since the break came from the American side, the case for short-run benefit and long-run detriment from American influence might seem good indeed. Not only did Maritimes exports greatly expand between 1831 and 1865 but the proportion going to the United States steadily grew,[42] as can be seen in Table 1.

But a rather closer look may raise some doubts. Shipbuilding prosperity was only partly American-stimulated (although very strongly so during the Civil War). Commerce also brought in good earnings as Maritimes' skippers followed the New England pattern of freighting around the world. Internal improve-

41. Perhaps the most thorough recent study of such efforts is that of Irene W. D. Hecht, "Israel D. Andrews and the Reciprocity Treaty of 1834: A Reappraisal," *Canadian Historical Review*, XLIV (1963), 313–329. Andrews, however, is believed to have drawn financial support for his activities from Canadian and British, as well as American sources. His public account is given in *Report of Israel D. Andrews on the Trade and Commerce of the British North American Colonies*, Senate Executive Document No. 112, 32nd Congress, 1st. Session (Washington, D.C., 1853), pp. 843–845.

42. These are abstracted from official returns compiled by S. A. Saunders and are most readily available in the collection of his essays, *Studies in the Economy of the Maritime Provinces* (Toronto, 1939). The relevant article, "The Maritime Provinces and the Reciprocity Treaty," first appeared in the *Dalhousie Review*, XIII (1934). The following table of imports from and exports to the United States as percentages of those of 1853 suggests the great importance to the Maritimes of trade with the United States just before Confederation, whether or not the provisions of the Reciprocity Treaty were the cause.

	Imports	*Exports*		*Imports*	*Exports*
1853	100.0	100.0	1861	124.8	124.1
1854	129.0	101.9	1862	123.5	139.4
1855	152.2	149.9	1863	153.9	174.0
1856	140.6	144.6	1864	159.1	195.6
1858	115.8	149.8	1865	154.9	284.2
1859	127.8	183.8	1866	161.8	248.2
1860	135.9	182.3			

The proportions of exports going to the U.S. fluctuated widely in the 1830's and 1840's. In two different years of the latter decade, we have the following returns: In 1844 of a total value of exports recorded of £734,319, £78,227 went to Great Britain and £96,115 to the United States; in 1847, when exports were up to £1,031,069, the respective portions were £71,804 to Great Britain and £474,950 to the U.S. See, respectively, C.O. 217/190, pp. 210–213, and C.O. 217/199, pp. 270–301.

**Table 1. *Percent of Total Exports Going to the
United States***

	Nova Scotia	New Brunswick	Prince Edward Island
1831	9	4	1
1851	21	11	30
1860	34	27	39
1865	41	31	43

ments (especially railway building) had important stimulating effects. And the demands created by the Civil War as well as the burgeoning urban-industrial revolution in the Republic might have accounted for much of the increase without the benefits of Reciprocity. Certainly there is no doubt that half a million Maritimers were doing pretty well out of their relationships with 20 to 25 million Americans to the south. But whatever the logic of the various constructions put on the evidence, the coincidence of the winding up of the Civil War, the ending of Reciprocity, Confederation, the beginning of a persistent economic decline, and the marked deceleration of immigration and acceleration of emigration, have combined to create one more strong hook on which to hang the theory that, even in their century of greatest prosperity, Maritimers *who stayed in the Maritimes* suffered more economically from American influence than they gained from it.

8

Samuel Gompers and the Berlin Decisions of 1902

Robert Babcock

At first glance the title of this paper might lead some to conclude that Sam Gompers, the labor leader and founder of the American Federation of Labor (AFL), was somehow involved in European politics. Certainly the ghost of Gompers would delight in such speculation, for Sam never shunned the limelight, and in later life he relished his largely self-appointed role as statesman and presidential confidante. Historians of Canada, however, know that the Berlin decisions refer to actions taken at the convention of the Trades and Labor Congress of Canada (TLC) at Berlin (now Kitchener), Ontario, in 1902. At that epochal meeting the TLC relinquished its birthright to the status of a Canadian national labor center and hitched itself firmly to the AFL's star. TLC leaders agreed to expel any of their affiliates who refused to join an AFL union claiming jurisdiction over the same job categories. The AFL promised an annual grant of $500 and the continued services of an organizer. In effect, the Congress was transformed into the equivalent of an American *state* federation of labor, and ceased to threaten the Federation's claim over the whole North American labor movement.

Early in his career Gompers learned to fear and hate socialist-inspired dual unions, which competed with Federation affiliates by organizing the same classes of workers. Paradoxically, as the AFL prospered in the early years of the 20th century the dangers from dual unionism loomed still larger. Millions of new members had not built up the stake in union benefit funds which would ultimately serve to guarantee their loyalty in times of challenge. The evidence presented here suggests that dual unionism in the Canadian trade-union movement threatened the power and authority of American craft-labor organizations in the months prior to the TLC convention of 1902. By then the AFL possessed a valuable stake in Canadian labor—and was afraid of losing it. Federation leaders, reacting to danger signals on both sides of the forty-ninth parallel, set out to combat dual unionism and bring greater unity to the structure and policies of organized labor throughout North America. The Berlin decisions seem to have been coordinated with that goal.

The foundations of continentalism in North American labor stretch back to the middle of the 19th century when American trade unions began to forge links with Canadian workers. At first the overwhelming struggle to survive prevented most American union leaders from concerning themselves with labor in other countries. By the 1890's, however, Gompers felt secure enough to devote some of his energies to a projected federation with European trade unions. He cast a glance northward for the first time and tried to enlist the support of the Trades and Labor Congress, but the whole scheme miscarried and was immediately followed by new challenges. A wave of industrial mergers, the erection of branch plants in other countries, and a rash of technological changes suddenly disrupted the job market. Union leaders were provoked into a flurry of organizing activity, and Gompers, fearful of the export of American jobs to Canada, hired a Hamilton unionist to serve as AFL organizer in the Dominion.[1]

John A. Flett, a suave, witty, forty-year-old carpenter who sported a giant walrus mustache, had served as a delegate to several TLC conventions, and had been elevated to the Con-

---

1. Lewis L. Lorwin, *Labor and Internationalism* (New York, 1929), pp. 117–120; Gompers to AFL Executive Council, Sept. 8, 1896, in Gompers Letterbooks, Library of Congress, Washington, D.C.

gress vice-presidency in 1898. In his first organizing tour in Ontario for the AFL in 1900, Flett set up fourteen locals in only seven weeks and quickly won the trust of Federation leaders.[2] Over the next three years, the AFL, by allocating over six thousand dollars to Canadian organizing and legislative work, enabled Flett to form hundreds of new locals aggregating several thousand dues-paying members.[3] Trade-union membership rolls mushroomed between 1900 and 1903. A Guelph printer, commenting upon these changes in the Canadian labor picture, cited Flett's efforts as a major factor after giving credit to favorable economic conditions.[4] There seems little doubt that the AFL contributed significantly to a Canadian trade-union movement numbering perhaps 60–70,000 men and women by the end of 1902.

The growth of the AFL's stake in Canadian labor brought Gompers and Frank Morrison, the Canadian-born AFL secretary, into close contact with another Canadian, a young Ottawa unionist who had become the guiding genius of the Trades and Labor Congress in 1900. Patrick M. Draper, a bilingual printer at the government printing office, brought ideas, vigor, and volubility to the TLC at a critical moment in its history. While Flett was building up the AFL's stake in Canada, Draper labored hard to make the Trades and Labor Congress a functioning national trade-union center. The TLC's revenue more than doubled within two years, and Draper was able to set up a tiny office with a couple of desks and a typewriter. It should be noted that Draper did not oppose the Federation's organizing activities in Canada, since many of Flett's newly created locals affiliated themselves with the TLC and paid dues to the Cana-

2. H. J. Morgan, editor, *The Canadian Men and Women of the Time* (Toronto, 1912), p. 406; Trades and Labor Congress, *Album of Labor Leaders* (Ottawa, 1909); Trades and Labor Congress, *Convention Souvenir* (Ottawa, 1901); *American Federationist*, VII (April, 1900), 107.
3. From Nov., 1899, to Oct., 1902, the AFL spent $6,134.22 on Canadian organizing and legislative work. Of that amount, 88 percent was allocated to Flett. By 1902 the Federation was devoting roughly seven percent of its total organizing expenditures to the Canadian field. (The dollar figures were compiled from monthly financial statements in the *American Federationist*, 1899–1902.)
4. O. R. Wallace, in *American Federationist*, X (Jan., 1903), 13.

dian organization as well as to their own craft-union headquarters and the AFL in the United States.[5]

Speaking to the AFL convention in 1900, Gompers revealed a firm belief that the AFL was destined to achieve predominance over the whole continent. He claimed that "the labor movement in Canada is part of our own; and we have endeavored to encourage our fellow workers by advice and such practical assistance as was within our power." [6] These words dovetailed with the outlook of business and political leaders at the turn of the century. Continental unification, many believed, was both desirable and inevitable, and only time would tell whether economic expansion presaged political union. Perhaps it is not surprising, then, that American labor leaders stressed the similarities between the American and Canadian trade-union movements. "They are, like us, a cosmopolitan people, having workers of all nationalities to contend with . . . ," W. D. Mahon told his fellow Americans upon returning from a TLC convention. Yet significantly, Mahon also claimed that "the Congress compares more nearly to our State Federations than it does to the American Federation of Labor, as the object of the Congress is to secure legislation for the workers, and it does not deal with any trade disputes . . . ." [7]

Draper did not see things quite this way. While he was no enemy of international unions in Canada, Draper hoped to transform the TLC into an effective national center with a status similar to that of the AFL. The Trades Union Congress of Great Britain, he asserted in 1901, represented the working people of that country in the same manner that the AFL personified the wage earners of the United States. The TLC was "equally independent, important and necessary . . . within its own scope and realm. . . ." [8] It quickly became apparent that Draper

5. Trades and Labor Congress, *Proceedings* (1900), pp. 27, 37; *Encyclopedia Canadiana*, III (Ottawa, 1966), 302–303; *The Canadian Who's Who* (Toronto, 1937), p. 313; Trades and Labor Congress, *Proceedings* (1902), pp. 14, 18, 64.

6. American Federation of Labor, *Proceedings* (1900), p. 28.

7. *American Federationist*, VII (Nov., 1900), 347. For American attitudes toward Canada at the turn of the century, see Albert Weinberg, *Manifest Destiny* (Chicago, 1963), pp. 355–381.

8. Trades and Labor Congress, *Convention Souvenir* (Ottawa, 1901). Since the papers of Draper and the Congress have not survived, the secretary-

envisioned the TLC as something considerably more potent than a state federation under AFL domination. Draper began to use the one vital power possessed by the Congress, but not by American state federations—the power to charter unions and central labor bodies. By 1902, he had issued some forty charters to federal labor unions and city centrals in Canada.[9]

Draper met Gompers for the first time when the latter journeyed to Toronto in June of 1901. Draper and Flett conferred with the famous American at his rooms in the Palmer House. The young TLC secretary was doubtlessly flattered by Gompers's invitation to visit the Pan-American Exposition in Buffalo with him. Gompers was probably given some advance warning at this time about the major political threat to international unionism in Canada which was to erupt at the TLC convention at Brantford in September of that year.[10]

Canadian labor had began to attract the attention of the politicians, especially after the TLC president, Ralph Smith of Nanaimo, British Columbia, had been elected to the House of Commons in 1900. Smith seemed to have become the chief agent in a plan by Laurier and Sir William Mulock to nationalize the Canadian labor movement.[11] Smith dropped a bombshell into the

treasurer's views have been inferred from other evidence. One of the most important is a letter from John Tobin to Gompers in 1910, in which the Boot and Shoe Workers' International Union leader said in passing: "While at one time Draper's loyalty to the American Federation of Labor was of a very doubtful character, I believe that of recent years he has been developing and has seen the error of his former ways. The last time I saw him [in 1909], . . . he told me how much he had learned during recent years and that he had gotten entirely over his idea that Canada should have a Federation co-equal with the American Federation. . . ." Tobin to Gompers, Sept. 14, 1910, National Union Files, Reel 2, AFL-CIO Archives.

9. Trades and Labor Congress, *Proceedings* (1901), p. 71; (1902), p. 64. A federal labor union accepted a variety of skilled workers into one unit in areas with insufficient numbers to set up separate craft locals. A city central united various craft locals within an urban area in pursuit of the general interests of organized labor.

10. *American Federationist*, VIII (July, 1901), 258; Gompers to Draper, (telegram) June 5, June 11, 1901; Gompers to Flett, June 3, 1901, Gompers Letterbooks. The AFL reimbursed Draper by $29.60, which was charged to "organizing expenses." *American Federationist*, VIII (Aug., 1901), 328.

11. Both Laurier and Mulock condemned the international trade-union tie. "If we must have Labor Associations in this country," Laurier wrote, "—and [I] think they are produicve [*sic*] of some good in some respects—we must endeavour to organize them on National lines." Laurier to Mulock, Feb. 5, 1902, Laurier Papers, Correspondence, Public Archives of Canada. Mulock expressed

delegates' laps by proposing to set up a Canadian Federation of Labor: "A federation of American union[s] represented by a national union [the AFL] and a Federation of Canadian unions represented by a national union [a CFL], each working with the other in special cases, would be a great advantage over having local unions in Canada connected with the national unions of America."[12] The Trades Congress president also suggested that American citizens should not participate in the settlement of Canadian industrial disputes. The Congress delegates decided to set up a special panel to investigate Smith's proposal and report back to the Congress at its convention in 1902. Before adjourning, the delegates chose to send Draper as their fraternal delegate to the forthcoming AFL convention in late 1901.[13] The stage was set for the momentous deliberations at Berlin.

When he learned of these events, Gompers invited Draper to meet the AFL executive council before the AFL convention had assembled. Draper recited Ralph Smith's call for a Canadian national trade-union structure, and made it clear that he had no desire to see the TLC become an appendage of the Liberal party. Later Draper was told that he had made a strong impression on the AFL directors. But the politicians' schemes were only one of a number of challenges that menaced international unions at the turn of the century.[14]

For a number of years AFL leaders had faced a serious contention with their enemies in western North America. In the spring of 1902 the socialist-oriented Western Federation of Miners created a new labor federation for the expressed purpose of challenging the AFL throughout North America. Federation leaders learned that their new rival, the American Labor Union (ALU), had successfully crossed the Mississippi and had issued charters to shoe trade supply workers in two Massachusetts towns. "There is talk of organizing a Central Labor Union

---

even stronger sentiments in a letter to Laurier, April 4, 1903. Smith's indebtedness to the Liberal party is revealed in Smith to Laurier, June 30, 1900, *ibid.*
   12. Trades and Labor Congress, *Proceedings* (1901), pp. 8–9.
   13. *Ibid.,* p. 77.
   14. American Federation of Labor, *Proceedings* (1901), p. 116; Gompers to Draper, Oct. 12, 1901, Jan. 24, 1902, Gompers Letterbooks.

under a charter from the American Labor Union," their informant added.[15] At the same time a new ALU-associated industrial union, the United Brotherhood of Railway Employees (UBRE), widened the continental division between eastern and western labor. Leaders of the UBRE set out to band together into one trade union the thousands of men employed on American railroads and on the Canadian Pacific and Canadian Northern lines. Locals had been planted in Winnipeg and Vancouver by the end of June, 1902, when Winnipeg machinists decided to strike against the Canadian Northern. Although the conservative running-trade brotherhoods remained at work and eastern unionists offered little sympathy to the strikers, the UBRE promptly joined the contest. When the new industrial union, struggling alone, failed to win a clear-cut victory, the Trades Congress bore the backlash of western anger.[16]

The failure of eastern trade unionists to come to the aid of the United Brotherhood of Railway Employees prompted a secessionist movement in British Columbia. The Phoenix Trades Council withdrew from the TLC and endorsed the socialist party. The Fernie central body refused to affiliate with the Congress. Then the Victoria Trades Council withdrew from the Trades Congress and took out a charter from the American Labor Union. "The old-time [trade union] workers," two AFL volunteer organizers reported later, ". . . have temporarily stepped aside and allowed the political socialists to run their course. . . ."[17] Little appeared to block a steady march by the United Brotherhood of Railway Employees across the continent toward Ontario. The form of this challenge to the AFL, as well as some of the tactics, were revealed by the president of the United Brotherhood. He told his organizer to write articles designed to win public sentiment for industrial unionism, and split the rank and file in the AFL from its leadership. "In this way you will constantly stimulate and augment a great public sentiment

15. John Tobin to Frank Morrison, June 27, 1902, National Union Files, Reel 2, AFL-CIO Archives, Washington, D.C.
16. *Labour Gazette,* III (Aug., 1902), pp. 110ff.; Trades and Labor Congress, *Proceedings* (1902), p. 47.
17. Trades and Labor Congress, *Proceedings* (1903), p. 32.

for the U.B.R.E.—for Industrial Unions, for the A.L.U., and for Socialism (but don't use the word) and against capitalism and the Gompers faction which is working in harmony with Marcus A. Hanna and the infamous civic federation to keep down the masses of the people." [18]

Clearly, the AFL faced a real threat from left-wing dual unionism in 1902—perhaps the biggest menace since de Leon's challenge in the 1890's. The ALU and the UBRE were contesting international craft unionism on both sides of the 49th parallel. If the leftist dual unionists captured or destroyed the Trades Congress, they could launch an attack on the international craft unions in the United States from their Canadian haven. Gompers personally wielded the power to keep these groups at bay in the United States, but he had no assurance that Draper and the Trades Congress would survive a left-wing assault.

In addition to the machinations of the Liberal party and radical unionists in Canada, the American craft unions were troubled by rumors of secession among Canadian laborites. These difficulties were linked to the rapid expansion of the craft unions in Canada during the preceding years. Some locals chafed under the new restrictions that devolved from their affiliation with international union headquarters in the United States. Others resented the high level of dues, and feared that their hard-earned money would be squandered or misspent by union officials. This danger appeared even greater to Canadians because the international boundary separated union leaders in the United States from their Canadian dues-paying supporters, and legal recourse for the latter was thereby complicated. One Liberal party unionist reported strong sentiment in Vancouver against the flow of union money to the AFL. "Our Local International Unions get no benefit from the American Federation of Labor," he insisted, "but they do get help from the Dominion Trades Congress, through legislation they get enacted for the benefit of the workers." He declared that international union

18. Canada, Parliament, Report of the Royal Commission on Industrial Disputes in the Province of British Columbia, *Sessional Papers*, No. 36a (1903), p. 8.

payments to the Federation on their Canadian membership should have been directed instead to the Trades Congress.[19]

Dissatisfaction broke out in some of the Canadian branches of one of the most powerful AFL affiliates, the United Brotherhood of Carpenters and Joiners. Members in Nelson, British Columbia, argued that Canadian locals of the Carpenters' Union would have flourished far more if they had been directed from a Dominion headquarters. Acting on this notion, they went so far as to try to reorganize the United Brotherhood's Canadian locals into a national union. "We would suggest that a convention be called to meet at some central point, say Winnipeg, Toronto or Ottawa, each organization agreeing to send delegates with instructions to do all they can to help form a central body in Canada, and to discuss other matters of importance." The Nelson men opined that ". . . the membership of all organizations would be doubled in one year if all the unions should be brought under one independent Canadian head." They called for immediate action, and then asked the Trades Congress to grant them a charter.[20]

While Draper wanted to see the TLC become a full-fledged national labor center, he refused at this point to incur the bitter emnity of the AFL by recognizing the dissident carpenters. His failure to grant this charter provoked criticism. "I think the time has arrived," one man asserted, "when the Canadian Trades Congress should . . . allow unions not wishing to belong to an International Union, to become Federal Labor Unions, chartered by the Congress." [21] This was precisely what the AFL began to fear might occur. If it did happen, the Trades Congress would undermine the authority of every international union headquarters to deal with Canadian locals. Instead of obeying a jurisdictional decision, or a dues assessment, or a contract clause, a Canadian local might be tempted to abandon its international

19. Trades and Labor Congress, *Proceedings* (1902), p. 39.
20. R. Robinson, Chairman, Geo. Flemmin, and A. Lackey of Nelson, British Columbia, to W. J. Frid, Hamilton, Ontario, April 6, 1901, National Union Files, Reel 2, AFL-CIO Archives.
21. Trades and Labor Congress, *Proceedings* (1902), p. 38.

headquarters without temerity and find refuge within the Trades and Labor Congress.

Just such a complication appeared to be arising among shoe workers' locals in the province of Quebec. TLC leaders from that province had been trying without success to amalgamate the Canadian Federation of Boot and Shoe Makers, a dual union composed predominantly of French-speaking members, with the Boot and Shoe Workers' International Union. Accepting their failure as final, they persuaded the Canadian dual union to apply for admission into the Trades Congress, and expressed the hope that the independent shoeworkers would be seated at the next convention beside representatives of the international union locals. Indeed, the Quebec labor leaders went even further and asked the Trades Congress to grant a charter to *any* local that applied for it. That suggestion, if acceded to, would have removed the deference paid by the TLC to international union jurisdictions and would have led to a plethora of dual unions throughout Canada.[22]

In eastern as well as western Canada, the AFL craft unions faced disruption within their ranks. Remnants of the Knights of Labor assemblies in Montreal captured control of the central body in that city in 1897. Locals of craft unions affiliated with the AFL then seceded from the Central Trades Council and set up a rival body, the Federated Trades Council, which received Gompers' blessing.[23] Both groups sent delegates to TLC conventions, but the Federated Council campaigned to obtain the expulsion of the Knights' representatives, partly because the presence of a competing central body in Montreal gave encouragement to secessionist movements within the international locals of that city. Moreover, the competition for new affiliates made it doubly difficult for the craft-dominated Federated Trades Council to adhere strictly to jurisdictional lines. In the fall of 1901 Gompers received a complaint that the AFL-char-

22. *Ibid.*, p. 36.
23. Gompers to P. J. Ryan, April 19, 1897; Gompers to A. Gariepy, May 4, May 27, 1897; Gompers to Joseph Ainey, May 27, 1897; Gompers to John Cantwell, July 31, 1897, Gompers Letterbooks.

tered Federated Council was harboring an independent group of lasters in violation of the AFL constitution. The Shoe Workers' International Union had affiliated three locals to the Federated Trades Council and expected to add three more, the informant stated, but their efforts were hindered by the lasters. The Federated Trades Council, it seems, had originally admitted the lasters in order to keep them from moving over to the Central Council. But instead of imbibing the international spirit, they were "corrupting such International feelings as may have heretofore existed in the Council." [24]

The rivalry between these two central bodies, augmented by the ancient friction between the crafts and the Knights (whose organization was based upon industrial-union principles), created a situation favorable to the Liberal party's schemes. Gompers was told that some of the locals affiliated with the Federated Trades Council were leaning toward the Canadian Federation of Labor ". . . as outlined by Ralph Smith . . . at the recent session" of the TLC.[25] Then, in May or June of 1902, Congress secretary Draper put the stamp of legitimacy on the Central Trades Council when he issued that body a TLC charter.[26] Montreal now had the distinction of possessing two central councils, one holding an American and the other a Canadian charter. The situation was not very conducive to harmony between the Federation and the Trades Congress.

Draper's grant of TLC charters to Canadian central bodies provoked a confrontation with the AFL. Draper argued that Canadian city centrals, because of their legislative concerns on the municipal level, required Canadian charters. In May of 1902 he requested some thirty-five trades councils to take out Congress charters. Within a few weeks the Toronto District Council, the Windsor Trades Council, and the aforementioned Central Council in Montreal complied.[27] On the other hand, since 1897 when the AFL had issued its first charter to a Canadian central body (the Montreal Federated Trades Council),

24. John F. Tobin to Gompers, Oct. 22, 1901, National Union Files, Reel 2, AFL-CIO Archives.
25. *Ibid.*   26. Trades and Labor Congress, *Proceedings* (1902), p. 64.
27. *Ibid.*, p. 18.

Federation organizers had set up councils with American charters in Revelstoke and Victoria, British Columbia, Brockville
and Galt-Preston, Ontario, and Charlottetown, Prince Edward
Island. Whereas Draper saw city centrals in terms of their legislative functions, Federation leaders considered city centrals to
be vital agents enforcing AFL jurisdictional lines at a time
when the latter were under great strain from shifts in technology. In order to carry out American labor leaders' orders,
city centrals throughout North America were routinely expected to ostracize recalcitrant locals. If an AFL-chartered
council dared refuse, Gompers invariably threatened to revoke
the council's charter. But what could the AFL do if the rebel-
lious council held a Trades Congress charter? After all, trade-
union discipline has always rested upon the threat of expulsion.

In 1902, the first serious conflict between AFL-chartered and
TLC-chartered bodies arose on Prince Edward Island. The
Congress had chartered the first trade union on the Island when
it had formed Federal Labor Union No. 10 from a number of
railway employees. In 1901 the local pleaded with the TLC for
the services of a Canadian organizer, but only weeks later John
Flett arrived in Charlottetown and organized several locals for
the AFL.[28] Then a trades council was chartered by the AFL.
When the TLC-chartered local presented its credentials and
asked for a seat on the council, that AFL-chartered body, acting
on the advice of the Federation secretary, refused "on the
ground that they did not belong to an International Union of
the American Federation of Labor and, consequently, could not
form part of the general labor movement." It was a very undesirable state of affairs, the secretary of FLU No. 10 told TLC
officers, and he hoped the convention of 1902 would solve the
issue. "Personally," he added, "we are strongly of the opinion
that Canadian Trade and Labor Councils should be chartered by
our Trades Congress."[29] Referring to this issue, Draper told the

28. American Federation of Labor, *Charter Book* (1902), AFL-CIO Archives.
29. Report of the P.E.I. executive committee, in Trades and Labor Congress,
Proceedings (1902), pp. 18–19, 44.

Congress delegates that the time had arrived "when the powers, rights and privileges of this Congress, as the national organization for legislative purposes of the Canadian wage-earner, must be defined." Until the AFL recognized TLC chartering rights, he thought it useless for the Congress to expend more time or energy on organizing endeavors. Draper believed that the Trades Congress needed, at minimum, the power to continue chartering both central bodies and federal labor unions.[30]

Similar uncertainty as to the line between TLC and AFL jurisdictions provoked an outburst from western Canada in 1902. A Vancouver-based freight handlers' union, chartered by the Trades Congress, had embarked upon an effort to organize Canadian railway freight handlers into a national union. At the same time the International Longshoremen's Association had begun to grant charters to workers in this field. John Flett had granted Longshoremen's charters to railway freight handlers in Ontario and the Maritimes, and the Vancouver freight handlers were furious. They "had spent a lot of time and money in communicating with Freight Handlers in Canada, but now their time and labor are lost." Flett could not serve two masters, the Vancouver unionists argued, and should resign either his Trades Congress vice-presidency or his AFL organizer's post. The Trades Congress was warned that it had little time left to establish a Canadian Federation of Labor. "If we are going to do anything for the Trade Union movement in Canada, we must do it at once, or else all our organizations will become American organizations, which I, for one, do not wish to see."[31]

Besides the TLC-AFL dispute over chartering authority, the organizations disagreed on a major policy issue—compulsory arbitration. The rash of strikes which accompanied the technological changes and trade-union expansion after 1898 provoked widespread public debate throughout North America on the "labor question," as it was euphemistically called in those days. One segment of public opinion, influenced by favorable reports from Australia and New Zealand, called for compulsory

30. Trades and Labor Congress, *Proceedings* (1902), p. 18.
31. *Ibid.*, pp. 38–39.

arbitration of industrial disputes. Proponents of this method assumed that civil servants could intervene impartially and expose the issues to the light of public opinion in order to secure a fair settlement. Gompers, mindful of the damage government intervention did to organized labor during the railroad strikes of 1877 and the Pullman struggle in 1894, bitterly opposed compulsion from whatever quarter. He feared that strikes would be compromised by legislation subject to a judge's whim. Then again, the AFL stance coincided with the social Darwinist outlook of its leaders. Big Capital could only be tamed by Big Labor; the remedy to industrial conflict would germinate in the industrial, not governmental, garden.[32]

Organized labor in Canada had experienced no such hostile treatment at the hands of government, and a plank demanding compulsory arbitration was included in the first TLC platform of principles without much controversy at the convention of 1898. By 1901 Ralph Smith publicly noted the divergence between the AFL and the TLC on arbitration. He admitted that Gompers's opposition to compulsory arbitration was "worthy of consideration" in the American political arena. However, conditions were different in Canada, Smith pointed out, and he was convinced that compulsory arbitration was worth a trial in the Dominion.[33]

The Liberals, in a move to satisfy the political demands of organized labor, brought down a compulsory arbitration bill in May of 1902. The measure proposed to introduce compulsory arbitration on railways when the disputants were unable to reach a voluntary agreement. It provoked a mixed reaction among trade unionists. While the Hamilton Trades and Labor Council endorsed it, the Brotherhood of Locomotive Engineers, meeting in convention in Toronto, expressed decided opposition. The Brotherhood, with a membership spread over the

---

32. For Gompers's opinions on arbitration, see his autobiography, *Seventy Years of Life and Labor*, II (New York, 1925), chapter 30; his article in the *Annals of the American Academy of Political and Social Science*, XX (July, 1902), 29–34; numerous editorials in the *American Federationist* during this period; a letter to Miss Mary Roberson, Mound City, Illinois, March 19, 1914, Gompers Letterbooks.
33. Trades and Labor Congress, *Proceedings* (1901), p. 3.

United States, Canada, and Mexico, had already negotiated contracts with ninety percent of the railroads on the continent, and feared that the Canadian bill would be taken up by other governments in North America to their disadvantage.[34]

Since Gompers shared the fears of the Engineers, he reacted strongly to the Canadian government's moves. First he asked Draper to forward copies of the *Labour Gazette* which had discussed the bill; then he dispatched fifty pamphlets to Draper setting forth the hostile AFL view to the compulsory idea. "It would be well to distribute these among your organizations," Gompers told the Canadian, "and should your [*sic*] desire more, I would be glad to send them to you." A few weeks before the Trades Congress met in convention, Draper ordered another batch.[35] The AFL leader clearly desired to secure the defeat of any compulsory arbitration legislation in Canada. Not only would the proposed legislation directly affect Canadian locals of the international unions, but it would bring the "New Zealand approach" a giant step closer to the United States. It was important to the AFL that the Trades Congress abandon its endorsement of compulsory arbitration and actively oppose the Laurier government's measure.

The growing divergence between the Canadian and American labor movements was publicly acknowledged by the American Federation of Labor at its convention in 1901. A committee regretted the secessionist tendencies among Canadian workers. "Movements of this character not only vitiate Labor's forces but cause general confusion, friction, and sometimes bitter antagonisms—all resulting in injury to our cause and danger to our integrity." The committee endorsed Gompers's proposal that the AFL send ambassadors to the Western Federation of Miners and to the Trades and Labor Congress, ". . . with a view to bringing about the unity so essential to the welfare of the toilers of America." It was necessary, one unionist said, to show "our Canadian Brothers [that] we recognize no imaginary boundary

34. *Labour Gazette*, II (June, 1902), 738–741, (Aug., 1902), 69, 80, 81, 214.
35. Gompers to Draper, Aug. 28, 1902; R. L. Guard (Gompers's secretary) to Draper, Sept. 6, 1902, Gompers Letterbooks.

line and believe all should be under one grand banner march-
ing on together for the protection and assistance of all wage-
workers on this Continent."[36]

During the spring of 1902, Gompers laid plans to counter the
dual-unionist threats that had begun to challenge the Federation's supremacy in North America. Matters said to be of the ut-
most importance, and "involving the largest interests of our organization and our movement generally," were placed on the
agenda of the AFL Executive Council.[37] Gompers invited TLC
secretary Draper to come to AFL headquarters and participate
in some of the discussions. Draper reached Washington, D.C.,
on April 14th and attended some of the Executive Council sessions. He told AFL leaders that the labor movement in Canada
was making splendid progress, and attributed the gains to the
work of John Flett and the international union organizers who
had been put in the field by the American craft organizations.
But the TLC secretary admitted that a "small element" in Canada was opposed to international unions, and recommended
that Gompers or Frank Morrison attend the next Trades Congress
convention, which was to be held in Berlin, Ontario, in September. Meanwhile, in order to carry the battle against dual unionism into the American west, the Executive Council agreed to
hold a summer meeting in San Francisco.[38]

On their journey to the Pacific Coast in July, the Federation
leaders conducted a vigorous six-week tour through the heart
of the Western Federation of Miners–American Labor Union
region. At every stop Gompers stressed the need for unity in the
labor movement. He publicly hoped that the AFL leaders
would accomplish "the absolute unity of the labor forces in
America." Such unity was essential, he maintained, because of
the growing concentration of capital. Boasting of the AFL's two-
million-plus membership figures, he intimated that only the
Federation could guarantee labor's future prosperity.[39]

36. American Federation of Labor, *Proceedings* (1902), pp. 184, 217.
37. Gompers to Executive Council, March 8, 1902, Gompers Letterbooks.
38. Gompers to Draper, April 7, 1902, Gompers Letterbooks; *American Federationist*, IX (June, 1902), 331, 336, 338–39. The AFL paid Draper $97.00 for expenses connected with his attendance at the session. *Ibid.*, p. 350.
39. *Denver Times*, July 9, 1902, reprinted in *American Federationist*, IX (Sept., 1902), 509.

Gompers did not hesitate to criticize the AFL's rivals. "If a Western labor union is a logical argument," he reasoned, "so is a Northern and a Southern and Eastern Federation of Labor. Our employers do not divide on sectional lines and stop at state boundaries."[40]

Had Gompers spoken in Canadian cities in mid-1902, he undoubtedly would have used the same argument against the proposed Canadian Federation of Labor. But events unfolded in such a way as to make a personal appearance in Canada by Gompers unnecessary. In June, Draper corresponded with Flett about dual unionism in Canada, and the AFL's Canadian organizer forwarded the letters to Gompers. Then the AFL affiliates in Montreal enlisted their Toronto brethren in their war against the Knights-dominated Central Labor Council of Montreal. At the same time the president of the Boot and Shoe Workers' International Union argued before the Toronto Trades and Labor Council against any affiliation of independent locals of the shoeworkers to the TLC. The Toronto unionists, although they listened to Draper's side of the case, cast their lot with the international unions.[41]

The fact that dual-unionist challenges to the AFL's predominance in North America were discussed by Draper, Flett, and Gompers and in the Toronto Trades and Labor Council only a few months before the Trades Congress convention suggests that the decisions made at Berlin may not have been purely spontaneous events. There is evidence from the convention itself which points to the same conclusion. When the delegates gathered at Berlin, those from the international unions clearly outnumbered other factions. Twelve Canadian delegates from the Boot and Shoe Workers' International Union sat with none other than John Tobin, the international president who had journeyed from his union headquarters in Boston and mobilized them to wage war against the dual Canadian union in their trade.[42] Most of the large delegations of international unionists,

40. *Denver Post*, July 11, 1902, reprinted in *ibid.*
41. R. L. Guard to Flett, June 28, 1902, Gompers Letterbooks; Minutes of the Toronto Trades and Labor Council, July 24, Aug. 28, 1902, Canadian Labour Congress Library, Ottawa.
42. Trades and Labor Congress, *Proceedings* (1902), pp. 5–7.

such as the Shoe Workers' and the Cigar Makers', voted unanimously in favor of the Berlin decisions. In fact, no less than fifty-one of the sixty-seven delegates who represented Canadian locals of international unions threw their support to the international cause. Twenty-one of the thirty Trades Council representatives, most of whom carried international union cards in their pockets, stood solidly behind the changes. One delegate publicly admitted that he had been instructed to vote against dual unionism.[43] Two Winnipeg delegates later explained that the Congress had been "packed with delegates who through their respective internationals are affiliated with the AFL, and further organizing and lobbying had been going on for months" to achieve the desired ends.[44] Perhaps it should not be surprising, then, that the dual unionists were overwhelmingly defeated by an 87 to 32 vote. Draper, incidentally, voted against the internationalist majority, though he did support the motion withdrawing TLC endorsement of compulsory arbitration.

The triumph of the craft internationals was sealed by the election of John Flett, the AFL organizer, to the presidency of the Trades and Labor Congress. In a light-hearted if rather malodorous moment, the convention wound up its proceedings by presenting the AFL fraternal delegate with a generous slice of locally-made Limburger cheese. The recipient, D. D. Driscoll, promised to recommend to his fellow Americans that all the international unions send organizers into Canada as quickly as possible. While the delegates celebrated their decisions at a German supper cooked by the Women's Label League, the expelled dual unionists gathered in another part of town to set up a rival group called the National Trades and Labor Congress. They made speeches and passed resolutions deprecating the drift toward internationalism at the expense of "nationalism." It seemed clear to them by the end of that fateful week in Berlin that the east-west axis of Canadian nationality was crumbling before the new north-south chains binding Canadian workers to American labor organizations.[45]

43. E. S. Jackson of the Toronto Typographical Union, in *Toronto Globe,* Sept. 17, 1902, p. 9.
44. *Winnipeg Voice,* Oct. 3, 1902, p. 1.
45. *Toronto Globe,* Sept. 19, 1902, p. 2; Sept. 20, 1902, p. 11.

Flett reported the good tidings to the American who paid his salary. Sam Gompers was delighted with the accounts of the TLC convention given in Flett's newspaper clippings. "They are mighty interesting reading," he told Flett,

and I want to congratulate you and organized labor of Canada upon the splendid stand taken by the recent Congress of the Trades and Labor Unions of the Dominion . . . The spirit of the labor movement is growing toward the recognition that our interests are identical regarding the arbitrary geographical lines. . . . Those who would preach the policy of isolation are absolutely inconsistent. The aim of the labor movement is to associate the workers in our trades in the various localities, then national, and the next step is international trade unionism. Let me congratulate you and the Congress upon your election as its president and wish you every success.

In a postscript, Gompers added that the "declaration for international trade unionism was splendid as well as the unqualified protest against compulsory arbitration." [46]

The representatives of the 2,287 dual unionists expelled at Berlin, whether motivated by personal ambition, by the vision of a Canadian Federation of Labor exercising full autonomy, or by a French-Canadian fear of drowning in a sea of Anglo-Saxons, failed to defend the TLC's shadowy autonomy. Instead the Congress was consigned to a rank among the American state federations. The bulk of Canadian unionists probably agreed with the Berlin decisions because they wanted assurance that the full weight of the AFL affiliates would always be available to assist them in their struggles on the economic front. Yet by wedding the TLC so tightly to international unionism, and by accepting the supremacy of the AFL in Canada, they forfeited influence over the shape and direction of the Canadian labor movement.

The continental unity so dear to Gompers enhanced the authority of the Federation, but not its responsiveness. After 1902 the French factor in Quebec, the strong Canadian tradition of positive government, and the desire of many Canadian unionists to build a social reform movement were filtered out or warped by an organizational structure and system of values which had grown out of the experience of the AFL and its leaders in the

46. Gompers to Flett, Sept. 29, 1902, Gompers Letterbooks.

United States. Consequently, after 1902 there would always be a group of grievance-ridden Canadian toilers who would respond to appeals couched in the sentiments of Canadian nationalism. There would always be a few Canadian labor leaders who were willing to lead a national labor movement against the ramparts of international unionism. Perennially, someone could be heard announcing that "the time . . . has arrived when the Canadian workmen should have their own sovereign congress, co-equal with the . . . American Federation of Labor and all other national organizations." [47] The Berlin decisions also paved the way for a separate trade-union movement in Quebec—an event foreseen by Daniel O'Donoghue, the venerable, white-bearded father of Canadian trade unionism, when he warned that the Berlin decisions "would be disastrous to the interests of labor, and would practically shut Quebec Province out of the congress." [48] Ironically, Gompers's strenuous efforts to unify labor on a continental scale resulted in several deep and long-lasting divisions within the trade-union movement of Canada.

47. T. J. Griffiths, at the first session of the National Trades and Labor Congress, *Toronto Globe*, Sept. 20, 1902, p. 11.
48. *Toronto Globe*, Sept. 17, 1902, p. 9.

9

American Unionism, Communism and the Canadian Labor Movement: Some Myths and Realities

Irving M. Abella

There has been very little written about the history of trade unions in Canada, but a good deal of what has been written should never have been; it has tended to confuse more than to elucidate. The purpose of my paper is not to condemn those who have written about the Canadian labor movement, but rather to question some of the basic premises which they have all unquestioningly adopted and which they have done much to perpetuate.

The history of the Canadian labor movement, at least as seen by almost all these authors, is based on three seemingly irrefutable truisms. Firstly, they all agree, as does almost everybody else who claims to know anything about the labor movement, that American unions had to move into Canada in order to create a strong, viable Canadian labor movement, that once we Canadians allowed in American industry, American unions necessarily had to follow. Thus the growth of international unionism was not only believed necessary, but beneficial as well, since Canadians were obviously not capable of building their own national union movement. Not one of these authors denies that American unions were absolutely essential in building the powerful trade-union organizations we have in Canada at the present time.

Similarly, it is the conventional wisdom amongst most knowledgeable Canadians that the contributions of the Communist

Party to the Canadian labor movement were largely, if not entirely, negative, that the Communists hurt the organization of labor in Canada more than they helped it, and that the Canadian labor movement would have progressed much more rapidly had it not been for Communist interference.

Finally, every student of the Canadian labor movement—almost without exception—concludes that, while the American Federation of Labor treated its Canadian affiliate, the Trades and Labor Congress, as an inferior dependant, the CIO's relationship with its Canadian affiliate, the Canadian Congress of Labour, was based on an assumption of equality between the two; in other words, the universal interpretation is that the CIO, unlike the AFL, recognized and accepted the autonomy of its Canadian affiliate, and indeed, encouraged the independent pretensions of the CCL.

These then are the three fundamental premises upon which the history of the Canadian labor movement has been built. So obvious and accepted are these axioms that few have questioned any one of them, let alone all three. For the rest of this paper, this is what I intend to do.

There are of course many reasons why American unions found Canada such a fertile territory for growth, but the primary reason, it seems to me, was that Canadian workers were so receptive. And why were they so hospitable? Simply because Canadian workers believed that American unions could do a better job for them than could Canadian unions. It wasn't that American unions were so imperialistic and aggressive; they were merely responding to pressing invitations sent by Canadian workers who had more confidence in the capabilities and strength of the American unions than they had in their own. But was this a feeling based on fact, or was it, as I suspect, based more on the typical Canadian belief that Americans can do things better than we can, that they are a more capable, aggressive people, and therefore that American unions could assure the "better life" the Canadian working man so desperately wanted, which was something he felt Canadian unions could not provide?

The most common explanation for the presence of American unions in Canada is that in a country the size and population of Canada, with the concomitant difficulties of communication, to create a strong nationwide trade-union movement would have been an impossibility. As Professor John Crispo, the recognized authority on international unionism in Canada puts it, "Canadian unions lacked any substantial domestic base." "The weak industrial base of the country and the sparseness of the population," he adds, "made it extremely difficult for any sort of national trade union movement to establish roots." He also argues that the "growing American-based unions had much more to offer the Canadian worker" than did "fledgling" unions started by Canadians. The reason Canadian workers joined American unions, according to Professor Crispo, was that these unions "could supply financial aid and experienced personnel that would have taken many years to develop through Canadian resources alone."[1] This, of course, is the traditional analysis. Perhaps the time has arrived to test this hypothesis. And what better way to test it than to study in some detail how specific American unions came into Canada to see if this thesis is, in fact, valid.

Since Confederation there have been at least five major so-called incursions of American labor organizations into Canada. First to come in were the various craft unions such as the iron moulders and printers who arrived as early as 1859 and later, as affiliates of the American Federation of Labor, formed the Trades and Labor Congress. In the late 1860's and 1870's the railway brotherhoods crossed into Canada. The next wave came in the 1880's when the Knights of Labor began organizing in Canada. In the 1890's and first decade of this century the Western Federation of Miners and the International Workers of the World invaded the Canadian labor scene. And finally in the 1930's and 40's the CIO entered Canada. In each of these periods, of course, Canadians joined these unions for various and quite different reasons. For purposes of this paper, however, I

1. J. Crispo, *International Unionism: A Study in Canadian-American Relations* (Toronto, 1967), pp. 12–14.

intend to look only at the most recent, and—I hope—the last, intrusion of a foreign labor center into Canada, that of the CIO. Perhaps the conclusions that may be drawn from such a study could also throw some light on the reasons American unions came into Canada in earlier periods of our history.

The CIO came into Canada at a time when almost half the organized workers in Canada belonged to national unions—the Workers Unity League, the All-Canadian Congress of Labour, and the Catholic unions in Quebec. The other half were members of AFL unions affiliated with the Trades and Labor Congress. This, it seems, was the one time in this century for Canadians to regain control of their own labor movement, because never before nor ever again would national unions have that high a percentage of the organized workers of the country. But the arrival of the CIO doomed that hope. And the most ironical aspect of that arrival was that the CIO didn't even want to come.

From the beginning, CIO activity in Canada was more the result of the forceful demands and activities of the Canadian workers than of the plans of the CIO hierarchy in the United States. Taking their example from fellow workers in the United States, Canadian workers started their own organizing campaigns. They looked for leadership to the Trades and Labor Congress, but instead, received little more than advice to wait. Because they felt no Canadian union was in a position to undertake any large-scale organization, by default, therefore, they opted for the CIO.

The reaction of the CIO was something less than encouraging. Like those of the TLC, the CIO leaders also urged Canadian workers to hold back. John L. Lewis and his colleagues were much too involved in the hectic labor scene below the border to give the Canadian movement more than a passing thought.

But Lewis had not taken into account the growing demands of Canadian workers for organization. These were most evident in Ontario. With the worst of the depression over, industry after industry began announcing record profits and issuing optimistic reports for the new year. Workers, on the other hand, were still being paid depression wages and were growing increasingly more restless. With the example of the CIO sit-downs just across the border, it was only a matter of time before Ontario workers would rebel both against their deplorable working conditions and their overcautious union leadership.

Dismayed by the apparent apathy of the CIO, Ontario workers took matters into their own hands. All over the province tiny locals were springing up, calling themselves CIO. Naturally the CIO in the United States had no knowledge of these locals. Throughout the province, a small group of dedicated men—most of them active Communists—were organizing for the CIO, though again, the CIO had never heard of them. Within a few months, the CIO found itself with scores of unions and thousands of workers it did not want, and even worse, did not know what to do with.

For the workers of Ontario the magic word was CIO. Wherever they heard it, they flocked; whoever used it, they trusted. Thus what Canadian organizers for eager Canadian unions had been unable to do, Canadian organizers for a reluctant American union succeeded in doing. Canadian workers obviously felt that the CIO magic would rub off on them; what the CIO was achieving for its members in the United States, it would also achieve for its members in Canada. Even though the CIO was not yet ready to expand into Canada, Canadian workers insisted. Thus a protesting CIO was dragged unwillingly into Canada. But even then it refused to do anything to help Canadian workers. It did not disown any of the unofficial CIO organizers in the country. On the other hand, neither did it assist them in any way. Indeed it was on the assembly lines of Oshawa and Sarnia, and not in the union offices in Washington and Detroit, that industrial unionism in Canada was born. It was not John L. Lewis nor any of his representatives who brought the CIO to Canada. It was the body-shop workers in Oshawa and the foundry workers in Sarnia who were responsible.

The first CIO sit-down strike in Canada occurred on March 1, 1937, at the Holmes Foundry in Sarnia. Actually the strike had little to do with the CIO. Some seventy of the plant's workers—

most of them recent immigrants from Eastern Europe—enraged both at the passivity of the CIO and at the company's refusal to negotiate with their new union, sat down at their machines. Within hours they were ruthlessly and bloodily evicted by a mob of Sarnia's "best" citizens, armed with such antiunion devices as crowbars, baseball bats, bricks, and steel pipes. The strike was soon broken, as were the arms, legs and heads of many of the strikers. The strikers were at once arrested and convicted of trespassing; no charges were laid against the strikebreakers.[2]

The Ontario Premier, Mitchell Hepburn, immediately denounced the strikers and those "foreign agitators" who had led the strike. Unfortunately for the premier's case, there were no foreign agitators. All the strikers and their leaders were residents of the province of Ontario. No one from the CIO, nor indeed, from anywhere outside the province had been involved in this strike.

The famous Oshawa strike one month later marks the birth of industrial unionism in Canada. This two-week walkout by some 4000 workers of the General Motors plant in Oshawa was the turning point in Canadian labor history.[3] On their own these workers organized themselves into local 222 of the United Automobile Workers of America, a CIO affiliate. With some initial assistance from Hugh Thompson, a UAW organizer from Detroit, the workers forced the G.M. management to negotiate with their new union. When General Motors, on the insistence of Premier Hepburn, broke off negotiations, the union called a strike and shut down the plant.

For two weeks, despite the unyielding pressure from both the company and the provincial government, the workers held out. At times these pressures were almost irresistible. Hepburn was determined to keep the CIO out of Ontario, not so much because he was concerned with the violence associated with the CIO, but rather because he was worried that the CIO would organize

2. For a more complete study of this incident, see I. M. Abella, "The CIO, the Communist Party and the Formation of the Canadian Congress of Labour, 1936–1941," *Canadian Historical Association Historical Papers* (1969), pp. 113–115.
3. *Ibid.*, pp. 115–119.

the gold mines in Northern Ontario, and thus would jeopardize the enormous profits of the Ontario "mine barons"—all of whom were his cronies and amongst his closest advisers as well. When the federal government rejected Hepburn's request for a large contingent of the Royal Canadian Mounted Police to intimidate the strikers, the Ontario Premier founded his own police force of unemployed veterans and University of Toronto students. These were the infamous "Hepburn Hussars," or as they were known in Oshawa, "Sons of Mitches." Hepburn also attempted to deport Thompson and other CIO agents in the province, but aside from Thompson, who was a British subject and could not be deported, he could find no other organizers from outside the province. He sent messages to General Motors executives in Detroit urging them to hold firm. He even cabled Colonel McLaughlin, the president of the company in Canada, who was vacationing in a yacht somewhere in the Caribbean, to order his lieutenants in Oshawa not to negotiate with the union.

But Hepburn's efforts were in vain. The strikers were determined and eventually the company agreed to sign a contract with the new union. The achievement of the Oshawa strikers in fighting and defeating both the power of big business and government inspired workers throughout Canada. It gave the CIO the impetus it so desperately needed to begin organization in the mass production industries of the country. The agreement at Oshawa, but particularly Hepburn's peculiar behavior, had suddenly turned the rather somnolent CIO organizing campaign into a violent crusade. The Oshawa strikers had won a great victory for themselves, but even more important, they had created for the CIO the psychology of success and enthusiasm needed for a massive organizing effort. What Akron and Flint had done in the United States, Oshawa was to do for Canada. It proved to be a landmark in Canadian labor history.

What is most significant about the Oshawa Strike is that it was conducted by Canadians without any assistance from the CIO. Although Hugh Thompson was ostensibly in charge of organization, most of the organizing was in fact done by Canadians. Whatever financial assistance the strikers were given came from churches and neighbors. Not one penny of aid came from the United States. Both the CIO and the UAW decided that they neither had the men nor the money to help the strikers. They also refused to call a sympathy strike of G.M. workers in the United States to support the strikers in Oshawa. Though the UAW had publicly promised to send one hundred thousand dollars, in the end all it delivered was its best wishes. Thus what the Oshawa strikers achieved, they achieved on their own.

In fact I suppose it can be argued that the CIO connection was as harmful as it was helpful. Hepburn and his mine-owning friends were not so much opposed to the creation of a union in Oshawa as they were to the possibility of the CIO gaining a foothold in Ontario. When reports filtered down to Queens Park from the North that the CIO was organizing the mines, the determination of Hepburn and his cronies to crush the strike hardened. The CIO had, however, nothing to do with the increased labor activity in the North. All the organizing there was being done by a small corps of dedicated amateurs, none of whom had any official connection with the CIO. The General Motors Company agreed to a settlement in Oshawa not because of the threats of the CIO but because it desperately needed cars for the Canadian and Empire market, and these could only be built in Oshawa. Fear of losing these markets to Ford and Chrysler, rather than fear of John L. Lewis and Hugh Thompson, forced General Motors to recognize the union. Negotiations with the company were carried on solely by Canadians, Charlie Millard and J. L. Cohen, though, of course, Hugh Thompson was available to advise, although by the time the settlement was reached, he was back in the United States.

Thus the role of the CIO in the Oshawa Strike seems ambiguous. The strike was conducted, financed and settled by Canadians. The CIO played no actual role, except in the minds of Hepburn, the mine owners, and, perhaps most importantly, in the minds of the strikers themselves. Caught up in the mystique of the CIO, they believed the international connection was essential. Even though half the organized workers of Canada at the time belonged to Canadian unions, the workers in Oshawa and across the country seemed to think that only American unions could provide the necessary muscle to protect and forward their interests. It was this attitude, based more on sentiment than fact, which, more than anything else, has doomed national unions in Canada.

Though the victory at Oshawa was a victory for Canadians it was immediately hailed across the country as a great CIO triumph. Because Hepburn had defined the enemy at Oshawa as the CIO, the CIO was given full credit for a victory it had done little to win.

Following the Oshawa strike there was a massive CIO organizing campaign amongst the industrial workers of Ontario. CIO organizers went into the textile mills of Eastern Ontario, the steel mills in Hamilton, the rubber plants in Kitchener, and the gold mines in the North. But again none of these men were American; in fact they were not even official CIO organizers. Rather they were largely a group of young, militant radicals, most of them members or supporters of the Communist Party.

Long before the CIO had undertaken the organization of the mass-production industries, the Communists had maintained an elaborate framework of unions, both inside and outside the Workers Unity League. Some of these had existed only on paper but they had been built around a faithful and militant nucleus of experienced party members who knew how to chair meetings, make motions, give speeches, print pamphlets, mimeograph handbills, and organize picket lines—all indispensable when thousands of workers without previous trade-union experience flocked to union halls. As Tim Buck, the Communist leader, put it: "Our party had trained and developed a whole cadre of people who knew about unions and knew how to go about organizing them. And the party members, even though they didn't work in the industry, would go out distributing leaflets, helping to organize the union." [4] When the order was given in

4. Transcript of an interview with Tim Buck, Oct. 3, 1960, United Electrical Workers Archives, Toronto, p. 8.

1935 to disband the Workers Unity League, the Communist unions moved directly into the Trades and Labor Congress and most of the Party organizers began organizing for the CIO. Without their aid CIO efforts in Canada would have been vastly circumscribed, and conceivably even aborted.

The weeks following the Oshawa Strike were euphoric for the CIO. Scores of new locals were started in plants and industries that had never before been organized. Thousands of new members were organized. Unfortunately, these halcyon days turned out to be sadly evanescent. Many of the workers who had signed up with the CIO in the first flush of enthusiasm soon drifted away. By August of 1937, CIO organization had come to a grinding halt.

The CIO failure following Oshawa was not surprising. With no funds and few experienced organizers organization campaigns were doomed. The CIO hierarchy below the border was just too involved in its own projects to lend much assistance or thought to Canada. Of even more significance, however, the CIO had made the strategic decision that organization in Canada would have to be undertaken by Canadians themselves. As Sidney Hillman, the "theoretician" of the CIO put it, "Canada must develop its own leaders if it is to have a sound labour movement."[5] Both John L. Lewis and Hillman felt that organization in Canada would have to wait until there was a body of Canadian personnel large enough to carry out the job.

Both Lewis and Hillman were admitting the obvious: that CIO organization in Canada was almost entirely the work of Canadians; little help had been given in the past, and now even less would be given in the future. Canadian organizers for the CIO would again be on their own, though they could still use the CIO label. Yet the advantages of using the CIO name were dubious. Whenever and wherever the three magic letters appeared, employer and government resistance stiffened immeasurably. Canadian union organizers would probably have been more successful had they dropped the CIO affiliation—an affilia-

5. Quoted in *Financial Post*, Oct. 30, 1937.

tion which at the time provided little of benefit to the Canadian organizers and workingmen.

By the middle of 1938 and into 1939, with the economy rebounding, the future of the CIO revived and new, more successful, organizing campaigns were launched. Again these were staffed and financed exclusively by Canadians. Most of these men had one thing in common: they were members of the Communist Party. In fact, so influential was the Party in the UAW that the union's headquarters in Detroit would send the weekly edition of its newspaper to Communist Party headquarters in downtown Toronto to be distributed to the various UAW locals in southern Ontario.[6] Indeed the entire CIO operation in Ontario was run by Communists. Thus when the militantly anti-Communist Charlie Millard was appointed by John L. Lewis to coordinate CIO activities in Ontario he found himself surrounded in the CIO head office in Toronto by Communists. Only on Saturday morning, when the Party held its regular weekly meeting, did Millard have the office to himself, and even then a Party member stayed behind, in Joe Salsberg's words, "to keep his eye on things."[7] There was thus a direct pipeline from the CIO offices to Communist headquarters; decisions made at the latter would shortly thereafter be made at the former, while those made at the former would instantly be known at the latter. It seems very obvious therefore that the Communists played a historic role in the development of the CIO in Canada. But more about that shortly.

From the evidence available to me it appears that all the major CIO unions in Canada—the UAW, the United Steelworkers, the United Electrical Workers, the International Woodworkers of America and the Mine Mill and Smelter Workers— were organized and financed by Canadians with little, and often no help from their parent organizations in the United States. Indeed it seems that one American union, the United Steelworkers of America, survived its first few years of existence only because of the funds flowing in from Canada. Dues collected from the Steel local in Sydney, Nova Scotia, made it

6. Interview, J. B. Salsberg.   7. *Ibid.*

possible for the International to meet its financial obligations. Without the regular monthly payment from Sydney, there is some doubt whether Steel could have kept afloat, especially after John L. Lewis split with Steel's president, Philip Murray, and turned off the subsidies flowing from his Mineworkers union into Steel's coffers.[8]

The United Electrical Workers union was organized in Canada by C. S. Jackson, a Canadian. And indeed since 1939 all the organizing for the UE in Canada has been carried on by Canadians. Because both the parent organization in the United States and the Canadian affiliate were thought to be controlled by Communists, it was almost impossible for the leaders of both sections to meet together, since as suspected Communists, none could cross the border. Thus the UE from the beginning has been on its own, and in fact is now a larger and more powerful union in Canada than the American dominated and subsidized International Union of Electrical Workers.

The International Woodworkers of America was in fact largely founded by a Canadian, Harold Pritchett. A one-time organizer for the Workers Unity League, he resigned the presidency when he was expelled from the United States for his Communist connections. He then devoted all his energies to organizing the IWA in British Columbia, and was so successful that, until 1948, the B.C. section of the union subsidized the much smaller and poorer American section. All the organizing in Canada for the IWA was done by Canadians and much of the money they raised went to the United States to support IWA activities south of the border.

Finally, the Mine Mill and Smelter Workers was also the work of Canadians. In fact the Sudbury local was the largest in the entire union and for a time it provided the bulk of the union's revenue. Such smaller CIO unions as the Textile Workers and the Packinghouse Workers were again largely organized by Canadians from Canadian funds with almost no assistance from American parent organizations.

8. Interview, Charles Millard; Philip Murray to Charles Millard, Feb. 18, 1940, United Steel Workers Archives, Toronto.

What conclusions can be drawn from this description of CIO activity in Canada in the 1930's and early 40's? If almost all the organizing for the CIO was done by Canadians, if almost all the money needed for this organization was provided by Canadians, and if all the leadership in the new unions was provided by Canadians, then who needed the CIO? What did the CIO do for Canadians that Canadians weren't doing for themselves? Was the CIO in fact necessary for the development of an industrial union movement in Canada?

I suppose the one deduction we can safely make is that, at the time, Canadian workers obviously believed that the CIO was necessary. For the Canadian workingman old traditions die hard. Because he felt that American unions had been essential in the past, despite the drastically changed situation of the 1930's he obviously believed they were still essential. Caught up in the "continentalist" ideology, and in the belief in the superiority of things American, Canadian workers were preconditioned to join American rather than Canadian unions; and having just suffered through a ravaging depression, they were understandably more concerned with material benefits than with national identity. They felt they had no choice but to join forces with their fellow workers in the United States. After all, their problems were the same, their traditions similar, and in many cases they worked for the same employers. Above all, the CIO seemed to have much more to offer than any Canadian union. It had the personnel, the large treasury, and, most important, the experience to provide Canadian workers with the organization they so urgently needed.

Or so Canadians thought. Yet in fact, the personnel, the treasury, and the experience were not provided by Americans but by Canadians. All the CIO provided was its name; and if this is all it provided then perhaps Canadians could have done the jobs themselves without any American assistance at all. If this is true for the CIO advance into Canada in the 1930's then perhaps it is also true of previous American union incursions into Canada. Perhaps international unions were, after all, not necessary for the development of a trade union movement in Canada. Perhaps, if the CIO example is the prototype, Canadians could have controlled their own unions right from the beginning. In any case, the nature of these earlier movements of American unions into Canada should be reexamined.

Surely it is also time to reexamine the contribution of the Communists to the Canadian labor movement. From my own research into the 1930's and 1940's it seems to me that on the whole their contribution was beneficial and perhaps even necessary for the development and growth of an industrial union movement in Canada.

In writing about the Canadian labor movement I have had the advantage of reading the penetrating study of Professor Gad Horowitz, *Labour and Politics in Canada*. Though in almost every respect this is a brilliant piece of work, it seems to me that, in attempting to apply the "Hartzian principle" to Canada, Professor Horowitz has done a grave injustice to the Communist Party. Because of his dogged loyalty to this concept, Professor Horowitz has seemingly found it impossible to see the Communist Party as anything but an abhorrent phenomenon. Instead of writing about what happened, at times Horowitz lapses into writing about what should have happened. Because the Hartzian theory—or the Horowitzian interpretation of it—does not allow for the existence of a viable Communist Party, Horowitz tends to ignore or denigrate it. In either case, it seems to me, he is mistaken.

Certainly in the Canadian labor movement the contribution of the Communists can neither be ignored nor denigrated, though their objectives and their tactics may most certainly be questioned. Although this paper is anything but a brief for the Communist Party, nonetheless, in the face of all the evidence, I find it impossible to accept Professor Horowitz's interpretation. In fact it was largely because of the Communists that the CIO took root in Canada as quickly as it did, for it was the Communists—when no one else was willing or able—who undertook most of the CIO's organizational "dirty work" in its first few years in Canada. It was the Communists who provided the necessary impetus and inspiration which enabled the CIO and the CCL to lay the permanent foundation for a strong and unassailable industrialunion movement in Canada.

Communists under the able guidance of J. B. Salsberg organized most of the CIO unions in Canada in the 1930s. The large CIO unions, Steel, Auto, Electric, Woodworkers, Mine Mill and Smelter, and Textile, were all organized at the beginning by Communists and were all, at one time or another in their history, dominated by the Party. Harold Pritchett, founder of the IWA, C. S. Jackson founder and still president of the Canadian UE, Tommy Church, George Anderson and Harvey Murphy, the first organizers of Mine-Mill, Harry Hunter, Dick Steel and Harry Hamberg, the first organizers for the Steelworkers, and Alex Welch, who started the Textile organization in Canada, were all active members of the Party, as were a host of other nameless young dedicated organizers who spread out the length and breadth of Canada to bring unionism to the unorganized under the most trying conditions. To show how dominant was the Communist Party in the CIO in the 1930's, when the CIO held its first Canadian conference in 1939, of the 105 delegates there, 82 represented Party dominated unions.[9] It was largely for this reason that the anti-Communist, pro-CCF forces in the CIO encouraged the merger of the Canadian CIO with the militantly anti-Communist All-Canadian Congress of Labour, which created the Canadian Congress of Labour in 1949.

Though on the whole they have been rather badly maligned by historians and commentators on the period, there seems little doubt that the contribution of the Communists to the creation of the CIO in Canada was invaluable. They were activists in a period which cried for activity; they were energetic, zealous, and dedicated in a period when organizing workers required these attributes. They helped build the CIO, and helped it grow until it was strong enough to do without them. They did the work that no one else was willing or able to do. Although there are many critical things one can say about the

9. Report of the First Conference of the Canadian Committee for the CIO, Ottawa, Nov. 4–6, 1939, UEW Archives, Toronto. The Party-dominated unions were the Auto Workers, Steel Workers, Electrical Workers, Shoe Workers, Fur Workers, and Mine Mill and Smelter Workers.

Communists, in building a viable industrial-union movement in Canada theirs is a contribution not easily matched. Their impact becomes even more admirable when it is realized that the Communist union leaders were under a constant searchlight of redbaiting hostility from the press, from employers, from government and especially from other unions. They therefore had to meet higher standards than most union leaders in respect to honesty, democracy, businesslike operation, militancy and results, that is, if they hoped to retain the loyalty of their own non-Communist membership.[10]

It seems to me that Communists were successful because they were dedicated and capable unionists who provided both first-class leadership and excellent service to their members. When they were expelled from the Canadian Congress of Labour in the late 1940's and early 50's, they were banished not because they were bad unionists but for political reasons which really had nothing to do with organizing workers. Caught up in the hysteria of the Cold War and the McCarthy period, the CCL proved its loyalty by banishing from its midst its Communist membership, that very same group of men who had contributed so much to creating the CCL.

Regarding the impact of the Communists on the Canadian labor movement, it seems to me that only one conclusion is possible. Though in many cases their objectives were questionable and their tactics reprehensible, on the whole their contribution to the growth of an industrial labor movement in Canada should no longer be overlooked, as it has been for too long. The Communists were certainly not saints, but neither were they always devils. The Canadian workingman owes many of these men a long belated vote of thanks.

Finally, let me deal with the relationship between the CIO and the CCL. Conventional wisdom has it that the relationship was between equals. As one noted student of the labor movement, Professor Paul Norgren, described it in 1951: "the CCL has been free of any domination by the CIO and the relationship

10. See Len De Caux, *Labor Radical* (Boston, 1970), for an admirable study of the dilemma of the Communist trade-union leader.

between the two organizations has remained entirely amicable." [11] After his exhaustive study of international unionism in Canada, John Crispo concludes that the CIO "appears never to have had . . . designs . . . to interfere in the affairs of the CCL," and that the CIO fully sympathized "with Canadian aspirations for independence." [12]

Unfortunately these analyses are simply not true. Between the CIO and the CCL there was always a great deal of tension and animosity. One would have thought that the CIO should have stayed out of the CCL's affairs, since the development of CIO unions in Canada was largely the work of Canadians. But right from the beginning the CIO was insistent upon showing the flag in Canada—the American flag that is. For a time it stubbornly refused to allow its unions in Canada to merge with the ACCL on the ground that they might sever their international connection. When the Canadian affiliates overcame this opposition the CIO then demanded that the newly created Congress devote all its energies to organizing workers into CIO unions. It also insisted that the CCL hand over to the appropriate CIO union its national and chartered unions, and to desist from organizing any more of these unions. This provoked a bitter squabble, since the CCL received most of its revenues from its national and chartered unions and not from its affiliated CIO unions, most of whose revenues went to the United States. Whatever funds dribbled back across the border from CIO headquarters in Washington to the CCL offices in Ottawa the CIO insisted be used for solely CIO purposes. In addition, over Congress objections, the CIO demanded that the CCL accept as affiliates all CIO unions in Canada, and that all jurisdictional disputes among Canadian CIO unions be settled in the United States. After lengthy acrimonious disputes, the CCL usually—but not always—got its way on all these matters. [13]

11. Paul Norgren, "The Labour Link Between Canada and the United States," in A. E. Kovacs (ed.), *Canadian Labour Economics* (Toronto, 1961), p. 37.
12. Crispo, *op. cit.*, pp. 111–112.
13. See I. M. Abella, "Lament for a Union Movement," in I. Lumsden (ed.), *Close the 49th Parallel* (Toronto, 1970), pp. 75–92.

222   *The Influence of the U.S. on Canadian Development*

The key man in warding off the designs of the CIO was the CCL's dynamic secretary-treasurer, Pat Conroy. He had been elected to this key position because he was a member of a CIO union—the United Mineworkers of America, but after a few short months in office he found himself spending a good deal of his time fighting the CIO. According to him, the aim of the CIO was to make the Canadian Congress of Labour its "satellite." Conroy felt that the Canadian labor movement had been for too long a satellite of American unions, and that it had finally arrived at a stage of its development where it needed a central labor body of independent decision-making authority.[14] It was his job, as he saw it, to give the CCL that authority.

On the other hand the CIO was not prepared to give the Congress that authority, at least not without a fight. To the CIO, the CCL was no different from any CIO state council; in other words the Canadian Congress of Labour in CIO eyes was no different than for example, the Nevada CIO Labor Council. It was for this reason that the CIO insisted at the founding convention of the World Federation of Trade Unions in London in 1945 that North America should have only one seat on the Executive Board, and that that seat should always be occupied by the United States. Conroy refused to support this measure on the sensible grounds that "no one could represent Canada . . . but Canada." Despite all the blandishments and ruses of the CIO, Conroy refused to budge. As the chief CIO delegate to the conference, Sidney Hillman, described it: "I came to London expecting trouble with the Russians. I have since discovered that I am to have more trouble with Canada, one of the CIO family, than anyone else in the Congress session."[15] Conroy got his way, and Canada was reluctantly given representation on the WFTU executive board.

Sometimes, however, the conflict between the CIO and the CCL took on ludicrous tones. In 1945, for example, when the CIO urged Congress unions in Canada to "communicate to their

14. See, e.g., Conroy to Millard, Jan. 12, 1942, Canadian Labour Congress Archives, Ottawa.
15. *Ibid.*, Memo from Conroy to Mosher, March 18, 1945.

senators their support of Henry Wallace as Secretary of Commerce," Conroy pointedly responded that Canadians had no desire to interfere in American affairs "though the contrary could not be said for some Americans." In 1949, when the CIO urgently wired Conroy that "vigorous action from your state supporting President Truman's fight to win Senate confirmation of Leland Olds to Federal Power Commission" was needed at once, Conroy good-humoredly replied that since Canada had not yet been admitted to the American Union, "it . . . should meanwhile accept and recognize the sovereign status of United States and refrain from promoting Canadian Imperialist tendencies in the internal affairs of the American people." Finally in 1950, after the CIO office had sent a barrage of wires urging the workers in Conroy's "state" to send telegrams and letters to their senators voicing their strong opposition to the policies of the American Congress, Conroy's patience ran out. He informed the CIO that the Canadian Congress of Labour was not a "state federation and could not be treated like one," that the 49th parallel was not simply a state line but an international border, and that after ten years it was "about time" that the CIO realized that Canada could not be treated like an American state. This was something the CIO was extremely slow to accept.[16]

Unfortunately, Conroy's attempts to eliminate the interference of the CIO in Congress affairs failed. After ten fruitless years of effort, Conroy sadly lamented the Congress was now "left without any authority . . . thereby reducing it to the status of a satellite organization." As he complained to a CIO leader:

My personal opinion is that I should resign from office, and let the Congress of Industrial Organizations and its International Unions take over the Congress. I am quite sincere in this, as I have been mulling the thought over for some time. The Congress is supposed to be an autonomous body . . . but . . . in matters of jurisdiction . . . the Congress is left without any authority, thereby reducing it to the status of a satellite organization at the mercy of its affiliated unions. These organizations choose to do whatever they want regardless of Congress

16. *Ibid.*, Haywood to Conroy, Jan. 24, 1945; Oct. 10, 1949; April 10, 1950; Conroy to Haywood, Feb. 1, 1945; Oct. 11, 1949; May 2, 1950.

desires, and in accordance with what their individual benefit may dictate they should do. . . . My own reaction is that I am completely fed up with this situation and within a few weeks it may be that I shall submit my resignation. . . . In short, the Congress is either going to be the authority in its field, or it is not. If it is not to exercise authority, then the more quickly the Executive Council appoints someone to hold a satellite position, the sooner the Congress will know that it is a purely subject instrument, with no authority and a servant of the headquarters of International Unions in the United States. . . . This thought has been running through my mind for the last three or four years, and I have not arrived at it overnight. It is just that as the chief executive officer of the Congress, I am in an untenable position, and I am not going to work in that capacity." [17]

Eventually, in 1952, frustrated beyond endurance, Conroy resigned. With his resignation the last lingering hopes for a purely Canadian autonomous labor organization disappeared. The centralizing efforts of the CIO had triumphed over the nationalist aspirations of the CCL.

It is worth noting, I think, that to most rank and file union members the conflict between national and international unionism was entirely irrelevant. It was amongst the leadership and not the rank and file that this battle was fought. The average union member, as almost all studies of the labor movement have shown, plays an unimportant role in the affairs of his union. Only at times when his own economic well-being is at stake— during strikes and collective bargaining negotiations—does he take more than a passing interest in the activities of his union. This was especially true of the unionist in the 1930's and 1940's when his immediate, and indeed sole concern was to achieve financial security.

American control of their unions did not concern union members as much as higher wages, better working conditions, and job security, all of which seemed dependent on the muscle provided by the American connection. Since most of them were working for American-owned companies, why should they be overly concerned if their unions were also American controlled? This attitude of the Canadian worker, more than anything else,

17. *Ibid.*, Conroy to Millard, April 21, 1950.

allowed the Canadian labor movement to be controlled by foreigners, the only country in the western world where this is the case. In more pointed words, perhaps we have American unions in Canada largely because of the colonial mentality of the Canadian workingman, a mentality, I might add, that was fully shared by the Canadian businessman. At the crucial times in the history of the Canadian labor movement, the Canadian workingman opted for American over Canadian unions, and refused to support Canadian leaders who were attempting to limit American control. In other words, the Canadian workingman has the union movement he deserves: large, powerful, rich, paternal, and American-dominated.

10

Salmagundi in Canada: Washington Irving, James K. Paulding, and Some of Their Contemporaries in Canada

Carl F. Klinck

My purpose in this paper is to provide footnotes to some of the chapters in one of my favorite books, *The World of Washington Irving*, by Van Wyck Brooks.[1] The jacket describes this volume as "the corner-stone" of the author's literary history of the United States, because it covers the important period "between the death of Washington in 1799 and the outbreak of the Mexican war of 1845," which saw "the slow birth of a specifically American literature."

This is also the period in which literary activity in the English language in the Canadas made an effective beginning. Its progress was slow at first, then rapid in Lower Canada after 1820, and in Upper Canada after 1830. The principal writers were travellers or immigrants dispensing information as journalists or imitating English models of gentility. Some of these authors adjusted quickly to the new environment and displayed themes, attitudes, and details patently Canadian; the native-born found it difficult to break out of the domination of British models and techniques. American periodicals were popular, but viewed with suspicion for political reasons.

There has not been enough study of early Canadian-American-English literary relationships to support broad generalizations, but I believe that popular, as well as superior, literature must be

1. London and New York, 1944.

investigated. I shall, to this end, examine a small number of rare books by contemporaries of Washington Irving on the common theme of the manners and culture of growing cities, New York, Quebec and Montreal. This is an exercise in parallel developments: I am attempting to illustrate the possibility of conducting comparative studies in English, Canadian and American literary history at ground level.

Salmagundi was a series of twenty issues of a collection of essays and poems which appeared occasionally in New York between January 24, 1807, and January 25, 1808.[2] The title signified a "hash," a *ragoût*, or, in the more formal language of the *Shorter Oxford English Dictionary*, "a dish composed of chopped meat, anchovies, eggs and onions, with oil and condiments." In literary usage the term signifies a mixture or miscellany. At least three New Yorkers wrote for this publication. Washington Irving was then in his earliest period as an essayist; he had published the *Letters of Jonathan Oldstyle, Gent.* in 1802–1803, and he would publish his comic masterpiece, *A History of New York*, in 1809. His later reputation overshadows that of James K. Paulding, but there are reasons for supposing that the latter may have been the chief contributor to *Salmagundi;* Paulding is said to have signed as the editor, writing from "the Elbow Chair of Launcelot Langstaff, Esq." Years later he would publish a second series of *Salmagundi.*[3] The original trio also included William Irving (a merchant and older brother of Washington) who was married to Paulding's sister. The "club," which they formed in the durable Addisonian coffee-house tradition, was a family affair; the authors met in the publisher's establishment, or in a mansion which they called "Cockloft-Hall."

William Irving was forty-one years of age, and Washington Irving and Paulding were in their gay twenties, but, in order to give the impression of mature wisdom, they caricatured each

2. David Longworth was the publisher. See Jacob Blanck, "Salmagundi and its Publisher," *The Papers of the Bibliographical Society of America*, XLI (1st quarter, 1947), 1–32. See also William L. Hedges, *Washington Irving: An American Study 1802–1832* (Baltimore, 1965).
3. 1819–20.

other, under pseudonyms, as old men: "Launcelot Langstaff, Esq." was "fertile in whim-whams and bachelorisms, but rich in many of the sterling qualities of our nature."[4] "Anthony Evergreen, gent.," "a kind of patriarch in the fashionable world," had seen "generation after generation pass away into the silent tomb of matrimony while he remain[ed] unchangeably the same."[5] "William Wizard, Esq." had resided a long time abroad, "particularly at Canton, Calcutta, and the gay and polished court of Hayti," and also had knowledge of China and the land of the northern American Indians. He was put in charge of "the territory of criticism," although his taste had "attained to such an exquisite pitch of refinement that there [were] few exhibitions of any kind which [did] not put him in a fever."[6]

Caricature of eccentrics—a favorite device of essayists at least since Addison and Steele—was the Salmagundians' principal method of providing amusing, but meaningful, satire. Cockloft-Hall was "a family hive" from which "a redundant swarm" were sent forth "to populate the face of the earth."[7] Christopher Cockloft was still a pre-Revolutionary Tory.[8] Pindar was an old bachelor and "an oddity" who ground out heroic couplets from his poetic "mill" to teach old-fashioned morality to young ladies.[9] The sterility of Tory reactionaries, however charming as antiques, was clearly demonstrated. Through the Cockney character of "Tom Straddle" the Salmagundians made quite clear their dislike of salesmen from Birmingham or Liverpool who acted and wrote as if Americans were barbarians.[10]

Jeremy Cockloft *the younger* was represented as a travel-monger who wrote only sketches of towns near New York. This passage is from "The Stranger at Home; or, A Tour in Broadway":[11]

Bowling Green—fine place for pasturing cows—a perquisite of the late corporation—formerly ornamented with a statue of George the Third—people pulled it down in the war to make bullets—great pity; it might, have been given to the academy—it would have become a

4. Washington Irving, *Salmagundi* (New York, 1883) p. 92. Hereafter cited as *Salmagundi* (1883).
5. *Ibid.*, p. 9.   6. *Ibid.*, p. 10.   7. *Ibid.*, p. 187.   8. *Ibid.*, p. 70–72.
9. *Ibid.*, pp. 24–29.   10. *Ibid.*, pp. 145–150.   11. *Ibid.*, pp. 46, 153.

cellar as well as any other.—Broadway—great difference in the gentility of streets—a man who resides in Pearl street, or Chatham Row, derives no kind of dignity from his domicil; but place him in a certain part of Broadway, anywhere between the Battery and Wall street, and he straightway becomes entitled to figure in the beau monde, and strut as a person of prodigious consequence!— Quere, whether there is a degree of purity in the air of that quarter which changes the gross particles of vulgarity into gems of refinement and polish? A question to be asked, but not to be answered— . . . Wall street—City Hall, famous place for catch-poles, deputy sheriffs, and young lawyers; because they have no business anywhere else.

Many of these essays gave other detailed descriptions of the people and scenes of New York, "this, doubtless, 'best of all possible cities,'" [12] with special emphasis upon "certain whims, eccentricities and unseemly conceits" of fashionable society.[13] The topics were "Theatrics—Containing the Quintessence of Modern Criticism," modern music, ladies dresses and "frippery," "style," "Plans for Defending our Harbor," "The Stranger in New Jersey, or Cockney Travelling," "Greatness," "The Chronicles of the Renowned and Ancient City of Gotham," "The Little Man in Black," and "Tea."

The most vivid presentation of scenes in the city was to be found in letters resembling those of Goldsmith in *The Citizen of the World*. These were attributed to a bewildered foreign observer, "Mustapha Rub-A-Dub Keli Khan," captain of a ship in New York harbor, whose communications addressed to officials back home in Tripoli hilariously described the strange ways of the Americans: their wives, the grand and most puissant bashaw (President Jefferson), a display by the local militia, government by words (a "logocracy"), slang-whangers (editors of newspapers), an attempt to secure a pair of breeches from a government source, an election, public festivals, the follies of women, and social dancing.

Jeremy Cockloft *the younger* was represented as a travelgoing to the South for the winter, enjoyed the fun in *Salmagundi*, although he believed that the authors were not positive enough in the realm of morality to be treated by the same critical laws

12. *Ibid.*, p. 7.   13. *Ibid.*, p. 9.

as British essayists.[14] Between the lines of the miscellany, however, he found clues to the manners of the American people;
in this "rich mine of information," "though it naturally partook
of caricature, the features of society [were rather] heightened
than distorted."[15]

The effect upon Lambert was to arouse a deep and serious
purpose, a moral responsibility to contradict the unfortunate
impression left in Britain by those commercial travellers whom
the *Salmagundians* called Cockneys from Birmingham;[16] his own
observation and reading had convinced him that rich and progressive America was competing with the Old World "in every-
thing that distinguished a civilized people from a nation of
barbarians."[17] His duty clearly was to scold the British for their
prejudices against Americans, people of their own stock. In two
books, therefore, he attempted to make his Old Country readers
"better acquainted with [American] manners than they [had]
hitherto been . . . [and] to conciliate the minds of [his own]
countrymen in favour of a people whose character [had] been
grossly misrepresented."[18] It should be noted that he published
just before and during the War of 1812–1814 between Britain
and the United States.

In 1810, after a year in Lower Canada and a six months'
journey in the eastern states as far south as Savannah, Georgia,
Lambert returned to England, and published in London his
*Travels Through Lower Canada and the United States of North
America in the years 1806, 1807, 1808*, in three volumes divided almost equally between the province of Lower Canada
and the republic.[19] From *Salmagundi* he had drawn material
for a chapter on fashionable life in New York. He described
elegant women, their fine figures, delicate complexions, and
their teeth ("bad teeth, a groundless charge"). Also, concerning
the city, he wrote about education, literature, taste in reading,

14. John Lambert, editor, *Salmagundi, or the Whim-Whams and Opinions of
Launcelot Langstaff, Esq. and Others.* Reprinted from the American edition, with
an Introductory Essay and Explanatory Notes, by John Lambert. (London, 1811),
p. xxxvii. Hereafter cited as Lambert's *Salmagundi.*
15. *Ibid.*, pp. xxxvii–xxxviii.   16. *Salmagundi,* (1883), p. 150.
17. Lambert's *Salmagundi,* p. xxix.   18. *Ibid.*, p. iii.
19. London, 1810. Hereafter cited as *Travels,* (1810).

Salmagundi, The Echo, Barlow's *Columbiad,* dancing, smoking, style of living, splendid marriages, and political parties. Mustapha, the Tripolitan "Captain of a ketch," was quoted with regard to "slang-whangers." *Salmagundi* was employed "as a specimen of American literature." [20]

Since these extracts were admired in England, Lambert published the whole of *Salmagundi* "from the American edition," as a book, in London in 1811, "with an Introductory Essay and Explanatory Notes." He had been in New York six weeks during December, 1807 and January, 1808, when *Salmagundi* was approaching its last issue. The whole of the miscellany was available before he returned to Montreal in May, 1808. The Introduction, fifty pages in length, was a reduced version of the American portion of the *Travels:* "a hasty review of the origin of the American union, and of the present state of the manners, customs and dispositions, of the people in that country." [21] As part of his study of literary progress, he commented upon *The Echo,* Barlow's *Columbiad,* and, with critical acumen and enthusiasm, upon *Salmagundi.*

A generous English review of this book appeared in *The Monthly Review* of August, 1811.[22] The anonymous critic agreed with Lambert (who was not identified) in deploring British and American prejudices against one another, and in recommending Addison's essays, which should tend "to cultivate the taste and improve the morals of a nation." [23] Americanisms and vulgarisms annoyed him. "Autumnal Reflections" was quoted at some length as an admirable example of the Salmagundians' "serious vein": [24]

There is a full and mature luxuriance in the fields, that fills the bosom with generous and disinterested content; it is not the thoughtless extravagance of spring, prodigal only in blossoms, nor the languid voluptuousness of summer, feverish in its enjoyments, and teeming only with immature abundance,—it is that certain fruition of the labours of the past, that prospect of comfortable realities, which those will be sure to enjoy who have improved the bounteous smiles of heaven, nor

20. Lambert's *Salmagundi*, p. ii.   21. *Ibid.,* p. ix.
22. *The Monthly Review* (Aug., 1811), pp. 418–423.
23. *Ibid.,* pp. 422–423.   24. *Ibid.,* p. 423.

wasted away their spring and summer in empty trifling or criminal in-
dulgence.

Does such over-writing, although praised by an Englishman,
not seem to be an American realist's burlesque of genteel essay-
English? If not, was even Launcelot Langstaff seriously dominated by some English models of literary prose? Lambert's rap-
prochment between the English and the Americans had evidently
not extended to understanding of one another's humor!

Lambert's concern with American affairs should not be seen
as neglect of Lower Canada. He had come to that province with
the intention of making a living there. His uncle had a farm at
Bécancour, across the St. Lawrence from Three Rivers, where
he was fulfilling his agreement with the British Government
to undertake the culture of hemp so that Great Britain might
become "independent of the northern powers for her supplies."[25]
Lambert served as his uncle's assistant. No other clue to this
young man's identity has been found, except a reference in the
Travels to the fact that he had been a school-fellow of Colonel
John By,[26] who was commissioned at the Royal Military Academy,
Woolwich, in 1799. If they were nearly the same age, it may
be assumed that Lambert was born about 1781 and was about
twenty-five years of age when he came to Canada in 1806.
"Lower Canada," he wrote, "seemed to be as little known to
the people of England, as the deserts of Siberia. . . . I therefore availed myself of this favourable opportunity to collect
information and to make myself acquainted with the present
state of Canada."[27] Lambert consulted such books as Peter
Kalm's *Travels into North America* (1753–1761; in English,
1770–1772) and Isaac Weld, Jr.'s *Travels Through the States
of North America, and the Provinces of Upper and Lower
Canada, during the Years, 1795, 1796, and 1797,* but he felt
that a new comprehensive survey of "the present state" would
be a valuable contribution:[28]

25. *Travels* (1810), pp. xiv, 443–452.
26. *Travels,* I, 2nd edition, corrected and improved (London, Edinburgh,
Dublin, 1814), 331. Hereafter cited as *Travels* (1814).
27. *Ibid.,* p. xviii.   28. *Ibid.,* pp. xviii–xix.

Every thing was of an interesting nature; for though the province belonged to the British Government, yet the majority of the people were
totally different from those whom I had been accustomed to see; their
manners, customs, language, and religion were all new to me; and I
found myself at once upon a strange soil, and among a foreign people.

One receives the impression that Lambert rendered his services to his uncle chiefly at Quebec City, for the information
gathered there was reported in six-sevenths of the Canadian
portion of the *Travels*. Three Rivers was given more attention
than Montreal, whose streets he found "extremely heavy and
gloomy" because the buildings were "ponderous masses of stone,
erected with very little taste and less judgement." [29]

The sixteenth chapter of the *Travels* is a much-prized early
analysis of "the state of literature, the arts, and sciences" in
Quebec in 1806, 1807 and 1808. Lambert felt obliged to admit
that these [30] "can scarcely be said to be at a low ebb, because they were never known to flow; and, from what I have
mentioned concerning the defects in education which exist in
the colony, it is not likely that they will, in our time at least,
rise much above their present level." He knew, of course, that
he was making a general statement, to which an old country
group of English officers and government officials and some of
the remaining upper-class French formed an exception with
respect to education.

The circulation of Lambert's *Travels* in his own day was
reduced because it "had scarcely been published two months
when one half of the edition was destroyed by a conflagration
at the printer's, and, ere [he] could receive the whole of the
money for the copy-right, [his] publisher became a bankrupt." [31]
The second edition, in two volumes, did not appear until 1814,
an inauspicious time when hatred and bitterness had increased
on both sides of the Atlantic because of the War of 1812–1814.
One can imagine prospective emigrants from the British Isles,
during the next decade or two, balancing the two portions of
the *Travels* and debating whether to settle in British Canada
or in the republican United States. Cultural comparisons con-

29. *Ibid.*, p. 516.　　30. *Ibid.*, p. 318.　　31. Lambert's *Salmagundi*, p. ii.

stituted one of the distinctions of Lambert's exposition and style. He preferred English ways, but he had "acknowledged and admired the *easy independence and happiness* of the Canadians, the *rising prosperity and freedom* of the Americans." [32] His book, being somewhat unfavorable to the French in Lower Canada, probably encouraged some of the British to venture into Upper Canada (now Ontario), the territory along the Great Lakes. The emigrants who possessed copies had, almost certainly, purchased them before boarding ship.

There is some mystery about *Cursory Observations Made in Quebec, Province of Lower Canada, in the Year 1811*, a separate booklet published in Bermuda; it was an urbane travel-essay [33] which bore an extraordinary resemblance to the account of Quebec given by Lambert in his *Travels*. The title-page, however, ascribed authorship to "Jeremy Cockloft the Elder, Esq., M.A.P.C." The pseudonym had evidently come into use as a generic name for a travel-writer. The author may have been Edmund Ward, a native of Nova Scotia, born in Halifax in 1787, who was government printer in Bermuda from 1809 until 1816. The identity of the author was made an intriguing problem by Salmagundian clues such as the pseudonym of Jeremy Cockloft *the Elder* (not Jeremy *the younger* who lived at Cockloft-Hall),[34] and the author's claim to have come "from the right horn of the Moon" ("Cockney-Travelling" in *Salmagundi* had opened with the words, "The man in the moon").[35] And the author of the *Cursory Observations* had hastened to explain that he was not (what the Salmagundians disliked) a salesman from Birmingham or Liverpool;[36] he was "no retailer,—except of a few extraneous ideas." [37]

Ward, if it was the Bermudian printer, may have found Quebec City lagging behind Halifax with regard to English culture. He agreed with Lambert: [38]

32. *Travels*, I (1814), xxiv.   33. No date of publication.
34. *Salmagundi* (1883), p. 44.   35. *Ibid.*, p. 46.   36. *Ibid.*, p. 150.
37. *Cursory Observations*, with a Preface by William Toye (Toronto, 1960), p. 38.
38. *Ibid.*, 30, 35.

The liberal arts either have been frozen in some severe winter, have deserted to a more congenial climate, or perhaps never visited the place. . . . Of the literature of Quebec I have seen but little, indeed nothing; except a few newspaper lucubrations, government proclamations, and obscure advertisements; . . .

The author's summary about Quebec City contained these lines: [39]

that the Theatre would be most enticing, if the building was convenient, and supplied with performers, dresses and scenery;—that the balls, assemblies and tea-parties, would be permanent amusements, and elegant recreations—*if* divested of ill-nature, envy, a struggle for procedure, gambling, and scandal;—that the *nunneries* of St. Roche's and St. John's might be useful, if the monks were more decorous in their devotions;—that the merchants would be all very honest and respected, if they acted as they ought to do;—that the crimps are incurable, and must continue so, whilst the police slumbers on its post;—that Stiles, the Yankey inn-keeper at St. John's Gate, would be a good subject, and an honest man, if he did not sacrifice so often at the shrine of Moloch; that he keeps good horses and carriages, if the former were well fed, and the latter in good repair;—that it wants only a few trifling things to make Quebec the Paradise of the Earth;— to wit; clean lodgings, honest undertakings, the abolition of scandal and backbiting, the introduction of rational amusements, an abhorrence of hypocricy, a milder climate, more industry in agricultural pursuits, and a more general urbanity towards strangers.

In the "slow-birth" of a specifically Canadian literature, travel books had a significant place. During the early years of the 19th century, when publicaton in the Canadas was largely confined to a few gazettes and newspapers, books had to be imported from Great Britain or the United States. Travel books —especially those written with accuracy, judgment, wit, and anecdotal finesse—vied with Addisonian essays for a position of respectability and moral approval half-way up the ladder toward creative literature.

A rather liberal view of what constituted general literature prevailed in Britain during the period which we are considering. The principal contents of the great new British literary

39. *Ibid.*, 40–41.

journals were not *belles lettres*, but rather essays and reviews, whether original articles or extensive quotations from current books. The situation may be understood if one looks through a file of the *Edinburgh Review* (established in 1802), *The Quarterly Review* (established in 1809), *The New Monthly Magazine* (established in 1814), or *Blackwood's Edinburgh Magazine* (established in 1817). In the United States the *North American Review* was founded in 1815. Two of the short-lived literary journals in Lower Canada, *The Canadian Magazine and Literary Repository* (1823–1825) and *The Canadian Review and Literary and Historical Journal* (1824–1826) would also serve as examples.

The next step, after descriptions, anecdotes and character sketches, might have been creative narrative, but a flood of cheap romances from abroad provided discouraging models, and the tale or short story was quite rare until after 1825, when maiden aunts could accept little gems of fiction in gift-books and annuals to be placed on their parlor tables. Sir Walter Scott and James Fenimore Cooper had not yet become famous in 1810, when Lambert in his *Travels* expressed regret that "novels and romances [were] most in request among the Canadian ladies, as they indeed [were] among the ladies of Europe." His objections were not only literary: he feared that the gentle hearts of these readers were in danger of being "influenced by voluptuous descriptions, revolutionary tenets, or impious dogmas."[40]

Imports were also opposed for nationalistic reasons in James Kirke Paulding's essay on "National Literature," as late as 1819–1820, when he published his own second series of *Salmagundi;* he called for native writing with an American sense of decency and morality.[41] Conservatives in Lower Canada held comparable views with "provincial" substituted for "American." There was a demand for stories that were "true." "Real life is fraught with adventures," Paulding wrote, "to which the wildest fictions scarcely afford a parallel."[42] A few years later,

40. *Travels*, I (1814), 325–326.
41. James Kirke Paulding, "National Literature," *Salmagundi*, 2nd series (Aug. 19, 1820).
42. *Op. cit.*

Samuel Hull Wilcocke, a Canadian reviewer, was bored by *Saint Ursula's Convent,* a romance by a Frederiction girl, and wished that the author had written a novel of the true story of six Canadian nuns from Sandwich, in Upper Canada, who were captured by pirates off Cuba, retaken by a British cruiser, and forwarded to New Orleans by an American vessel! [43]

As an alternative to the novel, the romance, or the short story, there were still the anecdote and the sketch. These traditional forms were related to fiction, on the one hand, and, on the other, to 18th-century creative descriptions of "real" life and experience. The British of Quebec—the military, the merchants, the fur-traders, and the social leaders—left literary activity largely to the journalists, who became the guardians of a tradition congenial to their profession and who were accustomed to make reports about human subjects. The persistence of a taste for such realism of human interest was natural and relevant.

As British news became more remote and impersonal, and as provincial affairs became more immediate and absorbing, improvisations grew out of the new situations. Such variations did not involve a "cultural lag"—that is, rejection of the rising English masters of romanticism—but rather positive cultural adjustment to local experience. Should they have been using natural scenery to image their disturbed psyches? Where scenery was so overwhelming, the survival of colonial man was more urgent, and a better subject for literature. His inner life demanded expression in action and interaction with other men. The first period of literature in Lower Canada was, therefore, realistic—British North American (that is to say, Canadian) in content and reference.

In the hands of journalists, this early writing was timely and urbane; it was not, as many Canadians still believe, reminiscent and tearful, about exiled wives condemned to live in shacks among stumpy fields while they dreamt of home. The journalists of the 1820's were centered in Montreal, a progressive city

43. *The Scribbler,* V, No. 125 (July 8, 1824), 234.

strategically placed where the Lake Champlain route from New York met the St. Lawrence route from Britain. Many new-comers accustomed to city life stopped here rather than pro-ceeding to less-settled Upper Canada. Their literary needs were met more easily from New York than from London.

Montreal reacted against the competition of American maga-zines, which had gained many subscribers in Lower Canada, "owing to their low price and facility of circulation." [44] Between 1821 and 1826 the city had at least three literary journals edited by old country immigrants, Samuel Hull Wilcocke from England, and David Chisholme and Dr. A. J. Christie from Scotland. Wilcocke's *Scribbler* was the first and had a longer run than *The Canadian Magazine* (1823–1825) edited by Chisholme and Christie or *The Canadian Review* (1824–1826) edited by Chisholme alone. The *Scribbler* was a notorious suc-cess because it mixed scandalmongering with literature; the Scots who attempted to produce colonial rivals to the popular *Blackwood's Edinburgh Magazine* elevated the tone of literary activity and soon failed, while *The Scribbler* went on its erratic way until 1827.

Wilcocke's model for *The Scribbler* may have been *The Monthly Mirror,* which had printed some of his contributions while he had lived in Liverpool. The subtitle of his own publica-tion was "a series of weekly essays published in Montreal, L.C. on Literary, Critical, Satirical, Moral and Local Subjects. Inter-spersed with Pieces of Poetry. By Lewis Luke MacCulloch, Esquire." The pseudonym referred to Wilcocke, who was also proprietor and principal author. He began with editorial essays of high calibre, more Johnsonian than Addisonian, because they were stern and dictatorial. Comparison between his miscellany and *Salmagundi* suggests that these two productions had an English ancestry proceeding from *The Spectator* by different, or parallel, lines. Both had been affected by newspapers, but the Salmagundians could afford to be genteel amateurs, at liberty to write feature articles and to "solicit no patronage," while

44. Quoted from "a Quebec paper" by *The Canadian Review,* II, No. 4 (Feb., 1826), 495–496.

Wilcocke, under stern necessity, had to work in the market-place, to amuse, to admonish, to raise subscribers from a non-literary level, and to keep their patronage for a literary journal by methods adjusted to the lowest newspaper practice. His amazing erudition, scholarship, public spirit, and idealism were tainted by the deliberate coarseness and irresponsibility of his satire and by his own subjective opportunism. He knew about "slang-whangers" from experience of politics in Liverpool, and fitted all too quickly into the scandalous behavior which Lambert had earlier observed in Lower Canadian society: [45] "Scandal was the order of the day; and calumny, misrepresentation, and envy seemed to have erected their standards among the greater portion of the inhabitants. The weekly papers teemed with abusive scurrility and malicious insinuations."

Wilcocke's satire was harsh and arbitrary in comparison with the mild Salmagundian characterization of those who differed from the norm in amiable eccentricities; his consisted rather of personal attacks upon those who were pretentious, vicious or morally reprehensible—or could be alleged to be so. His censure frequently took the form of capsule caricatures: nicknames were employed in gross fictions. The gossipy city easily made identifications, especially of the North-Westers, who "had been subject," Lambert reported in his *Travels*, "to the jealous and malignant observations even of those who [had] partaken of their hospitality." [46] The long list of *The Scribbler's* nicknames for the North-Westers, the officers of the Crown and the courts, the rich, the proud, the fashionable, the foolish, the flirtatious and the promiscuous still remains without a gloss. Anyone who can identify the originals will have an incomparable, if distorted, record of Montreal society of the 1820's. Who was Sir Frederick Brute, Dr. Chopit, Col. Dash-it-All, Mrs. Dripping, Dr. Drugwell, Lord Goddamnhim, Hon. Tory Loverule, Lord *Privy* Seal, or Spasm?

These exercises would seem juvenile, if they had not been so deadly in the context. One of the contributors who called him-

45. *Travels*, I (1814), 293.   46. *Ibid.*, p. 295.

self "The Amateur of Fashion" sent in an account of the Pic-Nic
dinner of the Driving-club at a small tavern about two miles
from Montreal. Military men and government officers were the
principal members. According to custom each guest brought
. . . "a good substantial eatable": [47]

The president exhibited a fine *Hunch* of venison, which, though lean,
had fair pretensions to the excellence of high flavour. The vice's *goose*
was very good of its kind, but it was remarked that it was not well
dressed, and wanted what, in culinary language, is termed polish.
The Loverule family sent a large *Turkey Cock:* this fine bird, the
emblem of pride and stupidity, was well worthy of being considered
a family dish. Mr. Nosy's *sheepshead,* dressed *a la blankette* was excellent; many of the ladies remarked that it looked quite dying. A
dish of *Cockscombs, en papillotte,* a joint contribution from the principal dandy-members was highly relished. General admiration was
excited by the Count Oldjoseph's *Calfshead without brains* quite *au
naturel:* it was considered the largest that was ever seen in Montreal,
and with the Countesses *highly pickled tongue,* pronounced a truly
Epicurean treat. Mr. McRobem McKillem McSlaughterem sent a pan
of *Kail Brose* accompanied with a handsome apology for such homely
fare, and an expression of his extreme regret that he could not fulfil
his intention of presenting the company with a *beaver's tail* dressed in
the Indian style, for that owing to recent events, which he would
never cease to deplore, he had been obliged to break up his grand
culinary establishment. A fine *Trifle,* highly admired by the ladies was
easily recognized as the contribution *en masse* of the military members.

Count Oldjoseph was probably a nickname for the Earl of Dalhousie, the governor-in-chief of British North America, who,
later (in 1824) founded the Literary and Historical Society of
Quebec.

Wilcocke had been a merchant, or an employee of a merchant,
in Liverpool from about 1797 until 1817. There is no record of
a meeting with Irving, who came to that same city in 1815.
Wilcocke was evidently of a different rank in society, although
he was a publishing littérateur, a lexicographer, poet, historian,
translator and geographer. The North-West Company had
brought him out to Canada in 1817 to serve as a public relations

47. *The Scribbler,* I, No. 29 (Jan. 10, 1822), 227–230.

man in Montreal while their violent dispute with Lord Selkirk raged about his colony on the Red River. Four of the principal pamphlets and books on the side of the Company were written by Wilcocke.[48]

When the North-West fur-traders were taken over by the Hudson's Bay Company, Wilcocke fell out of favor and was charged with embezzlement of valuable property. He escaped to Burlington, Vermont, but was seized there by strong-arm agents of the Company, brought back to Montreal, jailed for a year, acquitted, jailed again on an indefinite charge of debt, and released after ten months when officials of the United States government would no longer tolerate his illegal removal from its territory. He was freed, but forced to live in exile. *The Scribbler* was begun in prison to make money and win sympathy. It was continued while he lived across the American line at Burlington, Rouse's Point (1823–1825), and Plattsburg (1825–1827). His acknowledged mistress, Louisa A., acted as an agent, a reporter, and a messenger. The story of their sorrows is told in a thinly-disguised fiction entitled "Letters from Pulo Penang."[49]

The true value of *The Scribbler* lies in Wilcocke's initiation of Canadian literary journalism; the encouragement given in book reviews to new authors during the first period of such activity in Lower Canada; and his journal's vivid representation of the life of his chosen provincial city. He appeared at times as the sole author of a week's essays, and at other times as an editor overwhelmed by contributions from the amateurs, many of them young students-at-law, who responded to his invitation to indulge in conventional literary exercises or in uninhibited writing about local gossip. "You have, by example, taught us," one of his correspondents wrote, "that *gossiping* is no scandal, provided

---

48. *A Narrative of Occurrences in the Indian Countries of North America* (1817); *Report of the Trials of Charles de Reinhard and Archibald McLellan for Murder* . . . *Quebec* (1818); *Report of the Proceedings* . . . *at the Assizes Held in York* (1818); *Report of Proceedings* . . . *held* . . . *at Quebec* (1819); and the article on Benjamin Frobisher in L. R. Masson, *Les Bourgois de la Companie du Nord Ouest* (1889).

49. "Letters from Pulo Penang," *The Scribbler*, beginning I, 154, 177, 201, 235, 265, 389; II, 20, 346; III, 218.

it's all true." [50] This was the very stuff of literature, although applied as mischievously as Pope or Byron had done. The contributors were being encouraged to find material in *human* affairs, to search out motives by keeping their eyes on the actions of people. Honestly applied, the method held more promise for the future than rhapsodies about natural scenery could ever have done. So Wilcocke has a niche in Canadian literary history by pointing the way to independence through local and personal realism, even in fiction; romanticism, by contrast, was an exotic from abroad.

The Scribbler reached its highest level of local color in the fourth volume. Among the topics were the "Charrivari," the night-time riot in McGill Street; an elegant girl shopping at the Old Market, Humhaw & Co.'s bright stores, and others in St. Paul, Notre Dame and St. Joseph streets; the conversation of two St. Regis Indians at a public house near Chateauguay; domestic disputes; the Museum of Mount Royal; matrimonial and amatory intelligence; parties and fetes among the notables of Mount Royal; boxing matches; a muster of the militia; fashionable arrivals and departures; proposals for a Fire-society; the first hackney coach in the city; theatrical performances; musical concerts; foreign paintings; races; fairs; fencing; the Montreal General Hospital.

In a much more formal and conventional way, David Chisholme was providing a stimulus to native writers by mingling good foreign examples of historical and literary value with original contributions. His first volume of *The Canadian Magazine* (July, 1923) contained "original" articles on a proposal for "a well-regulated English Theatre in Montreal"; the Montreal Curling Club; the Quebec Literary and Historical Society; a biographical sketch of the late Alexander Henry (the fur-trader); and the Lachine Canal. There was also a review of *The Widow of the Rock* (1824) by Margaret Blennerhasset, who was living in exile in Montreal with her husband, Harmon Blennerhasset, both victims of Aaron Burr's wild expedition to conquer Mexico.

50. *Ibid.*, V, No. 121 (May 13, 1824), 123.

When Chisholme founded *The Canadian Review* in 1824, his first volume made an even better "Canadian" showing, with original articles on the settlement of the townships of Lower Canada; the education and duties of a Canadian merchant; the wars of Canada; a history of the aborigines of Canada; a brief account of the fur-trade of the North-West Company; a review of John Howison's *Sketches of Upper Canada*; and a review of Julia Beckwith Hart's *Saint Ursula's Convent* (1824), one of the first romances published in British North America.

Chisholme's chief "discovery" in his two journals was a contributor of "original" verse who was as "Canadian" as his devotion to Byron's poems would permit him to be. In Chisholme's *Magazine* and *Review*, this versifier, whom I have identified as Levi Adams, a young native-born Montreal Lawyer,[51] published "The Fall of Constantinople," "Ode to Spain," "Ode on Death and the Pale Horse," "Elegy on the Death of Lord Byron," and "Tecumthé." All of these reappeared, along with other poems, in an anonymous volume, *Tales of Chivalry and Romance*, certainly by the same author, published in Edinburgh in 1826.[52] The date of this volume gives it priority among collections of verse published abroad by a native of the Canadas. The long poem on Tecumseh showed Adams turning to Canadian subject matter.[53] Two small booklets, published in Montreal, may also be ascribed to him: *The Charivari or Canadian Poetics*,[54] and *Jean Baptiste*.[55] These are local-color poems, and both are about elderly bachelors, a favourite subject for character sketches. Here the bachelors, their brides, and their relatives are French-Canadians.

51. "The Charivari and Levi Adams," *Dalhousie Review*, XL (Spring, 1960), 34–42.

52. [Anon.], *Tales of Chivalry and Romance* (Edinburgh and London, 1826).

53. "Tecumthé," *ibid.*, pp. 75–178.

54. *The Charivari: or Canadian Poetics: A Tale After the Manner of Beppo* (Montreal, 1824). *The Canadian Magazine*, II (April, 1824), 378, attributes the book to Launcelot Longstaff. *The Scribbler*, V (May 27, 1824), 141–146, names the publisher, Jos. Nickless, and attributes the poem to Launcelot Longstaff, because the advertisements had used this name. Both spelled Longstaff with an o. *The Scribbler* said that "rumour has given this little piece to a gentleman of the Staff corps."

55. Levi Adams, *Jean Baptiste: A Poetic Olio, in Two Cantos*, (Montreal, 1825).

The stanza which I quote has been selected for its content rather than for any literary merit: [56]

> Now, good Baptisto, was an Epicure,
> And lik'd good living, such as soups and sauces
> Ragouts, and curries, —but could not endure
> Your meats plain boil'd and roasted; —his applauses
> Ran on made dishes, and no sinecure
> Did his cook have, amidst the doubts and pauses
> Of how to please the taste of one, who never
> Knew how to suit, the cravings of the liver.

The Canadian Magazine, edited by David Chisholme, an old world Scot, attributed *The Charivari* to "Launcelot Longstaff" (a likely-enough error in spelling). Samuel Hull Wilcocke, an old world Englishman, unable to resist a pun on "long" and "staff," deduced that "Longstaff" was a pseudonym for "a gentleman of the staff corps, to whose name the assumed appellation seems to have been made to assimilate." Here indeed was a "salmagundi," a *ragoût:* a tale about a French-Canadian folk-custom, told in colloquial English, written (very likely) by a native of Lower Canada, modelled upon Lord Byron's *Beppo,* attributed to a British officer, and bearing the American label of Irving or Paulding.

To present such a mixture is very nearly to define an English Canadian, or at least to reveal eclecticism as a significant characteristic of English-Canadian literature, both then and now. One might even venture to say,

Châcun a son ragoût.

---

56. "The Charivari, or Canadian Poetics," *The Canadian Review and Literary and Historical Journal,* I (July, 1824), 189. See also pp. 183–202.

11

The Americanization of French in Windsor

Alexander Hull

The French speakers in the city of Windsor and Essex Couny, Ontario, form an enclave separated by a distance of some 500 miles from the nearest French-speaking areas in Eastern Ontario and Québec.[1] The colony dates from 1701, but received many immigrants from Québec and Northern Ontario during the 19th and 20th centuries. Partially cut off from the modernizing trends taking place in Québec, these people have maintained in their language many older French-Canadian dialect features, but above all they have been subjected to an intense process of Anglicization which, in view of the preponderant influence of Detroit speech in the Windsor area, it is not improper to refer to here as Americanization. Since they constitute today only slightly over one tenth of the population of Essex County,[2] their numbers are insufficient to sustain the use of French to any significant degree outside the home and church. With increasing urbanization and resulting population mixtures, which tend to break up the formerly homogeneous French groups in certain suburbs and small towns, the pressure to use English increases yearly.

1. For details on the history and background of the Windsor French, see Alexander Hull, "The Franco-Canadian Dialect of Windsor, Ontario: A Preliminary Study," *Orbis*, V (1956), 35–60.
2. In Essex County, out of a total population of 258,218, there were 27,789 persons who declared their mother tongue to be French in the 1961 census. These represent about half of the 55,337 who declared themselves to be ethnically French. A figure of 31,580 persons who can speak both English and French suggests the low incidence of bilingualism among persons whose mother tongue is English.

Almost all the Windsor French are bilingual,[3] and have had most of their education in English. The result is that their speech is often incomprehensible to a monolingual French Canadian from Québec. They are cut off from the French-Canadian homeland in the St. Lawrence Valley by a psychological barrier as effective as the physical distance, and similar to that experienced by the Franco-Americans of New England when they travel to Canada. Many tales are told of frustrations experienced in the attempt to communicate with monolingual natives of Québec. A Windsor traveller who wanted a French-Canadian waitress to bring him an ash tray and said, as he would naturally have done at home, "Donnez-moi un ash-tray, s'il vous plaît," received only a bewildered stare as an answer. He had never heard the word "cendrier." A boy who rather unwisely took a job in a local firm which required him to answer letters written in French soon discovered he could neither understand them nor write an acceptable answer. Of course, similar problems occur in other parts of Canada wherever bilingualism is prevalent, and a certain degree of Anglicization or Americanization is characteristic of all Canadian French.[4] Enclaves such as the Windsor area are much more vulnerable, however, because of the lack of such corrective factors as French-language radio and television, all-French schools, and solidly French neighborhoods.

When two languages come into contact in an intimate way, due to widespread bilingualism, some type of "interference" is likely to occur, affecting usage in one or both systems.[5] In such situations, one language is usually "dominant": that is, in some

3. Only 2,081 persons in 1961 declared they spoke French but no English. These must be mainly from the 4,822 residents of Essex County who were born in Québec.

4. See most recently Gaston Dulong, "L'Anglicisme au Canada français: Étude historique," in Jean-Denis Gendron and Georges Straka (eds.), *Études de linguistique franco-canadienne* (Québec, 1967), pp. 9–14. Dulong stresses the importance of the temporary emigration to the United States of young men from Québec families, who would return to Canada after working for some years in the textile mills in New England, bringing back with them American habits and Americanisms of speech.

5. The standard treatment of the subject is Uriel Weinreich, *Languages in Contact* (The Hague, 1964). See also Einar Haugen, *The Norwegian Language in America,* 2nd edition (Bloomington, 1969).

sense psychologically more important to the bilingual person than is the other language. This may reflect various sociological factors: relative numbers of speakers of the two languages in the area; relative social status; and many less tangible value judgments concerning the speakers of each tongue, their personality, and their worth as human beings.[6] In the case of Windsor, all these factors combine to ensure the absolute dominance of English. This means, first, that English speakers will not learn French willingly nor easily, and therefore that only those of French native tongue will be bilingual. It will be important for such a bilingual speaker to maintain his English as free as possible from any French influence, whereas there is virtually no block in the other direction. In Québec, of course, English has also been dominant, but by no means as strongly so (except in the Montreal area), and current nationalistic feeling there reflects in part a struggle to reverse the psychological dominance status of the two languages.

The first type of interference which may be expected in such a situation is phonetic. The sound system of the dominant language may affect the system of the subordinate one in various ways, usually subtle and hard to detect. Often such influences occur at weak points in the language structure, where changes might in any case have taken place in the natural course of events, and it is difficult or impossible to prove that they are really due to bilingual factors. American English and Standard French[7] are far apart phonetically, both in general traits and in specific features. Standard French is a tense language, in

6. For some fascinating insights into the way English and French speakers in Montreal view each other and themselves, see W. E. Lambert, *et al.*, "Evaluational Reactions to Spoken Languages," *Journal of Abnormal and Social Psychology,* LX (1960), 44–51. Here both English and French young people rated speakers of English (as heard on a tape) superior to speakers of (Canadian) French in such traits as height, good looks, intelligence, dependability, ambition, and character. This type of stereotyped value judgment has a direct effect on language behavior. Note that a person speaking with a European French accent was judged quite differently.

7. The term "Standard French" is here used as in Pierre R. Léon, *Prononciation du français standard* (Paris, 1966), to refer to a norm of usage in France which reflects the habits of educated Frenchmen throughout France, permitting a certain amount of leeway for regional and social variants. Not all Frenchmen speak "Standard French," needless to say.

which each phonetic element present in the surface structure is clearly and precisely enunciated, there are few overlappings between successive phonemes, few assimilations, no diphthongization of vowels, no aspiration of consonants, no reduction of unstressed vowels, full release of final consonants, full voicing of voiced consonants, no tendency to voice voiceless consonants in intervocalic position, and generally weak and predictable stress. American English, a very lax language in this respect, is at the opposite extreme on almost all the above points. It would therefore be tempting to ascribe the relative laxness of Canadian French[8] to English influence. But this is almost certainly not the case: a similar laxness is normal in many patois spoken today in northern and western France,[9] inherited from late medieval French, and it is certain that the western regional or maritime French of the 17th and 18th centuries, from which Canadian French originated, possessed in essence most of the phonetic traits which distinguish Canadian speech today from that of France.[10] At most, one can speculate that English influence may have contributed to the preservation of these features, and may constitute an additional barrier to the adoption of a more standardized pronunciation.

One or two features of Windsor French, however, are certainly of American English origin. One of the most interesting is the tendency to introduce a [j]-glide[11] in such words as *nous* 'we,' pronounced [nʲu] or *soue* 'pigpen' [sʲu]. (This is apparently confined to younger, more urbanized speakers, and is clearly of recent origin.) Paradoxically, this feature is due

8. See Jean-Denis Gendron, *Tendances phonétiques du français parlé au Canada* (Québec, 1966). Gendron is measuring urban upper-class speech, however, and country speech, as he himself admits, may be much laxer than the variety he describes.
9. See, for example, Lars-Owe Swenson, *Les Parlers du Marais Vendéen* (Göteborg, 1959).
10. See Alexander Hull, "The Origins of New World French Phonology," *Word*, XXIV (1968): 255–269.
11. The phonetic transcription used here is basically that of the International Phonetic Alphabet. Hence, [j] = *y* in English *you;* [y] = *u* in French *vue.* A colon [:] is used for vowel length, where this is distinctive. Special signs include [ɹ] for the American retroflexed *r* ([r] is an apical trilled *r*) and [å] for a low back rounded vowel, similar to *aw* in English *law.* The open *o* [ɔ] in Windsor is fronted and weakly rounded, often tending to fall together with [a]. [i] is a high central unrounded vowel. Small capitals ([ɪ], etc.) are used for open, lax varieties of the high vowels.

to a kind of hypercorrection: upper-class Canadian-English speech generally makes a careful distinction between such words as *do* and *due;* most American English does not, pronouncing both as [duʷ] or [dɪ]ʷ. In the attempt to imitate prestige speakers, however, many Canadians (and Americans) "correct" both to [dʲuʷ]. This socially significant feature may be transferred to the French dialect also. Beyond this, final vowels in Windsor seem more lax than in Québec and diphthongize more commonly. A tendency to aspirate certain stop consonants can be noted. Otherwise, it is impossible to point with certainty to any English influence on the phonology of Windsor French: the fact that the word *chaîne*, for example, is pronounced there [ʃɛjn], and hence sounds to the ear in some ways more similar to English *chain* than to Standard French [ʃɛn] is largely, if not entirely, a coincidence.

Grammatical and syntactic interference is another possibility in bilingual situations. Although the morphology of most languages seems relatively resistant to outside influences (except that it may break down completely under sufficiently strong pressure, as happened to the Anglo-Saxon declensional system, for example, under Norman-French domination), syntax (word order, tense usage, and the like) is much more vulnerable. But here again caution must be expressed. For instance, Windsor French distinguishes (along with much of Canada) between *je parle,* corresponding roughly to the English simple verb 'I speak', and *je suis après parler,* equivalent to the progressive 'I am speaking'. The latter form does not occur in Standard French, where *je suis en train de parler* exists, but is relatively infrequent. This is a deviation from Standard French striking enough to have received considerable notice, and one Windsor French speaker, who had had more contacts with other varieties of French than had most of his fellows, was quite positive that it derived from an Irish source ("I'm after doing something"). In fact, the construction was common in regional western French in the 18th century, where it was used in much the same way as in Canada today.[12]

12. Haitian Creole shows reflexes of this construction also.

Several syntactical features of the dialect may be ascribed none the less to English influence, with a fair degree of probability. One is the use of *aller* plus infinitive not only for the future but for a habitual present, where it corresponds to a use of English "will": *ils vont toujours dire ça* 'they'll always say that'. Asked for the name of some older agricultural implements, an informant shrugged his shoulders and replied, *Par icitte ils vont user des tracteurs* 'Around here they (always) use tractors'. The passive voice is used much more frequently than in Standard French: *Le sarrasin est usé pour les crêpes* 'Buckwheat is used for pancakes'. English verb-plus-particle constructions are imitated, using either native words or borrowed English forms: *Je vais sortir dehors* 'I'm going to go out'; *J'y ai jeté des roches back* 'I threw some stones back at them'.[13] Verbs are constructed with nonstandard prepositions, in imitation of the English model: *dépendre sur quelqu'un* 'to depend on someone' (standard *compter sur* or *dépendre de*); *écouter à quelqu'un* 'to listen to someone' (standard *écouter quelqu'un*); *jouer une game* 'to play a game' (standard *jouer à un jeu*); *je reste sur la Wyandotte* 'I live on Wyandotte St.' (standard *j'habite rue W.* or *dans la rue W.*). But the total of such cases is not as great as might be expected, and it is remarkable that Canadian French in general has shown itself to be relatively resistant to such influences from English. It is here, above all, at the core of the language structure, that we discover the results of the pressure for *survivance,* for the maintenance of French identity, which has characterized the French of North America.

However, when we reach the next category of linguistic interference, we find quite another situation. This is the area which can be roughly labeled "lexical" or "semantic," and involves shifts in the meaning and use of individual words and idioms. Here the influence of English on Windsor French becomes deep and all-pervasive. The following categories can be drawn up: borrowing of individual words; shift of meaning of native words in accordance with the semantic pattern of the English language;

---

13. See text 2, below.

and loan translations, in which a compound word, expression or idiom is translated literally into French.

The most obvious result of Anglicization of the dialect is the use of English words in place of French ones. The borrowing of English lexical items has been continuous in Canadian French since the English conquest, and many words are by now so thoroughly integrated into the language as to be barely recognizable as English. Examples are: *buggy* [bɔje]; *steam* [stᵉɪm], *wagon* [wå:gɪn]. [14] Words of this type are common to all Canadian dialects, and are not especially characteristic of Windsor; they date from a time before bilingualism was usual. Some other examples are: *driver* [dravœ:r], *factory* [faktəri], *frame* [frɛm], *crow-bar* (reinterpreted as *gros-barre*) [grobå:r], *grocery* (*grosserie*) [gro:sri], *log* [lɔg],*peppermint* [papərman], *pudding* [putᵉɪn], *shed* [ʃɛd], *shop* [ʃɔp], *sleigh* [sle], *slush* [slɔʃ], *sulky* [sɛlkʲe], *team* [tᵉɪm], *yeast* [jɪs], *sink* [zɪŋk], *thrash* [traʃ] 'threshing machine'. Verbs are formed from nouns like *can* [kan], *drill* [drɪl], *frost* [frɔst], *match* [matʃ], *mop* [mɔp]: *canner, driller* [drile], *matcher, mopper.* Other verbs on English roots are *feeler* [file] 'to feel (of health)', *swinger* [swiɲe, swiŋe] 'to swing', *trimer* [trime] 'to trim'. Aside from the adaptation to the phonetic system of the dialect, some of these show the effects of popular etymology, by which they are attached to familiar French roots (hence, *sulky* [sɛlkʲe], affected by *selle* 'saddle'). *Pudding* [putᵉɪn] may owe its unexpected medial [t] to a hypercorrection: American English medial *t* in words like *putting* is often voiced, and the [d] of *pudding* was thought to be for *t*.

Most of these words derive from the earlier, pre-20th-century rural style of life: means of transport, foods, commerce, tools, common household items sold to the family by English-speaking salesmen. There are also a few common adjectives: *dull* [dɔl], *loose* [lʊs], *rough* [rɔf], *tough* [tɔf]. These may be explained as a convenient, short, easily pronounced way of expressing a concept

14. For details of the phonetic processes involved in adapting these words into French, see Jean-Denis Gendron, "Le Phonétisme du français canadien du Québec face à l'adstrat anglo-américain," in *Études de linguistique franco-canadienne*, pp. 15–67. He fails to take into account, however, some American English dialect variants which are the immediate source of many borrowings.

which in French is split up among a number of words, some rather long and difficult ones ('rough' is, for example, *rugueux, raboteux, accidenté,* and so on). Also, the common use of these words in lower-class and slang English must have made them stand out for the French: 'I've had a rough time'; Windsor *ça a été rough.* They are words with a somewhat pejorative connotation, and keep it in the French. It is less easy to account for a verb like *feeler,* but again the French word *se sentir,* irregular and reflexive, is replaced by a simpler form. (Compare, in contemporary France, the use of *réaliser,* an Anglicism, for *se rendre compte.*) In any case, this type of borrowing, common to Windsor and to the rest of Canada, did not materially contribute to the alienation of the Windsor French from their Québec counterparts until recent times, when the process of regallicization set in in Québec, rendering some of the above words more or less obsolete.

In contrast to the loans just treated, recent borrowings show less phonetic adaptation. More often than not, they are pronounced exactly as in English, even to the use of the retroflex fricative [ɹ] instead of the usual French trilled [r]. When incorporated into the sentence, they usually will have final stress, however, with lengthening of the syllable stressed in English, thus preserving the rhythm of the French sentence (so *fireplace* [faj:ɹplɛjs'], *peanut* [pi:nɔt] or [pi:nʌt']). They may also be signalled by a special intonation. This lack of adaptation corresponds to the present state of nearly complete bilingualism. Persons who still have an accent in English will, of course, reproduce these words as they pronounce them in English. Certain words may be pronounced in two different ways—one the old, adapted form, and the other the "modern" anglicized pronunciation. This is representative of a difference between generations, or between rural and urban habits. For example, the word *job* has the forms [dʒɑb] and [dʒɔb], the first representing the usual (American) English pronunciation among working-class people in Windsor, the second the French adaptation (or the more "elegant" English pronunciation of an older day). *Combine* (machine for harvesting) is pronounced [kõbɪn] or [kɑmbajn]. Uncertainty as to whether a word really is

French can lead to pronunciations such as [tɹɛjn] for *train,* instead of [trē]. (The word is comparatively recent in the standard language in this meaning, of course, and may never have reached Windsor in that form. Windsor does not use *char(s)* either for 'train' or for 'car', as a rule—the usual word for 'a car' is *un machine.*) Analogous to this are the semiadaptations of French words, such as [apriko] for *abricot,* [bulətē] for *bulletin,* [papəlje] for *peuplier* 'poplar', [pastʃørajze] for *pasteurisé,* or [samõ] for *saumon.* These show a characteristic blend of the two languages, reflecting an uncertainty as to whether the word is not really a badly adapted English one, which should be restored to a more "correct" shape. An interesting case is [mɛjl] for 'mail', replacing Quebec *malle,* itself an old French word preserved perhaps in part because of its similarity to the English. At times, the confusion is total, as when an informant, asked the word for 'bay', muttered, "We don't have one; we just say [bɛ]." Of course, "the real word," spoke up another man, "is *anse.*" (This word, although used in France, is much less common than *baie.*) The "real word," *le vrai mot* in Windsor usage, is the Québec word. This may be known passively: i.e., would be understood if heard but could not be produced on demand. The standard word may be completely unknown. For example, one informant, asked what he called a faucet, replied, "Par icitte on dit *tap.* Mais le vrai mot, c'est *champlure.*" The standard *robinet,* two degrees removed, would not be understood.

Here are some words of this recent stratum, merely a sample of hundreds which might be recorded by listening to a Windsor Frenchman speak:

Air vent, all right, angle, ash tray, baldhead (*c'est un baldhead* 'he's baldheaded'), bathroom, bike, binder, bluejay, bulb, bulldozer, chesterfield,[15] clothespress, coffee pot, couch, crib, crutch, crybaby, curb, cushion, fireplace, fumes, gas, ginger ale, grinder, hall, hedge, jacket, jar, jewelry, junk, lawn mower, light, lumber-

15. This word, in the sense of 'couch,' is probably a Canadianism, for once clearly distinguishable from an American English source. See Walter S. Avis, *et al.* (eds.), *A Dictionary of Canadianisms on Historical Principles* (Toronto, 1967).

yard, napkin, nickname, outlet, overalls, overcoat, peanut, pitcher, platter, pop,[16] porridge, radio, raincoat, scarf, screen, shower, sidewalk, soybean, stew, suit, sun porch, swamp, sweater, tap, teapot, wrench. (Some of these may be partially adapted to French, as *bluejay* [bludʒe] or [blǿʒe], *crybaby* [krajbebe], *teapot* [tipɑt] or [tepɔt].) Verbs in this category include *bail-er* [bɛjle], *decorate-er* [dɛkɔrete], *polish-er* [pɑlɪʃe], *rider-er* [ɹajde], *stand-er* [stæːnde] or [stɛ̃de] (*je peux pas le stand-er* 'I can't stand it'). English verbs are regularly adapted to the conjugation in *-er*.

All of these were actually heard in use, but it is difficult to say with assurance which are really stable in the dialect, and which are "nonce-forms" used on the spur of the moment to replace a momentarily forgotten French word. Many, however, are certainly the only words in use for the concepts involved. Some have a fairly exact French equivalent, but since one's interlocutor may not know it, it is safest (and less presumptuous) to use the English form. Outside the fields of agriculture (premechanized), religion, and the home (preappliance), where the traditional French vocabulary is preserved comparatively well, English designations predominate. Some people know passively the terminology of their own specialty (carpentry, for example) in French, but they never have the chance to use it, since the people they work with are usually English-speaking. Even one English speaker in a group makes it impossible to speak French. In general, one can say that most nouns, and some verbs, denoting concepts which are of 20th-century (or even 19th-century) origin are likely to be borrowings from English.

But even the commonest of objects and concepts, which certainly had French designations known to the people of the older generations, are often given English names (*fireplace, hedge, polish*). Various factors may be at work here. We have seen the importance of having a simple, regular verb to replace a more complex construction. This may extend to verbs like *polish-er*, which can be conjugated regularly and eliminate the complications of the *-ir* conjugation found in *polir*. This hardly explains

16. *Liqueur* in Windsor denotes only 'hard liquor,' and is not used for 'soft drink,' as in Quebec. This can be an important source of misunderstanding!

decorate-er for *décorer,* however, and a more decisive factor may simply be the English word *polish* on the can used. (There would also have been a French version, of course, but the Windsor French would normally read the English better, so would pay no attention to the French.) In the case of *fireplace,* another reason may be invoked. The older French word *chûnée* [ʃyːne] (for *cheminée*) designated both the inside 'fireplace' and the outside 'chimney.' Bilinguals feel the need to distinguish these. Similarly, throughout Canada, the word *can* has been borrowed for 'tin can'. In France, where the tin can has only recently begun to have much importance in the daily life of the household, the word *boîte* can serve without inconvenience for both 'box' and 'can'. Not so in North America, where the difference is vital. On the other hand, English, in the word *game,* has a single concept overlapping that of several French terms: *jeu, partie, match.* Hence Windsor *game* as in "j'ai joué une game de ping-pong." The English use of the word *coat* for both 'suit coat' or 'jacket' and 'overcoat' (French *veston* and *pardessus* or *manteau*) is reflected by the Windsor use of *coat* for both (also *capot,* as in Québec; one man spoke of his *capot de suit* [kapo d sjʊ/ːt], although it may be doubted that this is everyday usage).

At this point we are moving into another area of linguistic interference, the extension or restriction in meaning of a French word to correspond with the semantic sphere of the English word it "translates." Innumerable examples occur in Windsor, many of which are also usual in Québec. The word *place* is used in all meanings of the English 'place'. Hence: *C'est une bonne place* 'It's a good place'. *Plancher* 'floor' is used for *étage:* the Standard French *rez-de-chaussée* (American *ground floor* or *first floor*) may be spoken of as *le premier plancher.* English 'room' (Standard French *chambre, salle, pièce,* etc.) is *chambre* in all senses (*une maison de six chambres; la chambre de bain = le bathroom*). *Ouvrage* is 'work' (this may also go back to an older French usage): *je cherche de l'ouvrage* (standard *travail*). 'Number' is rendered by *nombre: mon nombre de téléphone* (standard *numéro*). One informant, translating 'towel' as *essuie-*

mains, spoke of an *essuie-mains à bain* 'bath towel' (again quite probably not everyday usage). The similarity in form of one of the words to the English term may be decisive: *aisé* replaces *facile* 'easy'; *chandelle* is used for *bougie* 'candle'. *Portrait* means all kinds of 'pictures', *trouble* is 'trouble'. *User* is 'to use' (often replacing the heavy *se servir de*). *Bureau* takes on the meaning of 'chest of drawers'.

The next stage is that of the loan-translation. Here each word of an expression may have basically the normal French meaning, but the combination, though usual in English, is not in French— or acquires a new meaning. Some sentences give the impression of having been thought out first in English, then translated. This is not necessarily true, however, in any individual case. Many of these loan-translations also appear in Québec, often among monolinguals. The process is simply more intense in Windsor. Often, too, Windsor replaces a common Québec loan-translation by the English word. (E.g., *cornet de crème à la glace* or *chien chaud* are simply *ice cream cone* or *hot dog.*) Here are a few typical examples of loan-translations as used in Windsor: [17] 'to fall in love' *tomber en amour* or *tomber en amitié* [amikʲe]; 'he's going on fifty' *il s'en va sur les cinquante;* 'the year round' *l'année ronde;* 'in seven years time' *dans sept ans de temps;* 'that made no difference' *ça faisait pas de différence;* 'I'm taking it easy' *je prends ça aisé* or *easy* [iːzi]; 'how are you' *comment êtes-vous;* 'someday' *quelque journée;* 'take a walk' *prendre une marche;* 'last name' *dernier nom;* 'the clock is going fast' *l'horloge va vite.* The list could be multiplied indefinitely. This type of interference is less obvious than the use of English words and harder to eradicate. On the other hand, being common to all parts of Canada, it does not serve as quite the isolating force that the other kind of borrowing does. (E.g., *chambre de bain* is more understandable than *bathroom* to a French-speaking monolingual.)

Following are two texts to illustrate the Windsor dialect. Text

17. See Edward Pousland, *Étude sémantique de l'anglicisme dans le parler franco-américain de Salem, Mass.* (Paris and Carlisle, Mass., 1933) for a detailed study of the loan-translation process in a very similar dialect.

1 was spoken by a mother; text 2 by her son (age 9?). Both were tape-recorded. The first one represents a person of the older generation, consciously attempting to avoid Anglicisms, but unable to do so entirely. The second one is perhaps more representative of what one usually hears in the street. English words used in unadapted or only slightly adapted phonetic form are here prefixed with an asterisk (hence *gas is to be read as [gæ:s], detached with high falling intonation in the original; in the second text, no intonational marker separated the English forms from the French ones).

Text 1:

J'avais parti une soirée pour aller à une danse avec mon
I had gone out one evening to go to a   dance with my

cousin. Puis [pi] on avait rôdé quasiment [kizimã] toute la
cousin. And   we had driven around almost   all

veillée en machine puis on avait pas pu trouver divou ce qu'était
evening in the car and   we had   not been able to find where the

la danse.   Et puis son machine avait quoi de mal avec qui . . .
dance was. And   his car   had something wrong with it . . .

il envoyait du *gas—des *fumes—en arrière divou que j'étais . . .
it was sending out gas—fumes—into the back where I was . . .

assis.   Et puis quand ce qu'on l—. . . était rendu sur la Sandwich
sitting. And   when   we   . . . had come onto Sandwich

Street, de l'autre bord de l'église Our Lady of the Lake, j'ai
Street, on the other side of the church Our Lady of the Lake, I

commencé à. . . . Il me parlait puis j'y répondais pas puis il s'est
began   to. . . . He was talking to me and I didn't answer him
            and he

aperçu qu'il y avait quoi de mal. Ça fait que . . . il a arrêté
noticed there was something wrong. So   . . . he stopped

entour du Pillette et puis . . . il m'a . . . il essayait arrêter des
around   Pillette and   . . . he   . . . he tried   to stop some

machines pour me débarquer de dedans le machine, parce que
cars   to   get me out of   the car   , because

j'étais pas mal pésante! Ça fait qu'après ça y a un couple de
I was pretty   heavy ! So   after that there were a couple of

machines qu'ont arrêté, puis ils m'ont couchée sur [sy] la . . .
cars   which stopped, and they laid me down on   the . . .

C'était le mois de février. Il a ôté son *overcoat puis il m'a
It was the month of February. He took off his overcoat and he

couchée   sur la neige et puis ils ont commencé . . . Quand je me
laid me down on the snow and they began   . . . When I

suis réveillée, ils étaient penchés par-dessus moi puis ils
woke up   , they were leaning over   me and they

pensaient que j'étais morte. Ça fait que la femme qui était
thought that I was   dead . So   the woman who had

allée à la maison leur [jøz] a dit qu'ils devraient m'emmener
gone to the house told them   that they should   take me

à hôpital. Mais je voulais pas y aller, ça fait qu'ils m'ont
to hospital. But I didn't want to go there, so   they

rentrée dans la maison, puis j'ai commencé à *feel-er malade,
took me into the house, and I began   to feel   sick   ,

ça fait qu'ils m'ont sortie dehors, puis quand j'ai rembarqué
so   they brought me out, and when I got back

dans le machine je *feel-ais pas le diable bien encore!
into the car I wasn't feeling too darn   well yet   !

Text 2:

J'étais après *ride-er mon *bike sur la Eastlawn quand
I was riding   my   bike on Eastlawn Ave. when

y avait deux petits gars qui me jettaient des roches. Ça fait
there were two little kids throwing stones at me.   So

que je me suis ôté sur mon bicycle [bisɪk], puis j'ai jetté des
    I got off   my bicycle,   and I threw some

roches *back. Puis j'ai manqué les petits gars puis j'ai
stones   back. And I missed   the little kids and I

frappé un gros châssis, et je l'ai cassé. Puis ça m'a coûté
hit   a big window , and I broke it. And it cost me

vingt-cinq piastres pour un neuf [nø]. *That's all.
twenty-five dollars for   a new one.

The result of the borrowings and adaptations mentioned above
is to render the ordinary speech of the Windsor French incomprehensible to anyone who does not know English. Since the

core of the language remains intact, it would be possible, with adequate schooling, French-language television, and sufficient motivation, to bring the dialect back in line with the rest of Canada. But one must reckon with the deeply ingrained inferiority complex, which caused one informant to lament, "Around here we use a hillbilly kind of French," and which makes so many of these people reluctant to speak French with any stranger. The future of the use of French in Windsor is very much in doubt, unless intense pressures can be applied to reverse the process of Americanization which has partially isolated it from the rest of Canada.

Index

DATE DUE

MAR 27 1974

FEB 25 1974

OCT 28 1971

DEC 11 1983

CT MAY 11 1992